Palgrave Studies in Economic History

Series Editor
Kent Deng
London School of Economics
London, UK

Palgrave Studies in Economic History is designed to illuminate and enrich our understanding of economies and economic phenomena of the past. The series covers a vast range of topics including financial history, labour history, development economics, commercialisation, urbanisation, industrialisation, modernisation, globalisation, and changes in world economic orders.

More information about this series at
http://www.palgrave.com/gp/series/14632

Jun Du

Agricultural Transition in China

Domestic and International Perspectives on Technology and Institutional Change

Jun Du
National University of Singapore
Singapore, Singapore

Palgrave Studies in Economic History
ISBN 978-3-319-76904-2   ISBN 978-3-319-76905-9   (eBook)
https://doi.org/10.1007/978-3-319-76905-9

Library of Congress Control Number: 2018934710

© The Editor(s) (if applicable) and The Author(s) 2018
This work is subject to copyright. All rights are solely and exclusively licensed by the Publisher, whether the whole or part of the material is concerned, specifically the rights of translation, reprinting, reuse of illustrations, recitation, broadcasting, reproduction on microfilms or in any other physical way, and transmission or information storage and retrieval, electronic adaptation, computer software, or by similar or dissimilar methodology now known or hereafter developed.
The use of general descriptive names, registered names, trademarks, service marks, etc. in this publication does not imply, even in the absence of a specific statement, that such names are exempt from the relevant protective laws and regulations and therefore free for general use.
The publisher, the authors, and the editors are safe to assume that the advice and information in this book are believed to be true and accurate at the date of publication. Neither the publisher nor the authors or the editors give a warranty, express or implied, with respect to the material contained herein or for any errors or omissions that may have been made. The publisher remains neutral with regard to jurisdictional claims in published maps and institutional affiliations.

Cover illustration: ping han / Alamy Stock Photo

Printed on acid-free paper

This Palgrave Macmillan imprint is published by the registered company Springer International Publishing AG part of Springer Nature.
The registered company address is: Gewerbestrasse 11, 6330 Cham, Switzerland

Contents

1	A General Theory Review	1
2	Economic Thinking on Chinese Agriculture	27
3	State-Led Changes: Failures and Successes	59
4	Trends in China's Grain Production	97
5	Agricultural Transition in Taiwan: Towards a Comparative Study with Mainland China	123
6	Agricultural Transition in Selected Asian Economies	151
7	Conclusion	175
	Index	185

Foreign-Language Words

按质论价   Anzhi Lunjia (Grain Pricing Based on Quality)
保本微利   Baoben Weili (Cost Plus Thin Profit)
超购价   Chaogou Jia (Above Quota Price)
大跃进   Da Yue Jin (Great Leap Forward)
倒三七   Dao San Qi (Reverse 30:70 Ratio)
德川幕府   Tokugawa Shogunate
多快好省   Duo Kuai Hao Sheng (Greater, Faster, Better and More Economical)
放卫星   Fang Weixing (Launching Satellite Campaign)
沸腾的广西   Feiteng De Guangxi
丰收曲   Fengshou Qu (Harvest Song)
高精尖   Gao Jing Jian (High-grade, Precision and Sophisticated)
耕者有其田   Gengzhe You Qi Tian (Land to the Tiller)
工作单位   Gongzuo Danwei (Work Unit)
公田   Gong Tian (Public Farmland)
购粮专款   Gouliang Zhuankuan (Special Funds for Grain Purchasing Purposes)
购销同价   Gouxiao Tongjia (Purchase and Sales at the Same Price)
国家定购   Guojia Dinggou (State Procurement)

viii   Foreign-Language Words

国家粮食风险基金	Guojia Liangshi Fengxian Jijin (State Grain Risk Fund)
国家专项粮食储备	Guojia Zhuanxiang Liangshi Chubei (State Special Grain Reserve)
合同定购	Hetong Dinggou (Contractual procurement)
户口	Hukou (Household Registration System)
集体化	Jitihua (Collectivisation)
价格双轨制	Jiage Shuanggui Zhi (Dual-Track Pricing System)
江戸幕府	Edo Bakufu
粳米	Jingmi
粮票	Liangpiao (Grain Ration Coupon)
粮食部门	Liangshi Bumen (Grain Bureau)
粮食省长负责制	Liangshi Shengzhang Fuze Zhi (Grain Provincial Governor Responsibility System)
米袋子	Mi Dai Zi (Rice Bag)
明治維新	Meiji Ishin (Meiji Restoration)
亩	Mu
南巡	Nan Xun (Inspection Tour to the South)
农忙假	Nongmang Jia (Busy Farming Holiday)
农民工	Nongmin Gong (Rural Migrant Labourers)
农业合作社	Nongye Hezuo She (Agricultural Producer's Cooperative)
糯米	Nuomi (Glutinous Rice)
蓬莱稻	Ponlai Rice (Japonica Rice)
去集体化	Qu Jitihua (Decollectivisation)
人民公社	Renmin Gongshe (People's Commune)
人民日报	Renmin Ribao (People's Daily)
三挂钩	San Gua Gou (Three Links)
三年大饥荒	Sannian Da Jihuang (Three Years of Great Famine)
生产大队	Shengchan dadui (Production Brigade)
生产队	Shengchan Dui (Production Team)
顺价销售	Shunjia Xiaoshou (Selling Grain at a Favourable Price)
统购价	Tonggou Jia (Quota Price)

| | Foreign-Language Words | ix |

统购统销	Tonggou Tongxiao (State Monopoly Purchase and Marketing System)
统派购	Tong Pai Gou (Unified Purchasing of Agricultural Products)
统销价	Tongxiao Jia (Rationing Price)
籼米	Xianmi
协议价	Xieyi Jia (Negotiated Price)
新华社	Xinhua She (Xinhua News Agency)
议购价	Yigou Jia (Negotiated Purchase Price)
玉米	Yumi
在来稻	Chailai Rice (Indica Rice)
政策性贴息贷款	Zhengcexing Tiexi Daikuan (Policy-Based Discounted Interest Rate Loans)
中国青年报	Zhongguo Qingnian Bao (China Youth Daily)

Name of People

邓小平	Deng Xiaoping
毛泽东	Mao Zedong
钱学森	Qian Xuesen
王明进	Wang Mingjin
温家宝	Wen Jiabao
朱镕基	Zhu Rongji

Name of Places

安徽	Anhui
板桥水库	Banqiao Reservoir
柴达木盆地	Qaidam Basin
城关	Chengguan
洞庭湖	Dongting Lake
福建	Fujian
甘肃	Gansu

谷城	Gucheng
广东	Guangdong
广西	Guangxi
贵州	Guizhou
海南	Hainan
和平社	Heping She (Heping Cooperative)
河北	Hebei
河南	Henan
河套	Hetao
黑龙江	Heilongjiang
红旗社	Hongqi People's Commune
湖北	Hubei
湖南	Hunan
环江县	Huanjiang County
黄河	Huang He River (Yellow River)
吉林	Jilin
江南	Kiangnan (also known as Jiangnan)
江苏	Jiangsu
江西	Jiangxi
江阴	Jiangyin
辽宁	Liaoning
麻城县	Macheng County
内蒙古	Neimenggu (Inner Mongolia)
宁夏	Ningxia
青海	Qinghai
塞什克	Saishike
三门峡大坝	Sanmenxia Dam
山东	Shangdong
山西	Shanxi
陕西	Shaanxi
上海	Shanghai
四川	Sichuan
淞江	Songjiang
苏南	Sunan (Southern Jiangsu)
苏州	Suzhou

遂平	Suiping
太仓	Taicang
天津	Tianjin
卫星农业合作社	Weixing Nongye Hezuo She (Weixing Agricultural Producer's Cooperative)
无锡	Wuxi
西藏	Xizang
西平县	Xiping County
溪建园一社	Xijianyuan Yi She (Xijianyuan No. 1 Cooperative)
先锋社	Xianfeng She (Xianfeng Cooperative)
新疆	Xinjiang
星光社	Xingguang She (Xingguang Cooperatives)
扬州	Yangzhou
扬子江	Yangzi Jiang (Yangtze River)
云南	Yunnan
长江	Changjiang (Long River)
长江三角洲	Changjiang Sanjiao Zhou (Yangtze/Yangzi Delta)
浙北	Zhebei (North Zhejiang)
浙江	Zhejiang
重庆	Chongqing
珠江三角洲	Zhujiang Sanjiao Zhou (Pearl River Delta)

Abbreviation

ADBC	Agricultural Development Bank of China
CCP	Chinese Communist Party
CPI	Consumer Price Index
FAO	Food and Agriculture Organisation of the United Nations
FPE	Factor Price Equalisation
GDP	Gross Domestic Product
GLF	Great Leap Forward
GNP	Gross National Product
HOS	Heckscher-Ohlin-Samuelson
HRS	Household Responsibility System
IIC	Induced Institutional Change
IR8	International Rice No. 8
IRRI	International Rice Research Institute
JCRR	Sino-American Joint Commission on Rural Reconstruction
KMT	Kuomintang
PBC	People's Bank of China
PRC	People's Republic of China
R&D	Research and Development
SOEs	State-Owned Enterprises
TFP	Total Factor Productivity
TJIA	Taiwan Joint Irrigation Association

xiv   **Abbreviation**

TVEs   Township and Village Enterprises
US$ United States dollars
USA   United States of America
USDA   USA Department of Agriculture
WW2   World War Two

List of Figures

Fig. 3.1   Wheat and early rice yields announced during China's 'Launching Satellite' Campaign, June 1958–October 1958   61

Fig. 3.2   China's rice production cycles and real purchase price change   65

Fig. 4.1   Output of four major grain crops in China from 1961 to 2011   100

Fig. 4.2   Urban population proportion changes in China from 1970 to 2011   101

Fig. 4.3   Trend in grain production in four major areas in China from 1978 to 2011   102

Fig. 4.4   Provincial grain production from 1978 to 2011   104

Fig. 4.5   Provincial per hectare grain yield from 1978 to 2011   105

Fig. 4.6   Per hectare grain yield change in Lower Yangtze Delta region from 1978 to 2011   107

Fig. 4.7   Per hectare grain yield change in Northeast China from 1978 to 2011   107

Fig. 4.8   Per hectare grain yield change in the middle and upper reaches of the Yellow River from 1978 to 2011   108

Fig. 4.9   Grain production change and provincial per capita grain sown area change in Northeast China from 1979 to 2011   110

Fig. 4.10   Link relative ratio of grain sown area of China from 1979 to 2011   111

Fig. 4.11   Comparison of total and grain sown area changes between national level and the Northeast China from 1978 to 2011   113

xvi   List of Figures

Fig. 5.1   Annual gross return and expenses of Taiwan agricultural
production   144

Fig. 5.2   Factor return in Taiwan agricultural production   145

Fig. 5.3   Revenue-cost ratio of mainland China's major type of
agricultural production   146

Fig. 5.4   Factor return in China's major type of agricultural production   146

Fig. 6.1   Per hectare paddy rice yield in selected Asian economies,
1961–2007   158

Fig. 6.2   Rice output in selected Asian economies, 1961–2007   163

Fig. 6.3   National GDP, agricultural GDP and total rice output in Japan   164

Fig. 6.4   National GDP/GNP per capita, agricultural GDP/GNP per
capita and paddy rice production in Japan, 1951–2009   167

Fig. 6.5   Paddy rice production and agriculture share in national GDP
from 1951 to 2009   167

Fig. 6.6   National and agricultural income per capita and agricultural
receipt per capita in Japan from 1975 to 2009   168

Fig. 6.7   National and agricultural GDP and rice production in China,
1977–2007   170

Fig. 6.8   National and agricultural population in China from 1970 to
2007   170

List of Tables

Table 3.1 Rural social labour force in China, 1985–1990   72
Table 4.1 Population change in Northeast China after reform   111

1

A General Theory Review

1.1 Introduction

In the late 1950s, food crisis was a worldwide phenomenon. In addition to China, South and Southeast Asian and Latin American countries were also subject to a potential risk of famine. But the results were different.

In 1953, Norman Borlaug[1] cross-bred the semi-dwarf Norin 10²-Brevor[3] with the disease-resistant cultivars to create new varieties of wheat according to the climatic conditions of Mexico.[4] Borlaug's synthetic hybrid improvement of wheat varieties from Central and South America marked the beginning of the famous Green Revolution. Along with the first wave of green revolution in Central and South America, hybrid improvement of new wheat seed technology spread to Asia. In 1962, the International Rice Research Institute (IRRI) produced a *rice* hybrid—International Rice No. 8 (IR8)—by crossing Dee-Geo-woo-gen

---

[1] Norman Ernest Borlaug (1914–2009) was an American agronomist and Nobel Laureate. He has been called 'the father of the Green Revolution'.

[2] A Japanese dwarf variety of wheat.

[3] A high-yielding American cultivar, Brevor 14.

[4] Hedden, Peter. 2003. 'The Genes of the Green Revolution.' *Trends in Genetics* 19(1): 5–9.

© The Author(s) 2018
J. Du, *Agricultural Transition in China*, Palgrave Studies in Economic History,
https://doi.org/10.1007/978-3-319-76905-9_1

with Peta. Its high-yielding nature has led to IR8 being hailed as a green revolution 'Miracle Rice'. In the Philippines, the IR8 technology created a 55 per cent[5] increase in rice output within ten years of the inauguration of the green revolution[6]; within 20 years rice output had more than doubled. The application of the IR8 'Miracle Rice' developed by IRRI enabled the Philippines to advance from mere self-sufficiency in food-grain production to the status of net exporter within a short period of time in the twentieth century.

In the thousands of years of paddy rice planting history, IR8 stands as one of the most important technological revolutions in rice production. Increased agricultural productivity brought about by green revolution technological innovations in Mexico and South and Southeast Asia promised a solution to the perennial threat of food insecurity, and fundamentally changed the nature of agricultural production. India and the Philippines took the lead in Asia in introducing new technology and began to adapt the new practices to their own local conditions. This sparked the diffusion of a green revolution in Asia.

However, China—the most populous country in Asia—failed to share in this process of external technology diffusion. In China, the Chinese Communist Party (CCP) and the Mao Zedong (毛泽东) regime sought to use political campaigns to raise agricultural productivity and total output, whilst resorting to state-enforced procurements to squeeze peasants' producer surplus. The culmination of these processes was the Great Leap Forward (*da yue jin*, 大跃进, hereafter GLF)—and the subsequent great famine. Meanwhile, the political framework in which China operated caused its technological exchanges with most other countries of the world to stagnate.[7]

These two results illustrate two basic elements of agricultural transition. The first relates to the source of agricultural productivity growth. In

---

[5] According to Food and Agriculture Organization of the United Nations (FAO) data, in 1960 paddy rice yield in the Philippines was 1.13 tonnes per hectare, increasing to 1.75 tonnes per hectare in 1970, and 2.21 tonnes per hectare in 1980.

[6] Within a decade of adopting the IR8 paddy rice variety, rice output in the Philippines increased from 1.13 to 2.21 tonnes per hectare.

[7] The exceptions were the Soviet Union and Eastern European socialist countries—though after 1960 even exchanges with these countries were constrained because of the Sino-Soviet split.

the 1950s, China and western scientists were aware that increasing factor intensification was not the only way to enhance the potential growth of agricultural output. They recognised that an even more important factor was technological innovation in agriculture, with its great potential for agricultural productivity growth. After the initiation of the green revolution, a series of breakthrough agricultural initiatives, in areas such as seed and fertiliser development and field management, marked the beginning of a new and transformative phase in the long history of global grain production.

The second and critically important element was the way in which technological innovation can be applied to agricultural production. In the 1950s, the CCP's introduction of central planning within a collectivised framework of farm production was the chosen means of trying to improve the institutions of agricultural production and thereby increase per hectare productivity. In the event, however, collectivisation and subsequent communisation failed to facilitate the adoption of new agricultural technologies. It is striking that while the GLF was being implemented in China, the impact of the green revolution was making itself felt throughout developing economies in Southeast Asia and Central and South America, as the new technologies were adapted to local conditions. China could also have benefited from the same process of technological diffusion. Instead, however, it was completely excluded from this process. With its existing indigenous agricultural technological base (including seeds, fertilisers and irrigation resources), it still failed to avoid the calamity of the great famine.

When Central and South America, and subsequent South and Southeast Asian economies, entered the era of high growth of agricultural production after the green revolution, agricultural technological change in East Asian economies, especially China and Japan, showed a different growth pattern. Irrespective of the timing, duration and the choice of technology changes, East Asian economies' agricultural technology transitions were very different compared to South and Southeast Asian economies. Inter-regional agricultural technology changes within the East Asian economies, even within China, also vary.

This work will follow the main clue of agricultural technology change to track down the particularities in East Asian economies' agricultural transitions, focusing on irrigated paddy-field rice planting regions such as China, Taiwan and Japan. The evaluation benchmark that this work used is the standard Induced Institutional Change (IIC) (Hayami 1969; Hayami and Ruttan 1970a, b, 1985, 1995) paradigm of technology change under a neoclassical economic framework. Furthermore, the work in subsequent chapters will try to gradually release the hypothesis of perfect market institutions and adequate factor accumulation, trying to extend the standard IIC theory to explain the agricultural transition under complex institutional conditions, with an application to China and selected East Asian economies.

The comparison of the experiences of China and other East Asian economies that have undertaken green revolution, as outlined above, highlights the importance of institutions as a factor shaping the different outcomes. When science and technology—the replacement of traditional inputs by modern inputs—have developed the potential for sustained agricultural productivity and output growth to generate sufficient food supplies to accommodate population growth, other factors may intervene to postpone or even prevent the application and diffusion of new technologies. Identifying such factors has become a key issue in understanding East Asian economies' agricultural transitions.

Two major questions define the main research thrust.

The first of these questions relates to the accessibility of technology. The comparative experiences of China and developing economies in South and Southeast Asia are a reminder that even when conditions allow for the universal adoption of new agricultural technologies, the time and place at which technology diffusion occurs may still differ between economies. Thus, for example, while the Philippines embarked on its green revolution in the early 1960s, China did not initiate its agricultural technological transition until two decades later, in the 1980s. What postpones or prevents the local agriculture from accessing the frontier technology is a vital question to understand the agricultural technological change, in short, the accessibility of technology.

The second question addressed relates to the choice of technology. In other words, at any given time when faced with a range of feasible technologies in the given technology set, which of these technologies will be selected, and under what specific conditions will the selection be made.

As Norman Borlaug's (2000) speech indicated, in most cases advanced agricultural technologies are already available for developing economies.[8] It follows that when technology has ceased to be a constraint on agricultural production, the most critical issue affecting farm output growth is how to make these technologies accessible to farmers. This work seeks to offer insights into those factors that determine differences in technological transition in agriculture between East Asian economies when the conditions and paths of technology choice simultaneously interact.

1.2 A General Theory Review

Classical economists regard it as axiomatic that the agriculture sector changes less rapidly than the manufacturing sector. This view has been strengthened since Adam Smith (1776 [1994]), and the difference between the agriculture sector and the non-agriculture sector is considered an inherent result of the difficulties of deepening labour specialisation in production. Ricardo (1817 [2006]) mentions the acceptance of improvement in agricultural production, but still sets a fixed level of technological development of the agriculture sector as a basic hypothesis in his fundamental models of growth, implying a common belief that agriculture usually cannot catch up with the pace of technical change in the manufacturing sector and is always inferior to other components of the economy. This basic classical economic notion of stagnant development in the agriculture sector is central to many theories of economic growth and has pervaded many consequent theories and studies. For instance, Karl Marx (1867 [1977]) dismissed the likelihood that the agriculture sector would be a possible source of economic growth, arguing that the development of capitalism in manufacturing would be the means of rescuing people from agricultural production and rural life. Even economists after World War Two (WW2), such as Lewis (1954), typically distinguish a dynamic modern manufacturing sector and an underdeveloped traditional rural sector.

---

[8] Please refer to Norman Borlaug's speech made on 8 September 2000 for the special 30th anniversary lecture in the Norwegian Nobel Institute, Oslo.

In contrast with research based on a view of the agriculture sector as stagnant, neoclassical economics incorporates the notions of 'rational individuals' and 'instant market clearance' hypotheses into the research framework and develops the evaluation benchmark of agriculture growth from the output performance to production efficiency. Schultz (1964) argues that the low price of rural labour relative to that of other inputs determines the input structure of agricultural production. In his view, in most cases, especially in developing economies, the agriculture sector was not backward, because the individual peasant is able to make every efficient use and choice of physical inputs and technologies available to him/her but lacks large-scale capital to make the agricultural investment with high payoffs—a vital problem in improving agricultural production.

Due to different natural endowments, patterns of agricultural development and adaptation to new technologies vary from country to country. Based on its basic assumption and hypotheses, neoclassical theory can be extended further. This work assumes that all current available agricultural technologies, as known by everyone, can be selected at any time with zero informative cost. This neoclassical theory extension holds only if: (a) one accepts that investment of human capital is included in the broader sense of technological investment, as well as of investment in physical capital. Thus, the cost of learning new technology or efficiency loss during the 'learning-by-doing' (Arrow 1962) process may be classified as investment in human capital; and (b) there are institutions that allow switches between different technologies at nearly zero cost—although this point goes beyond the horizons of neoclassical theory.

Therefore, two sorts of changes in conditions may determine the technologies and institutions used in the agriculture sector: (a) changes in relative factor prices, and (b) the application of newly developed technologies.

In theory, any change in the above two factors may result in changes in agricultural institutions and technologies, which may lead to a new economic equilibrium. Then it is possible to say that different endowments will impact on individual peasants who will make different choices of new techniques from the set of newly developed technologies available to them, and, similarly, institutions may be regarded as another set of choices left to society. The choice between the agriculture and non-agriculture sector sets is considered to have extremely important implications for the allocation of resources and for policy-making in an economy.

The economic development is a process of dynamic shifts in both institutional and technological factors, as well as in the inputs necessary to sustain production. This view is significantly carried into agriculture by Hayami and Ruttan (1985). Following the neoclassical approach, Hayami and Ruttan (1985, 1995) applied North and Thomas's (1971, 1973) theory and developed induced innovation theory (or the aforementioned IIC theory) to explain the institutional and technical changes that occur when agriculture faces market pressures and external technological development. They examined numerous successful instances of rapid institutional and technical changes in Southeast Asian economies' agriculture, emphasizing the importance of institutions and policies in agricultural transition. By expanding North and Thomas's (1971, 1973) research, Hayami and Ruttan took institutional change endogenously: institutions become less efficient in the economy with a change of both population and technological development in the long run. In addition, due to technological improvement and changes in labour supply, previous efficiently functioning institutions cannot keep pace with changes in population and technology, so that the corresponding institutional arrangements lack efficiency. A new institution will replace the former, this process leading to new efficient institutional arrangements. In induced innovation, resource endowments determine the difference in relative factor prices, which affects the direction of research and development in different economies. The induced innovation is thus thought to be optimal in relation to the existing relative price (with available labour and technology status as givens).

This induced innovation approach mainly focuses on technical and institutional changes influenced by the interaction between endowments and pre-transitional institutional conditions and the technological innovation that follows. Hayami and Ruttan's conclusion initiated much relevant research in developing economies and generated papers that sought to use their theoretical arguments to demonstrate and quantify the extent of the contribution of institutions to agricultural growth. However, because IIC theory is based on some critical neoclassical economic hypotheses, such as perfect market conditions, Southeast Asian economies'

8   J. Du

easy rural institutions to some extent satisfy such critical hypotheses. But when IIC applied to transitional economies (e.g., China) with complex market institutions, problems may arise. Chapters 3 and 4 will analyse this issue with empirical studies of Mainland China.

1.3   Institution and Technology Under a Neoclassical Framework

When analysts have sought to identify the leading factor in agricultural growth, they have usually asked: have technical change or institutional factors changed the main driver of farm growth? Basically, the answer to this question is contingent on two scenarios: the static scenario, in which technological innovation is absent; and the long-run scenario, in which technology develops in parallel with agricultural growth.

Under static conditions, technology is assumed to be fixed, with no new technology introduced (subject to the constraint of the current technological possibility frontier). In these circumstances, if current technology is at its optimum (which means that relative prices exert no pressure), the only requirement for agricultural growth is to adjust the capital–labour ratio or accelerate the factor accumulation. If, by contrast, there is a set of technologies available to choose from and the in-use technology is sub-optimal, the mechanism to assist choosing new technology will help to generate new agricultural growth. In this case, institutions will be more important in growth, although this is only the case in which, under static conditions, technological frontier is assumed to be unchanged.

Under long-run conditions, technology will develop to a higher level and enhance the available set of technologies. Along with technological development, if institutional factors (i.e., market institutions) can control the variety and direction of technological innovation, then the technological level, capital–labour ratio and factor accumulation may be adjusted to support an optimal economic order.

The long-run case approximates more closely to the real economy, where institutional factors help the economy to adopt newly developed technology. Technical change can lift marginal output to a higher level to generate growth; however technical change is not brought about by factor intensification. Rather, a factor always seeks to associate itself with techniques having the highest attainable average return, and this matching process finally leads to technical change. However, whether a factor can be successfully matched to the technique with highest return and its matching path is eventually determined by institutional arrangements.

In short, under real economic conditions, what is the leading factor in growth is an open question. Institutions and technology interact in the economic growth process, and only through empirical investigations of specific cases is it possible to identify the leading factor. Taking this question forward into the analysis of agricultural transition, the roles of institutions and technology in different agricultural contexts highly relies on the contexts in which transitions were undertaken.

1.3.1 'Induced' and 'Imposed' Innovation

Empirical study by Hayami and Kikuchi (1980) demonstrates the self-adjusting capacity of the economy that helps it to adopt new institutions and technologies in response to changing relative prices. However, studies of the USA and the Philippines derive from specific institutional arrangements: in the USA the agriculture sector was not regulated until after the boom period of WW2; similarly, Philippine rice farmers live in a comparatively free environment in which regulators hardly intervene in economic affairs at the local rural village level. As a result, institutional change, in the IIC definition, conflicts less with previous institutions comparing with other transitional economies, especially political institutions. Thus, a neoclassical type of IIC theory is more likely to be applicable to a less regulated economy. However, institutional and technical changes in most transitional economies, such as East Asian economies as aforementioned, are obviously not the case. Those economies where government is interventionist and applies massive regulations to the agriculture sector cannot easily be explained using IIC theory.

Under complex market institutions, agricultural transition usually undertakes in company with rural reforms through policies and political regulations. These policies are comparatively compulsory and seek to influence agricultural production in such a way as to have the most rapid economic impact and meet policy makers' expectations. IIC is a self-enforcing movement from old and inefficient institutions to a new and efficient institutional arrangement brought about by the interaction of political considerations and other factors. In contrast to induced innovation, in East Asian economies political intervention has played the leading role in agricultural transition. In the early stage of these economies' transitions, agricultural output has been increased in a short time by political regulations governing market institutions and pricing policy. Lin (1989) uses China's empirical study and calls this kind of institutional change 'imposed' institutional change.

Differences between 'induced' and 'imposed' innovations derive from one principal assumption: the policy-maker has perfect knowledge of the existing economy and is able accurately to forecast all other actors' and agents' economic behaviours and expectations. Scholars holding the view of imposed institutional change have the same problem as Lucas Critics with 'rational expectation' theories. In the real-world economy, nobody has all the existing information, nor can they forecast others' expectations accurately, which means that under conditions of imperfect decision making, policies may not achieve their original purpose. Those scholars holding the above viewpoint believe in the subjective impression that reform policies can always achieve the expected result. However, according to Critics this achievement only happens by accident, and even if the results are as expected result paths of institutional change are probably not always the same. Chapters 5 and 6 will look into different agricultural transitions in selected East Asian economies.

1.3.2 Productivity Research

In addition to institutional analysis on agricultural growth, since the 1970s neoclassical economists developed the total factor productivity (TFP) research (e.g., Fan 1991, 1997, 2000). The Cobb-Douglas production function is the most widely used modelling function, in which technology and institutions are introduced as variables. The TFP model is a methodology used to evaluate different factors' contribution to economic growth and works to illustrate the rate of technical and institutional change when used in individual economic units such as inter-sectoral research. In TFP studies of agricultural growth, regression results can show the existence of technical and institutional change in agricultural development, normally explained by the variables of increased quality and/or quantity of physical capital inputs. Thus, for various reasons, TFP estimation is likely to be useful for economic forecasting, policy-making and insight into economic growth.

Some TFP research suggests that productivity growth rates differ substantially across sectors and these differences have extremely important implications for future economic development (Krueger et al. 1992). Higher TFP growth rates in manufacturing may create an institutional arrangement that is more favourable to manufacturing than agriculture. The widespread failure of this developmental approach might be expected to raise questions about the validity of the underlying assumption of relative inferior productivity in the agriculture compared with that in the industry. But this is not always the case.

Under perfect market conditions, the agriculture sector as well as the industrial sector will make the most efficient use of the technologies available to them, and the economy should show a convergence trend between agriculture and industry. To put it simply, some strand of TFP method considers technologies in different sectors to be isolated from each other, and it ignores the possibility that Factor Price Equalization theorem (Samuelson 1948) might help to balance the inter-sectoral technical changes.

Although TFP is a widely applied method of interpreting economic growth, it has a few controversial points when used for purposes of evaluating technology changes. When considered an endogenous variable, technology is continuous but not homogenous. In Aghion et al.'s work (2001, 2005), technology change is considered as a burst of techniques that occurs within a short time. In his view, although technical change may appear to be continuous, only a few technological revolutions have been powerful enough to precipitate major economic breakthroughs. If technical change is not homogenous to affect growth, for example, the green revolution of the last century, this nature may raise questions to

TFP analysis on technology changes. Another common method of dealing with technical change is to decompose 'technology' into factors more directly correlated with agricultural growth. In some work (e.g., Huang and Rozelle 1996) technical change is considered to affect growth via some inner components, such as the application of seeds, chemical fertilisers and good field management. This evidence suggests that the recourse to indirect technology as the explanatory factor in driving growth is now widely accepted. It may describe the result of institutional or technical changes and even the directions of these changes, but not yet the mechanism whereby the changes take place. Chapters 3 and 4 will take Mainland China as a case study to show how policy-oriented institutional changes affect its total output and per capita productivity growth in the agriculture.

1.4 Three Phases in Chinese Agricultural Development

1.4.1 Phase One: The Traditional High-Level Equilibrium Trap

Chapters 2, 3, and 4 will focus on China's long-term agricultural development from pre-industrial to the industrial era. The traditional views treat the problems of stagnation in the pre-industrial Chinese agricultural development because of the absence of technical innovation. Chinese technical advances in agricultural production stood still during the medieval period, during which food-grain output just had grown almost *pari passu* with population growth and depletion of natural resources with the living standard fixed and unchanged. Breakthrough technologies did not generate in China despite an enlarged commercial sector, intensive agricultural production in the face of a population boom, and a continuous input to maintain the traditional agricultural production system.

This persistence of agricultural technology stagnation at the end of the pre-industrial China was explained by Elvin (1972, 1973, 2004) using the concept of the 'High-Level Equilibrium Trap'. The continued and sustained agricultural output increase to feed the growing population, without accompanying economic improvements, was, however, defined by Philip Huang (1990) as a growth pattern of 'Involution'.

Historians view the explanation of technical stagnation in Chinese agricultural development (Elvin 1973, 2004; Philip Huang 1990, 2002; Pomeranz 2000, 2002; Bray 1984, 1985, 1997; Li 1998, 2000) under one generic framework—the High-Level Equilibrium Trap. Their studies, in fact, present a series of inter-related economic phenomena: (a) Malthusian pressure on natural resources,[9] particularly the land constraint; (b) an excessive supply of low-cost rural labour, holding back capital-intensive technology change; (c) inefficiency and insufficiency of the market in Chinese pre-industrial economy; (d) a lack of available technologies which were technically feasible for adaptation and use by Chinese agriculture.

This traditional pattern of agricultural development, under the framework of a high-level equilibrium trap or the involution growth in Historian's view, describes an increase in grain output resulting from the excessive supply of low-cost labour that brought about high yield and total output in farming through labour intensification. Thus, labour-saving technologies could not be introduced. As a result, an involutionary production or a high-level equilibrium turned up with the abundance of low-cost rural labour and constrained the potential adoption and generation of more efficient technologies, which discouraged the economy from introducing new technology and innovation.

These traditional views of high-level equilibrium and involution theories imply that both labour- and capital-intensive technologies were available in the pre-industrial China; and suggest that the involutionary production in pre-industrial era is a typical example of the failure when the necessary pre-conditions of new technologies were absent from the economy.

However, in the pre-industrial era, labour was used not only in farming production, but also to provide national services and public goods such as national defence and irrigation. And in the world history, those countries with large population were usually more advanced. This points a positive correlation between increasing population and economic

---

[9] Here mainly refers to the population pressure on natural resources.

growth. But why did labour accumulation (population growth) do harm to economic growth at the end of pre-industrial economies, particularly China? Do the theories of high-level equilibrium and involutionary growth change according to the context? If paddy rice planting techniques could still absorb large amounts of labour input, what caused the pre-industrial stagnation in Chinese agricultural development? In Chap. 2, this work will consider whether the high-level equilibrium and involutionary growth theory identify a specific economic environment, or loosely fit a wide variety of different economic conditions from a dynamic view of a long-run technology change under the neoclassical economic framework.

1.4.2 Phase Two: Stalinism and Stagnation

From the foundation of the People's Republic of China (PRC) in 1949, agricultural production changed. The Chinese revolution was based on the peasantry, and therefore political elite attitudes could not be anti-peasant. Implicit was an affirmatory commitment to ameliorate Chinese agriculture and rural welfare.

But soon after 1949 China's overall economic problems dictated a fast-track urban industrialisation unconditionally at the expense of the agriculture. Given a stagnated yield level and a fast-booming population, the key issue facing the state was not a simple one-time squeeze of rural welfare, but a squeeze along with growth. This required Chinese government to provide adequate incentives to encourage agricultural production.

From the First Five Year Plan (1953–1957), Mao's China chose the Soviet—even Stalinist—path of prioritising enforcement of a tight agricultural procurement policy to support heavy industry. But an important difference was that Mao limited requisitions to maintain farmers' enthusiasm for agricultural production. However, from the eve of GLF, the state increased its procurement in harvest areas, precipitating fears and concerns in the agriculture sector. Together with the crisis years of natural disasters, the state suffered serious food shortages, resulting in the three-year 'great famine' and long-term stagnation.

Research into this stage of reform has usually fallen within the remit of traditional Chinese Studies, using descriptive policy analysis to make qualitative evaluations of the performance of the agricultural production, such as Walker (1984, 1988). Research into pre-1949 Republican agricultural development has tight connections with studies of rural China in the late imperial period (Duara 1988; Philip Huang 1990, 2002).

1.4.3 Phase Three: Post-1979 Reform

Since 1979, China has been undergoing a profound economic and social transition—transforming Soviet-style economic and social system into a market-oriented economy. Starting from the agriculture sector, Chinese agriculture has achieved an outstanding growth performance in terms of both total output and per capita output and has successfully fed the largest population in the world. Grain output in China increased from 304.7 million tonnes in 1978 to 546.5 million tonnes in 2010—a 79.4 per cent net increase. Meanwhile, during the same period, the population in China also increased from 962.6 million in 1978 to 1340.9 million in 2010, while the sown area of grain crops contracted from 120.6 million hectares to 109.9 million hectares (National Bureau of Statistics 2011).[10] In the face of a continuous increase in population, Chinese agriculture has kept pace with the population boom under the constraint of shrinking sown area of grain crops.

Given the land constraint, the only means of generating a large-scale output increase lay with increased yields per hectare. With tremendous growth performance, Chinese agriculture has attracted widespread attention among scholars. Most economists, as well as some historians, analyse agricultural growth by attributing the growth rate to various factors, especially changes in inputs, technology and institutions. Specifically, these papers discuss agricultural growth using capital accumulation, human capital accumulation, allocative efficiency and technological efficiency to explain the sources of such growth.

---

[10] *Zhongguo tongji nianjian (China Statistical Yearbook)*. National Bureau of Statistics of China. Beijing: China Statistics Press, 1981–2011.

1.5 A Comparative Study of Agricultural Transition in Selected East Asian Economies

Unlike previous research, this work will follow the clue of technology change to observe the different paths of agricultural transition in China and among selected East Asian economies. And the evaluation benchmark used throughout this work will be the standard paradigm of IIC technology change under neoclassical economic framework.

However, the IIC theory implies a critical constraint: 'factor accumulation' is a process independent from 'technology change'. Or this could be understood as that the agriculture sector has completed factor accumulation in terms of both 'absolute level of factor accumulation' and 'factor ratios' before technological and institutional changes begin. In short, factor accumulation in IIC theory is a pre-condition for agriculture to induce technology changes. But from the view of empirical studies, this pre-condition is very likely determined by Hayami's empirical studies of agricultural technological transition in Southeast Asian economies, such as abundant factor accumulation in Philippine agriculture and its relatively accommodating agricultural institutions: that is, a liberalised institutional framework and little government intervention. In short, models of agricultural technology change under the IIC framework are generally based on certain hypotheses relating to some key market institutions. However, if these key hypotheses are not satisfied, some specific questions arise:

1. when there is lack of a specific factor accumulation, will the technological transition circumvent this scarcity factor and turn to other possible technology choices in the given technology set? Or,
2. will the economy stagnate and wait for this specific factor to accumulate or will technology change get under way anyway? Further,
3. when this specific factor accumulation turns to be a long-term process, will the technology change correspondingly become a long-term evolution? And finally,

4. when short-term institutional factors (for example, policy changes) can influence factor flow not to be relative factor flow-based, then what will be the path of technological change in agriculture?

When we recall the research basis of Hayami's IIC theory—the empirical studies of Southeast Asian agriculture—it is easy to see that although the levels of economic development of Southeast Asian economies are below the Asian average, the economic institution and market structure in these economies are relatively accommodating. Therefore, the case of Philippines' agriculture, in theory, seems closer to a perfect market institutional framework, thereby minimising the distortion of agricultural technology changes from institutional constraint. However, when shifting the focus to technology changes in Chinese agriculture and comparing these with other East Asian economies, China's and other East Asian economies' agricultural technology change are significantly different from the Southeast Asian economies' standard IIC path. Given the premise of initial technology being determined exogenously (diffused from developed economies), differences of timing, duration and the choice of technology could not be fully explained by inter-regional differences in relative factor prices.

Therefore, East Asia's agricultural transition, with China as the representative case, is not based on relative factor price changes caused by exogenous factors under the traditional neoclassical framework. In other words, these hypotheses of critical institutional factors in neoclassical IIC theory have importance in shaping and determining East Asia's agricultural technological changes. Accordingly, this work tries to extend IIC theory to explain agricultural technological transition in China and selected East Asian economies, where some specific neoclassical hypotheses do not hold in the real economy.

1.5.1 Hypothesis 1: Duration of Technology Change versus Neoclassical Instant Market Clearance

The neoclassical paradigm assumes an instant clearance of factor mobility. This hypothesis is appropriate in dealing with problems under a demand and supply framework. But when it comes to discuss the duration—such as a long-term development—of technological and institutional transitions, it needs to be reconsidered.

Without regard to the importation of external technological innovations, technology change is, in fact, an issue of factor accumulation, requiring both absolute level of factor accumulation and factor ratios to satisfy the minimal criteria necessary to start technology change. Inherited from the neoclassical paradigm, the IIC theory also implies the critical pre-condition of adequate accumulation to induce technology change, ignoring the possibility of agricultural transition along with a continuing process of factor accumulation: factor accumulation and agricultural transition are not two independent processes, but are alternating all the time. Thus, the standard IIC model under the neoclassical framework only represents a special case of agricultural transition, in which the agriculture sector adjusts an existing level of factor accumulation (both absolute level and ratios) in accordance with the need to start technology change.

In the absence of impinging external conditions, agriculture can be viewed as an approximately closed sector. Under this condition, the source of agricultural factor accumulation is confined to the agriculture sector. Therefore, if the agriculture sector cannot provide adequate factors in the short term, both at the absolute level and in terms of relative factor ratios, to satisfy the criteria to induce new technologies, agricultural technological transition could evolve into a long-term process.

1.5.2 Hypothesis 2: Initial Value Problem of Factor Flow versus Relative Factor Price-Based Factor Flow

By relaxing the hypothesis of the absence of exogenous variables and when considering technological change influenced by external factors, the status of factor accumulation in the non-agriculture sector will be an important factor to observe agricultural technology change. Thus, with the hypothesis of the complex market institutions, research on technology change should take the inter-sectoral difference in initial value of factor accumulation into consideration. Due to the key hypothesis of instant market clearance, this inter-sectoral difference in initial level of factor accumulation is ignored. Therefore, factor flow in a neoclassical framework only comes from relative factor price changes. But in empirical studies, inter-sectoral difference in initial factor accumulation value and the resulting factor flow could possibly be a decisive reason to shape the path of technology change in one of the sectors, such as agriculture.

In IIC theoretic framework, the agricultural technology change does not involve the development in the non-agriculture sectors within the economy. In other words, a possible inter-sectoral competition for factors between agriculture and non-agriculture sectors is missing from standard IIC agricultural transition. However, in many developing economies, industrial and agricultural transitions begin almost simultaneously. Then when the agriculture sector starts technological transition without adequate factor accumulation, is it possible to release factors from agriculture to non-agriculture sector? Meanwhile, is this inter-sectoral factor flow based on difference in relative factor price? The above questions have not been explained in detail in IIC theory. But the release of factor from agriculture to non-agriculture sector has been apparent since the very beginning of China's agricultural transition.

Theoretically speaking, when we ignore inter-sectoral diffusion of externality and only consider the simplest form of factor flow, the sector with a higher level of a specific factor would release this factor to other sectors. But this factor flow is different from the standard neoclassical type, since even the sector with higher level of accumulation may still not reach the minimal criteria to trigger technology change. Thus, this factor flow stems from the inter-sectoral difference in initial level of factor accumulation, neither inflow and outflow sectors may have sufficient factor accumulation to start technology change. Especially for the outflow sector, factor may start to flow out before its factor accumulation completed.

Back to the neoclassical IIC paradigm. Agricultural labour outflow could increase the marginal output of labour in agriculture sector and therefore decrease the marginal output of land. However, when we observe the agricultural output during China's agricultural transition, both total output and per hectare output increase contiguously. Thus, given a continuous labour outflow from agriculture sector, increases in

20   J. Du

both total and per hectare output only imply that other forms of input have replaced the agricultural labour input. Put simply, labour-saving technology change occurred in Chinese agriculture.[11]

1.5.3   Hypothesis 3: Complex Market Institution versus Perfect Market Institution

In the case of China's agriculture, post-1979 marketisation changed the relationship between the agriculture and non-agriculture sectors under the former central planning system. This is not only an issue of factor redistribution; more importantly, the agriculture sector faced a greater choice of technology. However, in the discussion of China's marketisation, most of the literature ignores the market structure itself. But from 1979, every significant fluctuation in China's agricultural growth and technology changes are closely related to market structure change. This process in the neoclassical model is simplified. But when market links agriculture and non-agriculture sectors in different ways, the inter-sectoral arrangement of market structure is crucial to determine technology changes in agriculture.

First, from the view of factor mobility, the adjustment in market structure can change the price of a factor and the scale of associated factor inflows and outflows. As mentioned above, agricultural technology transition may depend on whether agriculture sector can achieve a certain level of factor intensity. Thus, the state's control over agricultural inputs may influence agricultural technology innovation. This distortion is not only a problem in neoclassical resource allocation but has the potential to further affect the dynamic technology arrangement in the agriculture, and even lead to long-term agricultural inefficiency.

Second, from the view of incentives, structural change in the agricultural market directly affects the technology set available to the agriculture sector. In developing countries, technology change in agriculture in many cases is achieved through purchasing technology-based industrial products, such as fertilisers and seeds. Thus, the agriculture sector's ability to

---

[11] Chapter 4 focuses on the regional technology change in China.

A General Theory Review   21

obtain specific agricultural inputs from industry may determine its capacity to select and induce technology change. From this perspective, there actually exists a technology market—the agricultural input market.

After analysing the above critical hypothesis in neoclassical economics, it is easy to find that East Asian economies' economic conditions differ from standard IIC requirements. When relaxing these hypotheses, discussion about East Asia's technology change in agriculture will bring us new findings of agricultural technology change under complex market institutions.

1.6   Structure of the Work

Following a theoretical review on Chinese agriculture and general agricultural growth, including its technological and institutional dimensions (Chap. 1), this work then embarks on an investigation of the role of economic institutions in determining China's agricultural technology changes from a historical perspective.

In whatever context, the shaping influence of history is profoundly important. To understand contemporary China's agricultural growth, we must look back to find the deep-rooted historical reasons and shaping forces behind these structures. Chapter 2 examines China's technical change in the pre-industrial era. The 'Great Divergence' debate and the 'Involution' model in pre-industrial agriculture will be used to support the argument that China's agricultural technology evolution was a typical case of technology choice determined by complex market institutions. Involutionary growth is an economic phenomenon shown at the end of a possible path of technical change that deviates from the standard IIC model, where factor accumulation fails to satisfy the criteria for initiating an ideal technological transition.

The analytical thrust of Chap. 3 is provided by an examination of the impact of agricultural policies on farm input and product markets under the impact of post-1979 reforms. The way in which post-1979 agricultural reform policies evolved leads us to observe that, in the short-term, the market structure determined by agricultural reform policies played the decisive role in determining the process of technology selection. For example, after 1983, when the agriculture sector was opened as a market for industrial products, such as seeds and fertilisers, to the industrial sector, there was obvious technological progress in Chinese agriculture. Chapter 3 also introduces new perspectives on the working of the 'Grain Bureau' (*liangshi bumen*, 粮食部门) in the Chinese grain circulation system. These insights throw light on the intentions of agricultural policies at the time of their formulation and implementation, as well as highlighting the shaping influence of agricultural policies on the evolution of market structures and institutions at different stages of the reform process. China's post-1979 reforms have generally been regarded as exemplars of adjustments towards a market-oriented economic system. However, on the basis of an analysis of the interaction between two major determinants of agricultural policy—the fiscal budget and food security— Chap. 3 will argue that China's post-1979 reforms are not so much examples of market-oriented reform as evidence of a state-oriented economic growth mode based on reform of the pricing system.

Chapter 4 is an exercise in empirical analysis that investigates the rate and direction of flows of agricultural labour in China in order to illustrate the decisive role played by the market structure—shaped by different regional institutional factors—during agricultural transition and in terms of technological innovation between the areas of factor inflow and outflow. Meanwhile, through an examination of the characteristics of China's inter-regional labour (factor) flows after 1979, Chap. 4 also explains how different market structures influence the inter-sectoral and inter-regional factor reallocations, given constraints such as inadequate labour accumulation. This chapter also investigates how this reallocation has affected the growth paths of the agriculture sector and the choice and adoption of different technologies and institutions in different parts of China during the economic transition. By analysing changes in paddy rice yield, total output and the corresponding level and ratio of factor inputs, Chap. 4 also uses regional output differences in order to identify the extent and direction of agricultural technological transition in different parts of China. With empirical studies within Mainland China, this chapter returns to the two main questions of this work with an emphasis on the first one to explain the market conditions under which a specific technology (labour intensive or capital intensive) will be chosen from the existing technology set.

Chapter 5 investigates technology selection and seeks to identify the existence of technical progress by analysing 'factor returns' with empirical studies on both Mainland China and Taiwan. Where there is no obvious increase in arable land and/or labour input, a stable and substantial increase in per capita output growth unambiguously demonstrates the existence of technological progress. Further, analysis of 'factor return' in relation to different factor inputs (i.e., the return to labour and land) can help us distinguish different agricultural growth paths, such as technology-based or factor intensification-based growth paths. In short, by observing different factor returns in agricultural production, Chap. 5 can demonstrate the existence of technical change in agriculture, as well as highlight the general trend of technical change. Although this approach cannot predict the choice of specific technologies from the existing technology set during agricultural technological transition, it serves to enhance further analysis of technical change and helps towards a fuller understanding of the conditions that affect agricultural transition.

Chapter 6 is a comparative study of the post-war technical and institutional agricultural transitions in China and selected Asian rice economies, especially Japan. After 1979, inter-sectoral competition for factors and resources—above all, labour—between the agricultural and industrial sectors in China increased sharply. However, during the post-1979 agricultural reforms, there was no major direct distribution of subsidies by the government to the food sector. Meanwhile, in the face of the same demands of technology diffusion, the experiences of China and some Southeast Asian economies show significant differences in terms of technology selection, localisation and the duration of green revolution initiatives. Compared with China, Japan is another good example of technology deviation during green revolution. Chapter 6 seeks to throw light on these issues by explaining the diversification in the same technology diffusion under different market structures and institutions between China and Japan.

The final chapter (Chap. 7) will retrospectively summarise the major findings of this work.

After literature review and methodology interpretation in this chapter, Chap. 2 will go back to the pre-industrial Chinese agriculture. From the features of technical changes in the pre-industrial China, Chap. 2 tries to identify the characteristics of market institutions in determining the path of old Chinese agriculture. Discussion will be carried out around a famous debate between 'involutionary growth' and the 'great divergence'.

References

Aghion, Philippe, Christopher Harris, Peter Howitt, and John Vickers. 'Competition, Imitation, and Growth with Step-by-Step Innovation.' *Review of Economic Studies* 68 (2001): 467–492.

Aghion, Philippe, Nick Bloom, Richard Blundell, Rachel Griffith, and Peter Howitt. 'Competition and Innovation: An Inverted-U Relationship.' *Quarterly Journal of Economics* 120 (2005): 701–728.

Arrow, Kenneth. 'The Economic Implications of Learning by Doing'. *The Review of Economic Studies* 29, no. 3 (1962): 155–173.

Borlaug, Norman. 'The Green Revolution Revisited and the Road Ahead.' Address to *Special 30th Anniversary Lecture*. The Norwegian Nobel Institute, Oslo, 8 September 2000.

Bray, Francesca. *Agriculture*. Part II of Vol. 6, *Biology and Biological Technology* (Vol. 41 Overall). In *Science and Civilization in China*, edited by Joseph Needham. Cambridge: Cambridge University Press, 1984.

———. *The Rice Economies: Technology and Development in Asian Societies*. New York: Oxford University Press, 1985.

———. *Technology and Gender: Fabrics of Power in Late Imperial China*. Berkeley: University of California Press, 1997.

Duara, Prasenjit. *Culture, Power, and the State: Rural North China, 1900–1942*. Stanford: Stanford University Press, 1988.

Elvin, Mark. 'The High-Level Equilibrium Trap: The Causes of the Decline of Invention in the Traditional Chinese Textile Industries.' In *Economic Organization in Chinese Society*, edited by W.E. Willmott. Stanford, CA: Stanford University Press, 1972.

———. *The Pattern of the Chinese Past*. Stanford: Stanford University Press, 1973.

———. *The Retreat of the Elephants: An Environmental History of China*. London: Yale University Press, 2004.

Fan, Shenggen. 'Effects of Technical Change and Institutional Reform on Production Growth in Chinese Agriculture.' *American Journal of Agricultural Economics* 73 (1991): 266–275.

———. 'How Fast Have China's Agricultural Production and Productivity Really Been Growing?: New Measurement and Evidence.' *International Food Policy Research Institute EPTD Discussion Papers* No. 30 (1997).

———. 'Technical Change, Technological and Allocative Efficiency in Chinese Agriculture: The Case of Rice Production in Jiangsu.' *Journal of International Development* 12, no. 1 (2000): 1–12.

Hayami, Yujiro. 'Sources of Agricultural Productivity Gap Among Selected Countries.' *American Journal of Agricultural Economics* 51 (1969): 564–575.

Hayami, Yujiro, and Masao Kikuchi. 'Inducements to Institutional Innovations in an Agrarian Community.' *Economic Development and Cultural Change* 29, no. 1 (1980): 21–36.

Hayami, Yujiro, and Vernon Ruttan. 'Agricultural Productivity Differences Among Countries.' *American Economic Review* 60 (1970a): 895–911.

———. 'Factor Prices and Technical Change in Agricultural Development: The United States and Japan, 1880–1960.' *Journal of Political Economy* 78, no. 5 (1970b): 1115–1141.

———. *Agricultural Development: An International Perspective*. Baltimore and London: Johns Hopkins University Press, 1985.

———. 'Induced Innovation Theory and Agricultural Development: A Personal Account.' In *Induced Innovation Theory and International Agricultural Development: A Reassessment*, edited by Bruce Koppel. Baltimore: The Johns Hopkins University Press, 1995.

Hedden, Peter. 'The Genes of the Green Revolution.' *Trends in Genetics* 19, no. 1 (2003): 5–9.

Huang, Philip. *The Peasant Family and Rural Development in the Yangzi Delta, 1350–1988*. Stanford, CA: Stanford University Press, 1990.

———. 'Development or Involution in Eighteenth-Century Britain and China? A Review of Kenneth Pomeranz's the Great Divergence: China, Europe, and the Making of the Modern World Economy.' *Journal of Asian Studies* 61, no. 2 (2002): 501–528.

Huang, Jikun, and Scott Rozelle. 'Technical Change: Rediscovering the Engine of Productivity Growth in China's Rural Economy.' *Journal of Development Economics* 49, no. 2 (1996): 337–369.

Krueger, Anne, Maurice Schiff, and Alberto Valdes. *The Political Economy of Agricultural Pricing Policy*. 5 Vols. Baltimore and London: Johns Hopkins University Press, 1992.

Lewis, Arthur. 'Economic Development with Unlimited Supplies of Labour.' *The Manchester School* 22, no. 2 (1954): 139–191.

Li, Bozhong. *Agricultural Development in Jiangnan, 1620–1850*. New York: St. Martin's Press, 1998.

———. *Jiangnan De Zaoqi Gongyehua* (Proto-Industrialization in the Yangzi Delta). Beijing: Social Sciences Academic Press, 2000.

Lin, Justin. 'An Economic Theory of Institutional Change: Induced and Imposed Change.' *Cato Journal* 9 (1989): 1–33.

Marx, Karl. *Capital*. Vol. 1. Trans. Ben Fowkes. New York: Knopf Doubleday, 1867 [1977].

North, Douglass, and Robert Thomas. 'The Rise and Fall of the Manorial System: A Theoretical Model.' *The Journal of Economic History* 31, no. 4 (1971): 777–803.

———. *The Rise of the Western World: A New Economic History*. New York: Cambridge University Press, 1973.

Pomeranz, Kenneth. *The Great Divergence: Europe, China, and the Making of the Modern World Economy*. The Princeton Economic History of the Western World. Princeton: Princeton University Press, 2000.

———. 'Beyond the East-West Binary: Resituating Development Paths in the Eighteenth-Century World.' *Journal of Asian Studies* 61, no. 2 (2002): 539–590.

Ricardo, David. *Principles of Political Economy and Taxation*. New York: Cosimo Classics, 1817 [2006].

Samuelson, Paul. 'International Trade and the Equalisation of Factor Prices.' *The Economic Journal* 58 (1948): 163–184.

Schultz, Theodore. *Transforming Traditional Agriculture*. New Haven: Yale University Press, 1964.

Smith, Adam. *The Wealth of Nations*. New York: Random House, 1776 [1994].

Walker, R. Kenneth. *Food Grain Procurement and Consumption in China*. New York: Cambridge University Press, 1984.

Walker, R. Kenneth. 'Trends in Crop Production, 1978–86.' *China Quarterly* 116 (1988): 592–563.

Zhongguo Tongji Nianjian (China Statistics Yearbook). National Bureau of Statistics of China. Beijing: China Statistics Press, 1981–2013 Editions.

2

Economic Thinking on Chinese Agriculture

2.1 Involution and Agricultural Intensification

In Chap. 1, we have briefly reviewed previous research on economic transition and transitional agriculture. Therefore, in this chapter we will move this theoretical review further to an application to agricultural growth with a focus on factors in China's agricultural development in the long run.

Various reasons attribute to the Chinese economic and agricultural growth, such as newly developed techniques, improvement in institutions, and so on. Obviously, the factors discussed in previous literature are important to China's economic and agricultural growth after 1979, but none of them was unique to China.

The contemporary China is the continuation of the old China. Although it is now triggering dramatic economic growth, whereas those deep-rooted reasons that influenced Chinese economy in the history is still functioning. Therefore, except for those factors discussed in detail in Chap. 1, there must be some deep-rooted reasons that support Chinese style economic and agricultural growth.

© The Author(s) 2018   **27**
J. Du, *Agricultural Transition in China*, Palgrave Studies in Economic History,
https://doi.org/10.1007/978-3-319-76905-9_2

28 J. Du

The key to understand Chinese style economic and agricultural growth lies in the findings of its major shaping force from the history. And this chapter will take the discussion back to China in the history through a famous debate on the 'great divergence'. The basic area selected for observation is Kiangnan (*jiangnan*, 江南) area.

2.2 The Great Divergence Debate

2.2.1 Definition of Kiangnan

'Kiangnan' literally means 'South of the River'. This region traditionally encompasses Jiangsu (江苏), Anhui (安徽), Zhejiang (浙江) and Jiangxi (江西) on the south bank of the Yangtze River (*yangzi jiang*, 扬子江).[1] The Kiangnan in the 'great divergence' discussion mainly refers the narrowly defined geographic area, that is composed by current southern Jiangsu (*sunan*, 苏南), northern Zhejiang (*zhebei*, 浙北) and Shanghai Municipality (上海)—the major area of the south bank of the lower Yangtze River. This region is also regarded as the core area of the Yangtze Delta (*changjiang sanjiao zhou*, 长江三角洲), or called Small Yangtze Delta. Nowadays, Small Yangtze Delta in agriculture mainly refers to the paddy rice planting zone, which consists of Suzhou (苏州), Songjiang (淞江), Taicang (太仓), Wuxi (无锡) and Jiangyin (江阴).

2.2.2 Kiangnan in Economic History

Kiangnan is a special socio-economic zone in the economic history. In the late imperial period, this area was the most developed and urbanised region in China. Consequently, many subjects in China's economic history were based on research of the Kiangnan area and many important findings of China's pre-industrial social and economic structure were built

---

[1] Yangtze River is also known as the Long River (*changjiang*, 长江). In its narrow meanings, Yangtze River only refer to the lower stretch of the river near Yangzhou (扬州).

on research in this region. For example, China's 'sprouts of capitalism' is mainly carried out on Kiangnan's regional economy.

According to Li (1998), there was only little change in arable land in Kiangnan area from the sixteenth century to the nineteenth century. The 1580–1583 government statistics, in Ming dynasty (1368–1644), showed that the approximate area of cultivated land in Kiangnan was 4.5 million Chinese mu (*mu*, 亩),[2] and this figure was only two per cent smaller than that in 1820 (Li 1998, pp. 26–27). That is, the total area of cultivated land could be regarded as near constant. Meanwhile, statistics of population in this area showed that total population increased from 20 million in 1620–1690 to 36 million in 1850 (Li 1998, pp. 19–20).

2.2.3 Kiangnan in the Great Divergence Debate

Kiangnan included most prosperous cities in the coastal China and its economic capacity remained world standard in pre-industrial era. Consequently, it became an important observation region in comparison studies.

Based on the character of decreasing land–labour ratio in this area, Li (1998, 2000), Huang (1990, 2002) and Pomeranz (2000, 2002) all made their arguments largely or even fully based on the Kiangnan area. A series of controversial discussion around 'Involution Theory' and 'great divergence' has become hot topics in the 1990s and 2000s. The major bifurcation could be stated as: if the economic growth indeed happened in pre-industrial Kiangnan.

Kiangnan had all similar economic features as England, with a highly developed agriculture sector, a free trading market, and emerging industry (i.e., the textile industry). All these features are comparable with those of England during the same period. However, divergence happened from the nineteenth century, where Kiangnan stagnated but England went to industrialisation. The ten years debate on great divergence shows the importance of Kiangnan in world economic history.

---

[2] Mu, short for Chinese mu, is a unit of area to describe a size of land used in China. One mu is equal to one-fifteenth of a hectare or one-sixth of an acre.

The reason why this chapter chose Kiangnan as the observation object is because the agricultural development history in Kiangnan provides a full version of rice production technology development. In China, the rice production technology was developed in Tang dynasty (618–907), but it was not well introduced to most Kiangnan areas during Tang. The modern Kiangnan agriculture mode was developed in late Song dynasty (960–1279) with the feature of double cropping combined with water field rice and winter crop. This specific agricultural technique requires massive labour inputs, and until late Song, Kiangnan did not have such a sufficient labour resource. Thus, the double cropping pattern had being developed over at least five centuries in this area until late Qing (1636–1912). But because of resource constraints of water and labour, a water field plough system had not been established in north China, which limited observation within the Kiangnan area.

Due to those above properties of Kiangnan and its agriculture development in the period of sixteenth to eighteenth century, it is very easy to establish a connection between our focus and the arguments in history of economic theories. Some reason has been shown by Huang (1990, 2002) and Pomeranz (2002), based on the economic similarities between England and Kiangnan. This chapter focuses on key factors in China's economic growth from a historical view and will argue that the pattern of Chinese agricultural growth resulted from the institutional and technical constraints. Further, this chapter will try to explain the importance of market institutions in pushing technology upgrading and per capita output growth. In addition, this chapter will introduce the evolution of economic theory in the way that indicates how economic growth was understood at different stages in the history of economic theory. And by doing this, it will be easy to find the roots of different theories on agricultural growth, including the involution theory and the great divergence, in economic thoughts.

2.2.4   Debate Between Divergence and Involution

In past two decades, pre-industrial Chinese economic history was dominated by the discussions around the economic development in late imperial Kiangnan comparing with England. The debate of 'Involution' against 'great divergence' was made between Phillip Huang (1990, 2002) and Kenneth Pomeranz (2000, 2002). The great divergence debate, except for Huang and Pomeranz, also involves other social scientists such as Myers (1991), Brenner and Isett (2002), Li (1998) as well as other Huang and Pomeranz's followers. The major disagreements in the debate are carried around concepts of 'rural living standard', 'agricultural productivity' and 'agricultural growth'. And basically, all these come from a major disagreement over the causality between 'sustained agricultural growth' and its shaping forces.

It is widely agreed that population growth from late Song dynasty (early thirteenth Century) to Qing dynasty has greatly reduced the land–labour ratio in China. This trend did not change during the entire pre-industrial era, as the agriculture sector did not have apparent evidence of increase in average farm size like British style 'agricultural revolution' in the eighteenth century. According to the fact that Chinese agriculture had achieved significant growth in output to keep pace with population boom throughout this period of time, Huang (1990), in his book *'The Peasant Family and Rural Development in the Yangtze Delta, 1350–1988'*, introduced the 'involutionary growth' initially to the study of China's agriculture history. The concept of 'involution' was however initially used by Geertz (1963), where involution was used to describe a society with increasing labour intensification.[3] But as a result of ambiguous definition of 'involution' and to further understand inner logic of debates between Huang and Pomeranz, all use of involution theory in this work only refers to the book of Huang (1990).

Against Pomeranz, Huang first argued that it was because the geographical constraints determined the maximum area of arable land in the Yangtze delta after long-term expansion, especially during Ming and Qing dynasties. Second, because of the increasing labour-land ratio in Yangtze delta, the growth of labour caused average arable area per labour to decrease continuously. Therefore, in general, the empirical phenomenon described in involution theory was correct[4]: for over five centuries, all newly added

---

[3] Geertz (1963) uses this term to illustrate an 'involution' society caused by external factors. In Huang's book (1990) reasons of involutionary society are endogenous.

[4] But the phenomena only.

labour was absorbed within the agriculture sector in Yangtze Delta, especially the small Yangtze Delta (Huang 2002; Brenner and Isett 2002).

Although Huang agreed the agricultural growth was taking place in the pre-industrial China, he argued that this growth was locked in a pattern: 'involution'. Involutionary growth only indicates a simple expansion in output, which implies a more intensified application of labour using unchanged basic planting technologies and a pattern of declining labour productivity in agricultural production. In addition, Huang's argument refers to the continuous declining marginal output on labour, which may lead to the decline in output per person—although total output increases.

Pomeranz also agreed that China did not follow a sustained economic growth path from late Qing, but he profoundly disagrees with Huang's involution theory when applying China's pre-industrial economic growth in Qing dynasty. Pomeranz compared Kiangnan with England and found the living standard and labour productivity were comparable between the east and west, and in his thoughts the low marginal output in Huang's argument was a common phenomenon in pre-industrial world; not unique in China. The rise of the western world largely benefited from its natural resources, which was a contingent, however accidental, factor. Pomeranz also pointed out that Huang did not pay much attention to the nature of farming between the east and west, to distinguish labour intensive or land intensive agriculture, which was also important.

In Pomeranz's book '*The Great Divergence*' (2000), economy in the sixteenth century's west Europe from the 'old' (pre-industrial) world was largely arising from accidental benefits, such as the location of coal mines. Because of these non-systematic factors, an industrial sector emerged from the body of the agriculture sector and pre-industrial commercials in the West, especially England. Because of the rise of industrial sector, the labour flowed out of agriculture sector due to high labour demand in the industrial sector, and this further enabled the economy of west Europe to grow along a resource-intensive and labour-saving path. Pomeranz also argued that although Chinese living standards and productivity levels in eighteenth century were comparable to European countries (especially England),[5] due to a different trajectory of resource re-allocation and other factors, the

---

[5] Actually, if we accept some economic estimations (e.g., Maddison 1998 [2007]), Chinese living standards were much better than in most Europe areas until nineteenth century.

divergence in economic growth still happened. However, in Pomeranz's thoughts, industrial technology change in England and in the British agricultural revolution were accidental events and the rise of the west was nothing about institutional divergence between the east and west.

Another important historian concerned with the 'involution' and 'divergence' debate is Bozhong Li. Li provides a solid economic history research on Kiangnan, which offers comprehensive and persuasive empirical evidence to the debate. Li's work (1998) on Kiangnan's pre-industrial economy makes accessing critics in the debate possible. And later in this chapter, we will move Li's findings in pre-industrial China to contemporary Chinese agriculture from economic thoughts.

If we go back to early issues in economic history theory, it is easily to find that the great divergence and the involution arguments all refer to the problem of the origin of capitalism. The debate is mainly carried surrounding 'living standard', 'productivity' and 'sustainable economic development'. However, what is the standard to evaluate 'living standard'? Was the rural labour productivity improved and in what way? And how could we define the development?

Therefore, because most criticism is relevant to above questions, it is more than necessary to clearly understand these concepts before reaching a conclusion. In the following part, Sect. 2.3 will take both sides' arguments into an economic framework to find the fundamental bifurcation in the 'involution' and 'great divergence' debate and make a counter debate to the involutionary growth from neoclassical economics.

2.3 Pattern of Chinese Agricultural Growth: Divergence or Involution

2.3.1 Involution Theory: A Classical Approach

After a brief review of Huang and Pomeranz's research on pre-industrial Chinese agriculture, we simply find both their views were clearly expressed in the way of classical economics, especially, that Huang's involutionary growth theory was a typical growth pattern in classical economics framework.

In classical economics, especially Adam Smith, specialisations were regarded as the source of productivity growth. Two consequences of specialisation were usually mentioned in classical works: first, physical capital stock per capita increases; and second, output per capita increases. Huang's argument was from the point of specialisation in classical economics, but if specialisation did not take place, how could growth be defined?

Huang's explanation was also a response to the high-level equilibrium trap theory (Elvin 1972; Chao 1986). High-level equilibrium trap theory argues that if specialisation and early industrialisation did not happen, labour would be cheap and labour-saving technology would not be introduced, then, without new technology and faster capital accumulation, capital stock per capita could not grow rapidly. Though there is slight difference between Elvin (1972, 1973) and Chao (1986), basically, they both shared the same thought, that the low labour cost is the cause of the trap. Huang's theory presents a race between capital accumulation and population growth. If capital accumulation is faster than population growth, then capital stock per capita increases, otherwise it decreases. Classical economists and historians paid special attention on agriculture because (a) it is the largest sector in the pre-industrial world and (b) the main capital good in the agriculture sector is land and, basically, cannot be accumulated by normal means.[6] Huang then concluded that, although agriculture in pre-industrial China had sufficient output growth compared with population increase,[7] there emerged no better-off economy because of a continuously decreasing marginal output per labour and an absolute decreasing trend in capital stock per capita (i.e., land) in the long run—involutionary growth occurred.

In views from recent literatures (e.g., Arrighi 2007), China in the pre-industrial era had possessed a similar initial condition as western countries, for example, a comparable income level or an even higher labour efficiency in the agriculture sector. Huang, Pomeranz and Arrighi view of China in the following phase did not go to the same development path as

---

[6] This is also known as a Malthusian trap.

[7] As it supported population growth during the whole Qing period.

taken in the European Industrial Revolution. Or in other words, China took an alternative route of growth which could not be fully explained by classical economic theories. As the pre-industrial Chinese economy lacked a characteristic feature of classical economic growth—namely, the specialisation—thus, it seemed reasonable for Huang and others to propose a new concept of 'involution' to explain the particularities of pre-industrial development in China.

Logically Huang and Pomeranz agreed with classical economic analysis based on specialisation, but they used a slight different methodology to reach a different growth path represented by Chinese agriculture. Thus, it is necessary to use a classical economics framework to trace the reason leading to this labour intensification growth path. Theoretically, classical economists believed the main factor powering output growth was specialisation and it was this specialisation since the seventeenth century that brought Europe from the pre-industrial into the industrial era. In Huang and some other classical economists' framework, such as Marx (1867), commercialisation was the reason leading to specialisation. The well-known Marxism causality, which was also taken by the great divergence debate, was that commercialisation encouraged selling-oriented production. This kind of selling-oriented production was different from medieval self-sufficient production, and this trend in long-term became the origin of specialisation in a Marxism view. However, classical economists did not clarify the concept of specialisation. They used this concept to describe specific labour application and labour working with specific physical assets.[8] And as observed by classical economists this process always came with a significant increase in physical capital per labour.

Like the view of classical economics, Huang argued that in a pre-industrial economy when commercialisation did not induce specialisation or no specialisation was observed in production, capital would cease to accumulate whilst labour was still increasing. The increased labour would stay within traditional sectors and caused physical capital per labour to decrease. Because of decreasing capital stock per labour, the output per capita would also decrease. In the case of China, it was agriculture.

---

[8] Assets that only designed for certain purpose, which is different from land and other simple tools.

2.3.2 Classical Theory

However, classical economic theory has two properties different from modern economics, and both these differences had impacted the theory of economic history deeply.

First, classical economists do not use the concept of marginal change. Therefore, most common tools in classical economics are in the form of 'average', such as average income, average profit, and so on. The direct result of this framework can also be seen from the analysis on specialisation in classical economists' works. Since Adam Smith, the concept of 'specialisation' was used to explain the intensification process to both labour and physical capital, and the increase in physical capital per labour was recognised as the process of 'specialisation' as mentioned above. Although classical economics noticed that in early stage of the industrialisation the output growth was highly related to the capital accumulation, however, classics had no constraint to either the capital labour ratio or the absolute figure of physical capital per labour—in its framework the relation between different types of factors are ignored, as only after the term of marginal change was introduced can we then compare the output of different factor; therefore the ratio of different factors.

The second concept classical economics does not have is the division of long-term and short-term economic changes. In neoclassical economics, most focuses are on short-term and in this case all inputs and products prices can be regarded as constant—one implication of this assumption is that technology can be seen as fixed in the short-term. But in classical economics as the analytical tool of time-division is absent, the tendencies of short-term economic changes (in logical) and (historical) real trends in the long-term are mixed. The best example given by classical economics is that many classical economists acknowledged the downward trend of profit rate on the scale of economic unit, but most of them also regard this as the weakening of profitability.

The above two special points of classical economics make classical economists view specialisation in their own way. Classical economists have observed two separate facts: one is that specialisation, as the beginning of industrialisation, has enhanced capital accumulation, and the improved capital accumulation level can be measured by both capital stock per labour and the scale of economic unit measures. Therefore, to follow classical economics, it is easily to conclude that the dramatic capital accumulation was an automatic result from specialisation. Another is, statistically, the trend of average profit of economic unit is declining on its scale. This view has been specially emphasised and developed by Marx, and partly succeeded from Ricardo. In another word, 'specialisation', as a tool of logic in classical economic thinking, had an underlying meaning that capital accumulation was a self-generated and self-consolidating process when certain initial conditions were met. In addition, the only working factor in classical framework was the physical capital—as Marx emphasised *'capital produces capital'* and the *'surplus-value'*.[9] Marxism historical materialism has great impacts in economic history theory, and it has been the theoretical foundation of involution and divergence theory.

In a broader sense, the core concept regarding capital–labour ratio in neoclassical economics can be expressed as follows. Resources including labour and capital are combined at a balanced level (which keeps both getting maximum marginal output) to form economic units, and this economic unit with such ratio can be duplicated in the whole economy. Here there are two implications from neoclassical economics to question involution theory—first, the capital labour ratio can be self-adjusted to a certain level, and second, this certain (or say optimal) level will spread out the whole economy in the long run. However, these two points were missing in classical economics.

Huang and Pomeranz both agreed to the classical type physical capital accumulation. As a direct consequence of the classical sole-capital-based growth assumption applied in their frameworks, both Huang and Pomeranz considered that capital accumulation in quantity was the critical condition to economic growth. In the case of Chinese agriculture, the degree of land distribution was selected as the indicator of capital accumulation to evaluate agriculture growth. Holding this point, Huang and Pomeranz made the crucial critic to neoclassical and

---

[9] This increment or excess over the original value called 'surplus-value"—from Karl Marx's Capital (1867 [1977]).

institutional economics—because Chinese agriculture[10] never developed into a capital-intensive method of development; then the neoclassical growth pattern could not be applied to explain Chinese agriculture, nor could the traditional classical growth pattern.

To respond to Huang and Pomeranz's viewpoints, it will be necessary to review the basic assumptions in neoclassical framework, and further compare the neoclassical assumptions with the classical assumptions used.

In the neoclassical framework, factors—typically labour and physical capital—cannot be combined freely, they must follow certain constraints which were initially called decreasing marginal returns. Back to simplified pre-conditions of neoclassical Solow–Swan model (Solow 1956; Swan 1956), capital and labour are only marginally substitutive. Considering an existing initial capital–labour ratio in a production, if one unit of labour was withdrawn, more than one unit of capital will be required to maintain the output level, and vice versa.[11] That is to say, although increase in output arises from more inputs applied, marginal output will be continuously decreasing on each additional unit of input. This pre-condition is essential in neoclassical framework, as it ensures a certain (optimal) capital–labour ratio could be captured in economic growth.

The nature of the neoclassical decreasing marginal return assumption presents the ability of output per capita limited by certain technical constraints. The increase in capital and labour within one economic unit is no longer a simple input gather-together to duplicate output quantity, but instead, it implies an improved technology applied in production whilst the marginal output of factors has also changed. Based on the neoclassical notion, the increase in labour or capital aggregation is a result of technical change: the technology change enables one or more factors to achieve higher marginal returns, thus such factors will be continuously put into production until marginal return reaches the equalised level as others. This notion in neoclassical theory is also an important change from classical assumptions. It declares that economic growth is a technology-driven progress, and the increased per capita capital stock resulted from improved

---

[10] And most of the world.
[11] Also see, Inada conditions (Inada 1963).

capital-intensive technology. Based on this, a crucial inference in neoclassical economics can be drawn—labour-intensive production shows no difference from capital-intensive production, if factors can obtain equal returns over the long-term.

Therefore, it needs to be careful to apply the classical economics theory into pre-industrial China. In the involution theory, not only the use of technology changes was missing, but also the conditions on which technology changes would happen. The involution theory lacks a set of theories to explain the mechanism of technology changes in growth. With the absence of technology change, those critics from classical assumptions could no longer hold when decreasing marginal returns were introduced into system.

2.3.3 From Classical to Neo-Classical: A Counter Debate to Involution Theory

In the above section, we have explained that the involution theory was originally from classical economics, and from this section we will attempt to discuss if it is necessary to use a different growth model beside main stream neoclassical theories on growth or if the 'particularities' in involution theory supports its distinguished status compared with neoclassical economics.

From the view of a neoclassical framework, a key point discussed in the great divergence debate, alternative to efficiency, is the capital labour ratio in neoclassical framework. We will start the analysis on this point from the neoclassical growth framework without technology change.

In the neoclassical framework before late 1980s, technology was isolated as an independent determinant to economic growth in the system, although technological change was still exogenous and considered as an accidental change from outside system. Besides, neoclassical growth model also assumed a changeable rate in labour and mainly argues savings through rational behaviours will make the capital accumulated at a matching rate in accordance with the fertility rate. In this version of neoclassical theory, capital accumulation in the long-term will grow at a matching rate as labour and shows a convergence trend in the economy.

Oppositely, Huang regarded pre-industrial China as a society without rapid technology change; technology was almost fixed regardless exogenous or endogenous in the long run. In addition to the absence of technology, capital accumulation—in the sense of capital stock per capita—was stopped in pre-industrial China as there was no added arable land after five centuries of exploration. Another important implication from Huang was the irrationality in peasant's behaviours, shown as the positive fertility rate given limited arable land scale. According to Huang, it was because Chinese agriculture has many particularities different from neoclassical economic assumptions, that involution theory reasonably came up. However, can we answer these particularities support involution? Hardly.

Empirically, in Huang and Pomeranz's theory, it was essential to view no capital accumulation in pre-industrial China as land was regarded as fixed assets with constant value. However, if we specify the nature of 'capital' in the context of agriculture in Kiangnan, especially in paddy rice planting areas, we will find this conventional viewpoint did not hold. Cropping system of water-field rice and wheat was introduced slowly in Kiangnan, and it was not fully taken in Kiangnan area until early nineteenth century. The reason why this process took so long was—if not all—largely because of the nature of double copping rice production, which required extra irrigation system besides a good control over soil quality and other field works. In this case, water-field planting would need the extra labour or labour efforts devoted into production. Take the irrigation system for example. The irrigation pipes under farmland in pre-industrial age are usually made of glutinous rice (*nuo mi*, 糯米), and such an irrigation system needs to be maintained quite frequently, and almost all villages regard this system as valuable agriculture assets. One curial question here is should we consider this improvement as capital appreciation, when labour was used to improve irrigation or land quality? If the answer is yes, then we say involution theory improperly defined land limitation as the only constraint to physical capital formation. As long as irrigation, soil quality and other factors improve, physical capital in rice production increased, although only slightly.

Regarding the issue of fertility rate, straight evidence from Li (1998) showed the birth rate in Kiangnan area is significantly lower than that in England and other Europe areas, except recovery age after wars or other natural disasters. That implies in fact China's fertility rate had done a corresponding change when facing physical capital constraints, which is an opposing argument to Huang's. According to Becker (1960, 1981) and Becker and Tomes (1976), the fertility rate was indeed a result of individual economic decision based on family utility maximisation. As the consequence of Becker's argument, together with Li's evidence, it seems rational that peasants in pre-industrial Kiangnan tried to keep the capital labour ratio by controlling their birth rates.

In Huang's 1990 book, he used the concept of 'marginal output' in his analysis. Originating from neoclassical economics, the 'marginal output' of labour was used as a measurement to evaluate the economic development in society. To further understand Huang's argument, it will be necessary to study the nature of decreasing marginal output in the neoclassical framework.

First, in a neoclassical framework, capital–labour ratio is not always at balanced level—defined as all factors' marginal output equal—in any economy, shortage of one (or two) factor may cause the economy biased from a balanced scale. Although a neoclassical approach assumes that economy can drive itself back to the balanced level through capital accumulation, it may take generations to achieve. The standard approach in neoclassical growth theory assumes that the economy will automatically search for and lock into the best capital accumulation rate, so does the growth rate of labour force.[12] A large portion of critiques on involution theory within historians (e.g., Pomeranz 2002; Wong 1997) is from the this approach: if economy has its self-adjustment function, then Chinese agriculture should also have the ability to seek its 'optimal' growth path,[13] or alternatively the economy had reached the balanced scale already but this capital–labour ratio was far from other economies. In other words, involution theory suggested that in pre-industrial China labour increased too fast to be related to capital accumulation. However, there is currently no supporting empirical evidence for this hypothesis. Oppositely, Li's argument is that the living standard in Kiangnan area did not suffer from an obvious downward trend.

---

[12] Known as golden rule in the Solow–Swan growth model (Solow 1956; Swan 1956).
[13] Which at least can allow factors to get the same price among all sectors.

Second, the neoclassical growth framework is a single-sector-based model, but in the real economy multiple sectors should be taken into consideration. According to Li (1998, 2000), the proportion of urban population in Kiangnan was at least ten per cent in the eighteenth century, and if we add the non-agriculture sector in rural areas (e.g., textile industry) to above figure, the scale of the non-agriculture sector must be larger than ten per cent. Thus, the development of the non-agriculture sector may cause resources flow in or out from agriculture sector and therefore affects the output margin in agriculture. Resource flow between sectors implied capital or labour was seeking a better level of capital–labour ratio to achieve higher output margin. Since Huang's theory was based on free factors markets in pre-industrial China, it would be difficult to say that capital or labour stayed within the sector with significant lower output margins.

Bearing the neoclassical decreasing marginal output assumption in mind, the standard Solow–Swan model implies labour and capital are two changing variables in time series while both factors can flow freely between sectors in the economy. However, in Huang's supporting description, he mentioned in some rural areas, return to female/child labour as well as part of male labour was less than their living cost or even far from maintenance. If so, why did these labours still stay in the rural sector? If this phenomenon was true, it only indicated that a low level of output per labour was common in pre-industrial Chinese agriculture sector, possibly with an extremely low-level labour price. In consistency with neoclassical assumptions concerning labour input and factor price equalisation, if the urban labour can get a better price, then a stagnant capital accumulation, growing labour supply, decreasing marginal output to labour, together with a low rural labour price must force agricultural labour to flow to non-agriculture sectors. This flow will not stop until labour price is equalised among all sectors. This was also confirmed by Huang (1990, 2002), Pomeranz (2002) and Wong (1997) that rural labour flow was with less restriction in pre-communist China. It is more logical to conclude that, in pre-industrial China both agriculture and non-agriculture sectors got the same problem of low level output per labour and the whole economy was sustained at a low level of economic return rather than only the agriculture sector. Thus, economic resources would not flow from agriculture sector to urban just because it had no chance to be better-off. At the macro level, this is known as Heckscher–Ohlin–Samuelson (HOS) theorem (Heckscher and Ohlin 1991; Samuelson 1953).[14] The factor price between sectors will be equalised as a result of factor flows. A strong argument of HOS states that, even when factor flow is forbidden by non-market reason, the factor price still will be equalised in the long-term, if there exists a free products market. In the light of factor price equalisation, we may conclude that if factor price in one sector is observed at a low level (because of less marginal products), and if there is no significant barrier to block factor flow or cross sector product selling, the same factor in other sectors must also suffers from the problem of low return. We could theoretically answer Huang's first problem: if the labour price, and marginal output, stays at a low level in one sector in the long-term, other sectors must have the same problem.

In the short-term, changes in demand and supply may determine the factor price in different markets, but in the long-term, supply and demand of factors will be decided by the optimal scale of production—in neoclassical theory this is given exogenously. So, the analysis of factor price equalisation theorem ensures factor price reflects optimal scale of production in the whole economy rather than a single sector. Based on factor price equalisation and given a relatively free capital flow between sectors in pre-industrial China. This statement holds as long as the sector is not completely closed. The argument that agriculture stagnation held back the whole economy and eventually led to involution was ignorant of the real reason: The agriculture particularities were only more representational to the underdevelopment of the whole Chinese economy in pre-industrial era. Here it is easy to compare Huang's argument on growth theory with classical and neoclassical approach: Huang argued that within the agriculture sector marginal output per labour was declining to zero or negative, like that of some classical economists (e.g., Karl Marx). However, neoclassical theory views the less marginal revenue as a problem of the

---

[14] This is also known as factor price equalisation theorem.

whole economy, otherwise the factor price equalisation mechanism would re-allocate resources from one sector to others to catch higher price. This process continues until factor price equalised.

Both agriculture and non-agriculture production were facing the same problem of lower marginal return in pre-industrial China, but this problem had not arisen from stagnation in agriculture production. Moreover, when all sectors were facing the same problem of lower return, the decreasing marginal output per labour and agriculture stagnation should indeed have no causation. This phenomenon in a pre-industrial economy was fundamentally arisen from the absence of some certain technology progress which was necessary to start industrialisation.

2.3.4 Main Stream Neoclassical Economic Theory on Growth

In the above content, we have made a comparison between involution theory—with its theoretical foundation classical economics—and neoclassical growth, correspondingly from the aspects of capital accumulation, labour stock, and capital–labour ratio in pre-industrial China. Differing from Huang, Pomeranz in the debate distinguished the west from other countries and considered the underdevelopment was in fact a common phenomenon in the rest of the world rather than only in China. But he also argued the continuous output per capita growth in economic development was largely an accidental event; it has little relation to the divergence in institutions between the east and the west. Back to the great divergence debate on growth path, we find the key point in the debate should be addressed to the definition of development, and if we translate the problem Huang and Pomeranz came across, this question should be 'what is development, how can we estimate and measure economic development?' Based on above inference of the debate logic in a classical economic framework, we will move the analysis further and mainly argue that both sides' evidence and theories in fact can be viewed and rethink under a neoclassical economics framework.

If we recall the basic neoclassical knowledge about production, we will find at the macro level, it is essential to keep labour and capital growing at a matching rate to maintain a constant output per capita, otherwise the marginal production of each additional unit of input would decline very quickly. Micro-foundation of the neoclassical assumption—the production capability—can be expressed by means of capital stock per labour. That is, under given technology constraints, the average capital per capita has its limitation, once too much capital was invested the exceed level can only produce little extra products. So, if the average capital per unit labour was lifted by external shocks, it will still go back towards the normal level automatically.

It is obvious that fundamental difference exits between neoclassical economics and involution theory.[15] Huang (2002) and Pomeranz (2002) argue that, because when average capital per unit labour grows, the final output grows, so the capital is the key to development. To the contrary, the neoclassical theory regards that the capital–labour ratio and capital stock per labour only reflect the current technology level, and if capital stock has been changed without technology support, in long-term it will move towards its original level. So, in the view of neoclassical economics, the reason leading to development is the change in technology, which in a broader sense means the way factors were combined to achieve higher level of production. Only if technical constraints are improved to adapt more capital stocks per labour will the economy experience the real economic growth. This will be the key argument in the following analysis over China's growth pattern in Chaps. 3 and 4.

Neoclassical approach considers that although given a similar pre-industrial capital accumulation level, whether and in which form innovation took place would be determined by market structure, which decides the level of technical and institutional innovation. The phenomenon of 'involution' does not conflict with the principles in economics, because it only reflects institutional constraint that blocks innovation within an economy from happening.

---

[15] Here, we consider Pomeranz's theory as an extended version of involution theory.

2.4 Market Role in Innovation

2.4.1 Specialisation as a Form of Technical Change

In previous research on Chinese agriculture, it is taken that Chinese agriculture output growth based on household small scale production form arose from intensified production with diminishing marginal output. The source of economic growth argued in the involution theory was classical economics style specialisation and the following boom in capital stock per labour, and the involution theory also claimed marketisation in pre-industrial China was relatively independent to specialisation and industrialisation (Huang 1990). However, marketisation, specialisation and industrialisation in fact interact with each other in economic growth, as the institution plays the key role in specialisation deepening process and contributes to industrialisation. The crucial difference between involution theory (also Pomeranz's argument in debate) and neoclassical economics should be addressed as what causes output per capita increase. This answer, however, is also the reason leading to these two different growth patterns.

First, we view specialisation as the division of cooperative labour in narrowly circumscribed jobs, aimed to enhance the efficiency of all factor inputs including labour itself. This improvement of a detailed division of labour is tightly related to an enhanced level of output and of the complexity of industrialisation processes. However, if we start from a simple question that specialisation could increase output but without extras inputs, it must imply specialisation could increase the marginal output of at least one input factor whilst the capital–labour ratio remains unchanged. When recalling the neoclassical production assumptions, output has still experienced increase even though both capital and labour inputs are fixed, it is easy to conclude that the only possible way to sustain this output increase should be the production technology change. Even without any change in physical conditions, such as tools and machines, technical improvement can take place in production by the effect of learning-by-doing (Arrow 1962). The nature of a learning-by-doing effect states labour can accumulate more human capital focusing on a narrow area of knowledge or skill through specialisation, and this accumulation in labour efficiency should be regarded as a type of technical change. If we extend this case further and know human capital is increased in fact, the physical capital could also be being enhanced to match the growing human capital level. Therefore, one of the results of such technical changes is the enlarged capacity to each economic unit, which means the optimal scale of each economic unit has been increased to accommodate more human and other physical capitals.

The logic of involution theory arguments differs. As specialisation could be regarded as a special form of technical change, it is necessary for us to return to the basic question why output per capita grows. Recall the neoclassical theory, in its assumption the parameter of technology is set as homogenous linear, which means technical progress can increase the optimal scale of economic units, and thus output margins could be increased. There are also critiques on the neoclassical model, among which the most famous is the Solow residual.[16] But neoclassical Solow model clearly shows in the long-term the source of economic growth—if we define growth as the improvement in quality, not only quantity—must be technical progress rather than capital accumulation in quantities.

Undoubtedly, technical change has an important role in agriculture, since the Green Revolution has proven both agricultural efficiency and output was largely promoted by technologies. We should consider it is the technical progress that powers the output per capita change in agriculture production, rather than capital accumulation explained in Huang and Pomeranz's theories of Chinese agriculture growth path. Also, empirical evidence (e.g., Li 1998, 2000) supports that even in pre-industrial China, the Chinese agriculture output growth was in fact powered by technical improvement (i.e., the rice and water-field technique in Kiangnan), then where this technical change was derived from should be the real reason drives Chinese agriculture to its particular growth path. But involution theory and divergence argument stopped here at the arguments about land distribution and specialisation.

---

[16] Solow residual means the part of growth that cannot be explained through the Solow model, which implies externalities between factors.

2.4.2 Commercialisation as a Phase in Marketisation

The core argument Huang and Pomeranz (and their followers) made is based on one common sense, that is, in pre-industrial China[17] a market institution has been well established and it was equivalent to the market institution in the UK during the same period. Based on this notion, it was easy that Pomeranz came to the conclusion that marketisation in pre-industrial world was common,[18] and it was not the sufficient condition to economic growth (just as neoclassical view insists). However, we argue that, market consists of a set of institutions, and the concept 'market' Huang, Pomeranz and other related literatures only refers to the narrow definition of market—the exchange of products. Here we define it as 'commercialisation' at the early phase.

Basically, commercialisation is a commercial process to introduce products to the market. This process is often confused with marketisation, however commercialisation does not equal to market or the process of marketisation. Commercialisation could be found in different economies, but always follows a different commercialisation path and results. Therefore, it is necessary to distinguish commercialisation from previous confusion and consider it is only a part of market and an early phase of marketisation.

The core concept of market is the delivery of incentives. Market as an institution can match demand and supply at a cost, and in this sense, commercialisation enables the needs of suppliers and buyers, and it should be regarded as one of the key functions of market institution. However, to keep incentives to be delivered with minimum bias, other institutions are also required as part of the market, for example, protection on property rights, rule of law, etc. If we view institutions in China we may find that in pre-industrial China, commercialisation emerging basis was different from the west, especially lack of sufficient protection to large-scale capital. On one hand at the very basic level, small-scale ownership of land can usually get type of protection

---

[17] Especially Qing and Ming dynasties.

[18] As we can see in the pre-industrial world, domestic and international trade and financial system also work, especially from the fifteenth to seventeenth centuries.

from the state, but on the other hand, large-scale ownerships, especially commercial and industrial capitals are less protected. Based on the different market conditions and institutions, most attention in current literatures was paid to commercialisation, but few of them viewed market institution in China as a whole. The pre-modern Chinese economy indeed had massive blocks of market institutions and they worked very well—just as in most other pre-modern economies, but almost all these institutions were low-cost institutions not concerned with the intervention of the state—in most cases the state was absent from areas in which state power was required to maintain an efficient market institution.

In the context of involution theory, the difference between commercialisation and marketisation was absent. In the involution theory context, the logic of economics describing the commercialisation was a sufficient condition to specialisation and enlarged the employment capacity, where in Marxism this process was interpreted as the origin of capitalism. In Marxism capitalist theory, it believed that exchanges of goods will lead to a capitalist production module that was the only source of economic growth from early industrial revolution world, and in this case, Marxism considered the commercialisation process arising as the capitalist and contributing to the specialisation. Involution theory has the similar argument when it described a widely carried commercialisation process in pre-industrial Chinese agriculture. But it also believes that given the small-scale family-based paddy rice production in Kiangnan area, agricultural development in China developed a different mode from western style, even though commercialisation had already started.

2.4.3 Market as an Institution and Induced Innovation

Braudel (1979) suggested that market components are not only those commercial links for products selling, but it should be a set of complex arrangements—we may say institutions.[19] With the rise of institutional

---

[19] However, Braudel may not agree that institution is the key to understand the rise of modern economy.

economics, commercial behaviours between individuals and economic associations are only a small part of the whole 'market institution', and the degree of marketisation in an economy could not be simply measured by the commercial behaviours or the commercialisation progress.

We recall the neoclassical growth theory, and the Solow–Swan model-based early versions. Economic growth has two different phases: (a) the economic units can duplicate so that the output scale in the societies will be enlarged, and (b) output of each economic unit grows so the society's total output increases. In the Solow–Swan model, these two kinds of growth are strictly distinguished. The first type of growth is endogenous; however the second type is determined by exogenous factors. Efforts of understand the mechanism of growth in the long-term were first made by North. According to North (1981), a well-functioning market should be supported with a set of institutions—a non-distortion pricing system, laws and property rights. Such a market would lead to efficient resource allocation and provide incentives both to make investment and techno-logical change that could increase output per capital. In particular, North clarifies that pressure from economy forms the demand of new institu-tions, and in long-term these demands must be fulfilled.

The North-type institutional theory also has been adopted to explain innovation that includes both technical and institutional progress. One example of the application is Hayami and Ruttan's work (1970a, 1970b, 1985, 1995) on Southeast Asia, as the induced innovation theory. Induced innovation theory suggests that if within an economy some certain factors are in shortage, then innovation will be taken towards technologies or institutions saving those shortage factors—as Pomeranz argues, in the early stage of English industrialisation the labour-saving technology was selected. From this point of view, there are two under-lying assumptions in the induced innovation theory. First, it assumes some factors may take advantage from the producing technology used in production. Thus, if innovation is introduced, it can reduce the usage of factors in shortage, or improve supply. Second, also impor-tantly, induced innovation theory assumes that there is no institutional barrier to block innovation—so factors can flow freely. In general, empir-ical evidence-induced innovation used to support its argument is all selected in areas or countries with less regulation, for example, agriculture in the nineteenth century USA, or middle twentieth century Philippines.

Thus, the core issue discussed here should be addressed to the use of market. Two functions of market institutions are discussed in North-type innovation. They are the institutions supporting market integration and the institutions generating technical change. Most of North's work refers to the first function where an institution provides the framework to enable private contracts for economic behaviour and to protect transferring resources from one group to another from extra expropriation. The second function of institutions is to support technical progress, which directly improves the economic capacity and makes an apparent output per capita increase (Landes 1969).

In the debate between Huang and Pomeranz, the use of market was almost absent. The argument made by Myers (1991) had targeted the use of market in adopting new technologies in late nineteenth century and early twentieth century. However, there was no direct response from Huang or Pomeranz's side. Myers's argument stated, even in early twentieth century's chaos in north China, Chinese peasants could still get their income lifted from addition of marginal capital and, their labour revenue increased, which indeed was the output per capita growth at neoclassical standard.

Theoretically, as we discussed previously, the determinant of output per capita growth is the capital stock per capita (both human capital and physical capital). The technical constraint determines the optimal scale of capital stock per capita, therefore determines the output per capita level in the economy. If institutional distortion blocks the expected income from scale economy, then the adoption of new technologies could hardly be done. This point also can be noticed on a neoclassical basis.

First, as shown in the Solow model, only improvements in technologies can enlarge the optimal scale of economic units and enhance the capacity of economic units further to accommodate more capital and labour. However, Solow's model cannot forecast the direction of innovation. Induced innovation shows the possibility that where innovation is most likely to be taken place: even under external shocks when the existing capital–labour ratio had been changed, innovation activities can make the current capital–labour ratio adjust towards the optimal. This is rather a fundamental adjustment to the neoclassical Solow model in which capital–labour ratio must be fixed at a certain path. The induced innovation can also explain why economy can adapt to changed situation (e.g., relative factor price) faster than neoclassical prospect.

Then, as shown in induced innovation theory, under a market institution with institutional constraints, the adjustments made by individuals to adopt external shocks must coordinate with institutional constraints. The central issue of Huang and Pomeranz's debate is about the capital stock per labour, or production mode in Marxism. But in the context of neoclassical based institutional economics this question will be diverted to institutional deviations which Huang and Pomeranz tried to swap off from agenda.

As we previously argued, in contrast to neoclassical style marketisation, the 'marketisation' Huang and Pomeranz used to describe pre-industrial China and Chinese market is actual commercialisation. The basic problem between commercialisation and marketisation could possibly be explained by the concept of market. In the debate between Huang and Pomeranz, the definition of market was not clear and the market was simply considered as commercial behaviours or transactions. Following this simplified but untested market definition, almost all arguments assume that China had a similar market institution to those working in England in the pre-industrialisation era. However, economic behaviours are often affected by other non-economic reasons, where circulation is only a part of all economic behaviours in the market. In early phase of pre-industrial China, commercialisation only offered free trading environment on product markets, but far from enough, its protection did not cover other areas except the circulation.

Market, besides the circulation, consists of a system supporting transactions, and a complex set of institutions, including some key components as the rule of law, common law, property rights and free trading rights. In pre-industrial China, junior level commercial behaviours were common in the market. Products like grain and textile were traded through business links and some part of the agriculture products were even outward market oriented (Li 1998, p. 108). However, these commercial activities with good economic performance only work at primary market level; the goods market. The other market institution components could only have the ability to protect small scale economic unit, whilst the corresponding market to protect large-scale capital operation was always incomplete and distorted. In this incomplete market, only those capitals under perfect protection could have the opportunity to expand and grow. Therefore, the distorted market in pre-industrial China determined only small-scale economic units and their development in both output and technology were preserved, whilst technology revolution in large capital operations faded away without proper market protection. This growth pattern, when applied to Chinese agriculture, shows continuously improved planting skill and cultivation methods, accompanied by a rapid population boom in pre-industrial China. One of the Chinese agriculture features came up— the intensified small-scale household-based production.

From the institutional aspect, commercialisation only ensures small-scale producers gain the payment of products from market. But in case that commercialisation does not come with solid base of protections over property rights, no market mechanism could assure large-scale income to be protected under the same institution. Or, we could say in general, the rent-seeking cost makes it very difficult to collect rents from individual peasants in rural China, but it is easy for government to infringe large ownership and income with distorted market institution.

A typical example could be represented by the traditional Chinese court. According to Ch'u (1962), court judge in county level was often held by a county officer, who usually did not have any legal training. This county officer always relied on his secretary who charged commission. If a lawsuit was based on obvious facts, for example, unfairness could be easily found, or a solution could be easily laid out to satisfy both parties. But when the case was related to complex business or property rights arrangements, the law became weak. Generally speaking, China's pre-industrial legal system only protected small-scale peasants and capital operations; it did not have sufficient support for large industry and farms. Thus, when legal action was taken, there was a great distortion as no clear expectation to the result of institutions, and individuals could not take legal system as their aid to business activities.

2.5 Conclusion

The proposed difficulty in Chinese agriculture in a California school framework is accommodating the modest population growth, however in reality the data cannot support arguments such as Huang (1990) that Chinese agriculture production experienced decreasing output since eighteenth century.

In the economic turning point in the eighteenth century, China went on a totally different growth path compared with pre-industrial Europe, and it was generally agreed that this growth path had its particularity to exist as complementary to other growth theories, known as 'Involution Theory', 'High-Level Equilibrium Trap', or 'Needham Question' (Needham 1954, 1969). Industrial revolution or involution has arisen a debate on the growth pattern from the pre-industrial world to industrialisation with specific application to east and west comparison studies.

Involutionary growth indicates an expansion in output which is from a higher intensified labour application in production, and with the population growth, an obvious decreasing trend is shown in the output per capita. Huang regarded the involutionary growth path as a character of pre-industrial Chinese agriculture. Nonetheless, Pomeranz thought this economic divergence was highly by accident, and the decreasing marginal output was a common phenomenon to all pre-industrial economies. Europe went to a labour-saving resource-intensive path largely by accident, not a result of the institutional divergence between the east and the west.

As implied in above studies on pre-industrial economy, especially the pre-industrial Chinese economy, it was considered no better off in Chinese agriculture due to a continuously decreasing marginal output to the labour. However, when placing the pre-industrial research further into the neoclassical economic framework, we find the factor of technology was missing in involutionary growth. It is simply because the classical economics does not distinguish the technical change from the specialisation process.

Starting from the debate between Huang and Pomeranz, this chapter brings research from recent China back to the pre-industrial era—Ming and Qing dynasties, and found the major reason causing a different economic growth pattern was the market institutions in pre-industrial China, rather than previous well-taken views of divergence or involution.

And when taking historical market conditions into consideration, debates comply with each other within a neoclassical economics framework.

This chapter mainly introduces the factor of technology into the analysis on growth, specifically to the agriculture sector. Importantly, it further discusses the connection between the market and technological progress in pushing economy to grow. China in the pre-industrial era had a similar capital accumulation level as western countries, but its protection over high-level specific assets was far from sufficient. Because high-level specific assets are necessarily needed in early phase industrialisation, Chinese market institution in the pre-industrial era could only support and protect those low-level technical changes.

In China, the market structure, especially in the countryside, was incomplete and highly affected by a combination of institutional and political constraints. Although China had a similar capital accumulation level with a similarly good institution of allocative efficiency in agriculture production as the west in a pre-industrial era, China still lacked some key market institutions that were not only specific to production, but also to protect incentives for technical change and possibly other endeavours, including the standardisation, property rights, judiciary, and so on. Because of a distorted market institution in stimulating and protecting large-scale high-payoff capital investment, epoch-making technology did not happen in pre-industrial China, meanwhile only those low-level technical changes on small-scale capital operation was protected to further stage. Chinese agriculture was a typical case that survived in the distorted market elimination.

This constraint of imperfect market institutions in China led to the Chinese economy and the agriculture sector growing into an alternative way, different from industrial revolution happening in England in the pre-industrial world. This constraint was not removed until early twentieth century, but soon the communist revolution again pulled the agriculture sector into the collective growth path. After studying China's market institutions of agriculture production in the history, we hopefully will find the importance of technology change in triggering agricultural technology change and this will guide us as an important criterion in the following chapter's agricultural growth analysis after 1949, especially the post-1979 agriculture reforms in Chap. 3.

References

Arrighi, Giovanni. *Adam Smith in Beijing: Lineages of the Twenty-First Century.* London and New York: Verso, 2007.

Arrow, Kenneth. 'The Economic Implications of Learning by Doing'. *The Review of Economic Studies* 29, no. 3 (1962): 155–123.

Becker, Gary. *An Economic Analysis of Fertility. Demographic and Economic Change in Developed Countries.* Princeton: Princeton University Press, 1960.

———. 'Altruism in the Family and Selfishness in the Market Place.' *Economica* 48, no. 189 (1981): 1–15.

Becker, Gary, and Nigel Tomes. 'Part I: Labour Supply and the Family Child Endowments and the Quantity and Quality of Children.' *The Journal of Political Economy* 84, no. 4 (1976): S143–S162.

Braudel, Fernand. *Civilisation and Capitalism 15th–18th Century.* London: Fontana Press, 1979.

Brenner, Robert, and Chris Isett. 'England's Divergence from China's Yangzi Delta: Property Relations, Microeconomics, and Patterns of Development.' *Journal of Asian Studeis* 61, no. 2 (2002): 609–622.

Chao, Kang. *Man and Land in Chinese History: An Economic Analysis.* Stanford: Stanford University Press, 1986.

Ch'u, T'ung-Tsu. *Local Government in China Under the Ch'ing.* Cambridge, MA: Harvard University Press, 1962.

Elvin, Mark. 'The High-Level Equilibrium Trap: The Causes of the Decline of Invention in the Traditional Chinese Textile Industries.' In *Economic Organization in Chinese Society*, edited by W.E. Willmott. Stanford, CA: Stanford University Press, 1972.

———. *The Pattern of the Chinese Past.* Stanford: Stanford University Press, 1973.

Geertz, Clifford. *Agricultural Involution: The Process of Ecological Change in Indonesia.* Berkeley: University of California Press, 1963.

Hayami, Yujiro, and Vernon Ruttan. 'Agricultural Productivity Differences Among Countries.' *American Economic Review* 60 (1970a): 895–911.

———. 'Factor Prices and Technical Change in Agricultural Development: The United States and Japan, 1880–1960.' *Journal of Political Economy* 78, no. 5 (1970b): 1115–1141.

———. *Agricultural Development: An International Perspective.* Baltimore and London: Johns Hopkins University Press, 1985.

Heckscher, Eli, and Bertil Ohlin. *Heckscher-Ohlin Trade Theory*. Cambridge, MA: MIT Press, 1991.

Huang, Philip. *The Peasant Family and Rural Development in the Yangzi Delta, 1350–1988*. Stanford, CA: Stanford University Press, 1990.

———. 'Development or Involution in Eighteenth-Century Britain and China? A Review of Kenneth Pomeranz's the Great Divergence: China, Europe, and the Making of the Modern World Economy.' *Journal of Asian Studies* 61, no. 2 (2002): 501–528.

Inada, Ken-Ichi. 'On a Two-Sector Model of Economic Growth: Comments and a Generalization.' *The Review of Economic Studies* 30, no. 2 (1963): 119–127.

Landes, David. *The Unbound Prometheus: Technical Change and Industrial Development in Western Europe from 1750 to the Present*. Cambridge, New York: Press Syndicate of the University of Cambridge, 1969.

Li, Bozhong. *Agricultural Development in Jiangnan, 1620–1850*. New York: St. Martin's Press, 1998.

———. *Jiangnan De Zaoqi Gongyehua (Proto-Industrialization in the Yangzi Delta)*. Beijing: Social Sciences Academic Press, 2000.

Maddison, Angus. *Chinese Economic Performance in the Long Run, 960–2030 AD*. Paris: Organization for Economic Cooperation and Development, 2007.

Marx, Karl. *Capital*. 1867. Trans. Ben Fowkes. New York: Knopf Doubleday, 1977.

Myers, Ramon. 'How Did the Modern Chinese Economy Develop? A Review Article.' *The Journal of Asian Studies* 50, no. 3 (1991): 604–628.

Needham, Joseph. *Science and Civilisation in China*. Cambridge, UK: Cambridge University Press, 1954.

———. 'Science and Society in East and West.' In *The Grand Titration: Science and Society in East and West*, edited by Joseph Needham, 190–217. London: Allen & Unwin, 1969.

North, Douglass. *Structure and Change in Economic History*. London: W. W. Norton & Company, 1981.

Pomeranz, Kenneth. *The Great Divergence: Europe, China, and the Making of the Modern World Economy*. The Princeton Economic History of the Western World. Princeton: Princeton University Press, 2000.

———. 'Beyond the East-West Binary: Resituating Development Paths in the Eighteenth-Century World.' *Journal of Asian Studies* 61, no. 2 (2002): 539–590.

Ruttan, Vernon, and Yujiro Hayami. 'Induced Innovation Theory and Agricultural Development: A Personal Account.' In *Induced Innovation Theory and International Agricultural Development: A Reassessment*, edited by Bruce Koppel. Baltimore: Johns Hopkins University Press, 1995.

Samuelson, P. 'Prices of Factors and Good in General Equilibrium.' *Review of Economic Studies*, 21 (1953): 1–21.

Solow, Robert. 'A Contribution to the Theory of Economic Growth.' *The Quarterly Journal of Economics* 70, no. 1 (1956): 65–94.

Swan, T.W. 'Economic Growth and Capital Accumulation.' *The Economic Record* 32, no. 2 (1956): 334–361.

Wong, Bin. *Transformed: Historical Change and the Limits of European Experiences.* Cornell: Cornell University Press, 1997.

3

State-Led Changes: Failures and Successes

3.1 Introduction[1]

3.1.1 The Early Narrative: 'Launching Satellite' Campaign

In 1957, the Soviet Union launched the first-ever artificial satellite in the world. This ground-breaking scientific accomplishment was propagandised by the Soviet Union as a political event that demonstrated the superiority of socialism. The 'satellite' became the glory of the entire socialist camp and a symbol of 'high-grade, precision and sophisticated' (*gao jing jian*, 高精尖) techniques. In subsequent years 'satellite' became a word with iconic status. In 1958, in pursuit of 'greater, faster, better and more economical' (*duo kuai hao sheng*, 多快好省) socialism in China, Mao Zedong initiated the GLF. During the Great Leap, almost all local governments publicised unrealistically exaggerated reports of agricultural output, which became 'satellites' showing the superiority of Chinese socialist agriculture. Practices in agricultural production, such as 'wheat

---

[1] This chapter is an early version of working paper Du and King (2016).

© The Author(s) 2018   **59**
J. Du, *Agricultural Transition in China*, Palgrave Studies in Economic History,
https://doi.org/10.1007/978-3-319-76905-9_3

60   J. Du

satellites', 'rice satellites', 'corn satellites', 'tobacco satellites', etc. were collectively referred to as 'Launching Satellite' (*fang weixing*, 放卫星).[2]

On 8 June 1958, *The People's Daily* (*Renmin ribao*, 人民日报) reported that Weixing Agricultural Producer's Cooperative (*Weixing nongye hezuo she*, 卫星农业合作社) in Suiping County (遂平县), Henan Province (河南) had sent off its first 'satellite'. It claimed that the wheat yield from the cooperative's five mu had averaged 2105 jin per mu (around 15.8 tonnes per hectare).[3] Subsequently, Qian Xuesen (钱学森) published an article entitled 'How much grain yield per mu?' in the *China Youth Daily* (*Zhongguo qingnian bao*, 中国青年报),[4] in which he suggested—on the basis of his own 'scientific' calculations—the grain yield could even reach 40,000 jin per mu (around 300 tonnes per hectare).[5]

After the publicity about launching the first satellite in the *People's Daily* and other media, all local governments began to launch their own agricultural satellites. On 12 June 1958, *People's Daily* reported that the Weixing cooperative had again sent off a second 'satellite', claiming that their 2.9 mu experimental field had increased its average wheat yield to a record 3530 jin per mu; on 16 June 1958, Xinhua News Agency broadcast the fact that the Wang Mingjin (王明进) experimental wheat field in Xingguang cooperative (星光社) in Gucheng county (谷城县) of Hubei (湖北) province had increased beyond the record to 4353 jin per mu; on 23 June 1958 another cooperative in the same county called Xianfeng (先锋) had increased the yield to 4689 jin per mu; on 12 July 1958, *People's Daily* reported that the two mu experimental wheatfield in Heping cooperative (和平社) of Chengguan township (城关镇), Xiping county (西平县) in Henan Province broke the record for wheat yield with 7320 jin per mu. On 13 August 1958, Xinhua News Agency (*Xinhua she*, 新华社) reported that the early rice yield of Xijianyuan No. 1 Cooperative

---

[2] Of these, 'wheat satellites' and 'rice satellites' were the most famous.

[3] According to China Statistical Yearbook of 1989, the 1957 national average level of wheat yield was 114 jin per mu, which is equivalent to 0.86 tonnes per hectare.

[4] Qian, Xuesen. (1958, June 16). Liangshi muchan liang huiyou duoshao (How Much Grain Yield per Mu? 粮食的亩产会有多少?) *Zhongguo qingnian bao* (China Youth Daily, 中国青年报), p. 4.

[5] The wheat yield of 1958 in the USA was 27.5 bushel per acre, which is equivalent to approximate 1.85 tonnes per hectare. (United States Department of Agriculture (USDA). *National Agricultural Statistics Services*. http://www.nass.usda.gov assessed on 15 May 2013.

State-Led Changes: Failures and Successes 61

(溪建园一社) in Macheng County (麻城县) of Hubei Province had reached 36,900 jin per mu (276.75 tonnes per hectare). To celebrate these agricultural miracles, China's media released a series of propaganda films, with titles such as 'Boiling Guangxi' (*feiteng de Guangxi*, 沸腾的广西) and 'Harvest Song' (*fengshou qu*, 丰收曲).

As a result, announcement after announcement increased per mu grain yields appeared. At of the end of 'Launching Satellite' by around 25 September 1958, China's highest officially-recorded wheat yield was the 8586 jin per mu (64.4 tonnes per hectare, as shown in Fig. 3.1), achieved by Saishike (塞什克) farm in the Qaidam Basin (柴达木盆地) in Qinghai (青海). The highest officially-recorded rice yield was 130,435 jin per mu (978.26 tonnes per hectare), achieved by Hongqi (红旗) people's Commune (*renmin gongshe*, 人民公社) in Huanjiang County (环江县), Jiangxi Province.

The 1958 'Launching Satellite' agricultural initiative eventually precipitated disaster for the GLF. Exaggerated and ultimately absurd claims of increased grain production were made by Chinese local governments. Only several months after the rice yield was said to have reached a peak of 978.26 tonnes per hectare at Hongqi People's Commune in Huanjiang county in Guangxi (广西), the 'Three Years of Great Famine' (*sannian da*

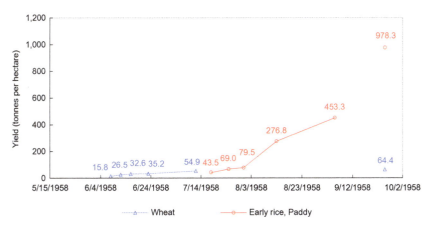

Fig. 3.1 Wheat and early rice yields announced during China's 'Launching Satellite' Campaign, June 1958–October 1958. Source: Compiled by the author with data collected from Xinhua News Agency and the People's Daily

62   J. Du

jihuang, 三年大饥荒) began.[6] This famine was to claim the largest number of fatalities in world history and was the biggest famine in the industrial era (Sen 1999).[7]

3.1.2   From Central Planning to the Market Reform

Contemporary China's agricultural transition alternates with social transformation. Therefore, different from other Asian countries, its agricultural technology transition is taken under a complex market institution. And this institution is basically formed by frequent agricultural policy changes.

After 1949, the changes in the agriculture sector that happened were dramatic: the re-organisation of China's rural society into people's communes, production brigades (*shengchan dadui*, 生产大队), and production teams (*shengcan dui*, 生产队) has fundamentally changed agricultural production form; and the land reform in early 1950s that preceded the communes helped the country to rearrange inter-sectoral welfare distribution and to transfer the agricultural producer's surplus to the industry (Ash 1976a, b, 1991; Wong 1973). Except during the period of great famine and much of GLF, these agricultural institutional changes through re-organising rural society and resultant labour mobilisation brought China increases in agricultural output. Throughout the late 1960s and the first half of the 1970s, total agricultural output increased steadily. Some scholars attributed the growth to the production form of the cooperatives (*hezuo she*, 合作社, 1955–1956) and of people's communes (1958) and the Dazhai (大寨) model of labour mobilisation (Zweig 1989), which tells a fact that pre-

---

[6] From the economic view of GLF, the deprivation of exit right of farmers from a collective in the 1959 can be viewed as a cause of the sudden declines in agricultural productivity during the commune regime, and this prolonged decline in agricultural productivity throughout China was a main factor that precipitated disaster for famine (Lin 1990).

[7] China's Great Famine is frequently claimed to have taken about 30 million lives. However, Dikotter (2010) argues that having taken four years to collect information on the number of deaths throughout China, from late 1958 to 1962 the number of deaths was around 45 million. A similar number is cited by Yang Jisheng, *Tombstone: The Untold Story of Mao's Great Famine* (墓碑: 一九五八——一九六二年中國大饑荒紀實) London: Allen Lane, 2012.

1979 agricultural performance was largely driven by intensive labour inputs mobilised by the new institutions that production decisions were made (Walker 1968; Ishikawa 1967). Another reason often used to explain China's pre-reform agricultural growth is the small-scale technical changes such as the construction of water control systems (Vermeer 1977) and the application of machinery and chemical fertiliser (Dawson 1970; Kuo 1972; Liu 1970; Stavis 1974, 1978). However, the question remains as to the important institutional changes, physical and intensive labour inputs still failed to lift China's per capita agricultural performance. Even if their contribution to agricultural growth is affirmative, these modern inputs and rural institutions have shown diminishing effects in stimulating output towards the 1970s (Perkins 1975). Between 1958 and 1978, per capita grain output was less than the bumper harvest of 1958, just before the launch of the GLF. China's agricultural output was in fact failing to keep up with the population growth. Since then, the country began spending huge sums of foreign exchange in the late 1970s on food imports paid for by the export of oil which the country could ill afford to export due to domestic energy deficits.

From 1979, China's agricultural reform began with the first stage of reform decollectivisation (*qu jitihua*, 去集体化) in the rural sector. By the mid-1980s the state had gradually phased out its mandatory procurement of non-grain farm products and replaced the state monopoly over grain purchase and marketing (*tonggou tongxiao*, 统购统销) with contractual procurement (*hetong dinggou*, 合同定购). In 1993 it started to reform the grain circulation system, which had been under tight control since the 1950s. After several attempts and reversals in 1994–1999, China's grain market eventually achieved basic liberalisation in 2003.

From central planning to the dual-track pricing system (*jiage shuangguizhi*, 价格双轨制) and then to the basic liberalisation of the grain market in 2003, China's agricultural reform has been cyclical. The intensions behind agricultural policy and the effectiveness of its implementation are particularly important when clarifying the facts and theories of contemporary China's agricultural transition. A successful policy outcome should generate sustainable, long-term per capita agricultural growth. However increased output is not in itself sufficient evidence of policy success; in other words, it is not the sole criterion by which to evaluate agriculture policy. Following sections will evaluate policies in China's agricultural reform from the relatively new perspective of the evolution of the grain circulation system, with discussion focused especially on the role of real grain prices and output in the implementation of annual agricultural policy.

Through an empirical study of the evolution of agricultural policies in the first 30 years of the reform (1979–2008), we find that running through the whole of China's agricultural reform are conversions of and alternations between two policy goals—Food Security (*liangshi anquan*, 粮食安全) and Fiscal Security (*caizheng anqua*, 财政安全)—and a pair of policy instruments—the grain bureau and the market. The state's biggest question has been whether to use the market or the grain bureau as the policy instrument to achieve food security in balance with fiscal security. China's food security includes not only the maximisation of grain output but also a rural-to-urban welfare transfer and grain monopoly interests; only the grain bureau can retain these monopoly interests and satisfy this grain-welfare transfer, not the market. However, using the grain bureau affects fiscal budget and reduces farmers' incentives, lowering the grain supply. Put simply, the Chinese government deals with grain issues in shock-response mode. When food security was threatened by the shocks of fiscal insecurity and the grain bureau's grain monopoly interest the state passively responded by strengthening the grain bureau's right to balance opposing policy goals to achieve food security. This finally resulted in the termination of the grain bureau and the exit of state from grain circulation. The effectiveness of food security and fiscal security as two mutually-restraining determination variables in agricultural policy-making was still strongly dependent on the state's choice of the grain bureau or the market as its policy instruments. The conversion of policy goals with alternating policy instruments eventually shaped complex market institutions and determined the cyclical growth pattern in China's post-1979 agricultural reform and transition.

3.2 Three Cycles in Grain Production After 1979

This section takes grain policy—especially on rice—as an example of China's agricultural policy for research. According to the changes in rice output and its real purchase price, the 30 years of reform (1979–2008) are divided into four stages.

The reasons for selecting rice policy as the research focus are that: (a) rice has been cultivated in China for thousands of years and the long-term evolution of rice-planting techniques has given Chinese farmers better knowledge of rice than of other crops, and correspondingly greater rationality in reacting to changes; and (b) rice is China's major staple food crop. Although the state has eased its control over other agricultural products, rice has always been under the highest level of state control. Thus rice-based studies can provide us with unbiased findings on China's post-1979 agricultural reform and institutional changes. Figure 3.2 plots the trends in paddy rice output and real purchasing price for the years from 1978 to 2008. It clearly highlights three complete cycles in rice output, which match exactly the changes in real rice purchase price.

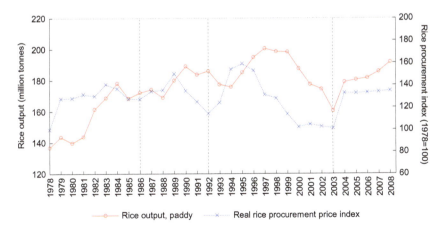

Fig. 3.2 China's rice production cycles and real purchase price change. Source: Du and King 2016

The first cycle of rice production, characterised by unprecedentedly rapid output growth, started in 1979 and ended in 1986. The second cycle lasted from 1987—the recovery from a slowdown in output—to 1992 (the eve of the 1993 grain circulation reform). The third cycle began in 1993—the year of an important grain reform initiative: its first phase, characterised by continuous rapid growth, ceased in 1998, when Prime Minister Zhu Rongji (朱镕基) announced another round of grain reform; but the cycle came to end in 2003, when the grain circulation system was deregulated further by the Prime Minister Wen Jiabao (温家宝).

From 1985 until early 1993, total rice output fluctuated, necessitating policy adjustments (a major feature of this period). From 1985, the state began to feel the fiscal pressure arising from large-scale expenditure (larger than anticipated) on several previous years of bumper rice harvests, and this gave rise to policy adjustment in 1985 whereby efforts were made to reduce the financial pressure by effectively abandoning total output maximisation. Alongside adjustment of the rice purchasing price policy, rice production fluctuated for several years until the institution of the famous '1993 Grain Reform' (*jiusan lianggai*, 93粮改).

The third production cycle is particularly important in Chinese agricultural institutional analysis. During these ten years—from 1993 to 2003—rice output reached its peak level, in 1997 (200.7 million tonnes) since 1979, only subsequently to fall into a rapid decline of 20 per cent by 2003 (160.7 million tonnes). The real rice price also showed dramatic fluctuations. From a policy perspective, this cycle is important because of three reform initiatives that took place during this period. The first was the '1993 Grain Reform', where policy measures successfully enabled rice production to reach the historic peak harvest of 1997. In the next year, Zhu Rongji instituted the '1998 Grain Reform' (*jiuba lianggai*, 98粮改), which sought to deregulate the grain system by reforming the grain bureau to reduce the large fiscal deficit. However, the impact of this initiative turned out to be negative, and, in response to a decline in the grain purchasing price (to relieve fiscal pressure), output fell. The third cycle ended in 2003, when the grain circulation system was further deregulated by Wen Jiabao government and finally opened China's grain system to the market.

Explanations of grain production cycles are usually given in terms of government regulation of grain circulation (e.g., Huang and Rozelle 1998). Another theme (e.g., Zhao and Gu 2004) is that formulation of food policy by the central government sought to fulfil multiple goals, including setting prices at levels that would reduce subsidies to the urban sector. But it proved difficult to achieve these multiple simultaneous objectives, not least because they were inherently mutually contradictory. In turn, these contradictions reflected the Chinese basic institutional framework and constraints in its agricultural transition.

The next section will review China's agricultural reform policies to trace the central government's attitude towards agricultural policy-making, with the key focus on some most important pressures that pushed it towards such policies.

3.3 Reforms on Grain Circulation System

In the mid-1950s China followed the Soviet Union in starting its own central planning system since its First Five-Year Plan (*diyi ge wunian jihua*, 第一个五年计划) in 1953. In this 25-year central planning economy strict state control over agricultural production and circulation set China's grain price far below the international level. The negative impact of the collectivisation (*jitihua*, 集体化) of grain production peaked in the Mao era.

After the death of Mao (1976) and the end of the Cultural Revolution (1966–1976), one of the most important issues faced by China's central government was how to feed the growing population and thus the food self-sufficiency. At the beginning of the reform the state used procurement pricing as the most direct and effective method of increasing grain production. In 1979 the quota price (*tong gou jia*, 统购价) and above-quota price (*chao gou jia*, 超购价) of all major grain crops were increased by 20 and 50 per cent respectively, which translated into a 50 per cent increase in the marginal revenue from grain production compared to 1978. The rapidly-increasing grain prices gave farmers' a major incentive to increase their grain production.

68   J. Du

On the other hand, to change the highly collectivised agricultural production under the central planning system, the CCP Central Committee introduced the Household Responsibility System (HRS) pilot policy in its Document No. 75 (1980) 'Circular on Several Problems in Further Strengthening and Improving the Responsibility System in Agricultural Production' (*zhonggong zhongyang guanyu jinyibu jiaqiang he wanshan nongye shengchan zerenzhi de jige wenti*, 中共中央关于进一步加强和完善农业生产责任制的几个问题).

3.3.1   Period 1: 1982–1983 and 1984–1986

The state consolidated the HRS as the major form of organisation in the agriculture sector, with further official endorsement in the CCP Central Committee's Document No. 1 in both 1983 and 1984.[8] With the grain purchase price significantly raised by the state, decentralisation strengthened early agricultural reform to produce an unbroken series of bumper harvests from 1982 to 1984 (inclusive).

The process of decollectivisation began in the agriculture sector in 1982. Successful decollectivisation combined with higher prices increased grain output by large margins, but at the cost of the emergence of a new problem for the state because of increased pressures on the fiscal capacity of the grain system and the central government brought about by rises in the amount of funds needed for the purchase of grain. Some governmental files published in 1982 and 1983 show that central government realised that the pressures on its fiscal budget reflected an over-supply of grain. It was for this reason that the shortage of food was no longer a determinant of policy for a few years after 1983.[9]

---

[8] State Council Central Document No. 1. 'Some Issues of Contemporary Rural Economic Policies' (*zhonggong zhongyang guanyu yinfa dangqian nongcun jingji zhengce de ruogan wenti de tongzhi*, 中共中央关于印发当前农村经济政策的若干问题的通知). Beijing: Communist Party of China, Central Committee, 2 January 1983; State Council Central Document No. 1. 'The Notice of CPC Central Committee about the Rural Area Work in 1984' (*guanyu 1984 nian nongcun gongzuo de tongzhi*, 中共中央关于1984年农村工作的通知). Beijing: Communist Party of China Central Committee, 1 January 1984.

[9] November 1982, the State Council Central Document 137, 'Circular on the diligent execution of all operations affecting grain' (*guowuyuan guanyu renzhen zuohao liangshi gongzuo de tongzhi*, 国务院关于认真做好粮食工作的通知). And January 1983, Central Document No. 1 [1983]. 'Some

In 1985, another significant adjustment in grain purchase pricing policy took place. The state shifted its monopoly over grain purchases to contractual purchases, with the new purchase price. This was known as the 'reverse 30:70 ratio' (*dao sanqi*, 倒三七), whereby 30 per cent of contracted grain was procured at quota price and 70 per cent at above quota price, based on the 1984 price level. Additionally, the State Council's Central Document No. 1 (1985) promised that the state would buy grain at a protected price equal to the 1984 quota price. The state's contractual grain purchasing policy foreshadowed the end of the complete state monopoly over grain purchases; however, comparing with quota and above quota prices, the new pricing method reversed the purchase price structure. In terms of contractual purchases, the state purchase price under contract increased with the 'reverse 30:70 ratio' policy. The name 'reverse 30:70 ratio' indicates that the new contractual grain purchase price consisted of 30 per cent of purchases being made at quota procurement price and 70 per cent at above-quota price (50 per cent higher than that year's quota price) based on previous year's price level. In general, the grain contractual purchase price increased to 135 per cent of the quota price in 1984. However, the extra production did not bring farmers a better income because the marginal revenue of production was reduced by the price protection policy, whereby the grain purchase price beyond contract was equal only to the quota price of 1984. With farmers' production incentives sharply weakened under the new pricing policy, output fluctuations set in, resulting in a significant post-1985 slowing in output.

While agricultural decentralisation was taking place, marketisation was beginning in the urban sector, starting with the first reforms of the state-owned enterprises (SOEs) (1983, 1984, and 1985–1986). Market-oriented reforms meant that the prices of industrial goods began to be determined by the market demand and supply, which obviously included all necessary inputs and consumables in grain system. Although state monopoly purchases had been replaced by contractual purchases, all other grain transactions were still under tight state control. Until 1986, the state

---

Issues of Contemporary Rural Economic Policies' (*zhonggong zhongyang guanyu yinfa 'dangqian nongcun jingji zhengce de ruogan wenti' de tongzhi*, 中共中央关于印发当前农村经济政策的若干问题的通知).

grain system remained in charge of grain storage, distribution and was responsible for all operational losses in annual grain circulation. This peculiarity of the Chinese grain system dictated that the cost of marketisation in the state-owned grain system should be borne by the central government.[10] With high inflation during 1988–1993, the running costs of the food circulation system increased sharply. When the fiscal burden became unacceptable to the state, it was eventually transferred to agriculture by depressing the contractual purchase price. As shown in the real purchase price index plotted in Fig. 3.2, the real purchase price of rice in 1986 decreased by 9.0 per cent compared with 1983, while the corresponding figure for wheat was 11.85 per cent. In this case, urban marketisation side by side with the increase in the grain bureau's running costs exacerbated the tension between agricultural reform and grain production.

Although policies depressed grain production, 1983 was a significant year, since it marked the first time that the CCP allowed individual farmers to engage in private trading of excess agricultural produce in local or cross-regional markets after the introduction of 'unified purchasing of agricultural products by the state' (*tong pai gou*, 统派购).[11] Although this policy was a response to the existence of excess supply of grain,[12] the 1983 Document No. 1 was the first document to legally sanction the free circulation of major grain crops (but

---

[10] The grain system, essentially the grain bureau, was an administrative department of government in charge of grain work. It may be regarded as part of the service sector located in urban areas. As a government, the cost of urban grain circulation activity was determined by the market, while the other, rural, part was still under state control. In respect to non-profitable grain transactions with increased running costs during marketisation, the final cost of the grain bureau's work was paid for from the government's fiscal budget. So, the expense to the grain bureau of marketisation was carried by the government.

[11] The CCP issued Central Committee 'Document No. 1' on 2 January 1983, entitled 'some problems of the current rural economic policy'. Article 7 of Document No. 1 indicated that excess agricultural produce after 'unified purchasing of agricultural products by the state' could be disposed of through multi-channel marketing. Such produce included all grains but excluded cotton.

[12] From 1979 to 1983, due to a favourable state monopoly purchasing price for major grain types, grain production in China had years' harvest in the first four years of the 1979 reform. However, with years' harvest, the state felt grain shortage was relieved, and considering the financial pressure brought by monopolising all grain output in rural China the state in 1983 first changed the state monopoly over grain purchasing to unified state purchasing with a contractual grain purchase policy. The harvest and central financial pressure promoted the policy allowing excess farms products to be directly traded on the market.

not cotton) without any intervention from the grain bureau. In the 1985 agricultural reform, selling grain on the market was further endorsed in State Council Document No. 1 (1985),[13] in which the 'market price' was highlighted as an important indicator to guide grain work and an important signal to grain producers.

Agricultural reforms during 1984 and 1985 successfully lowered the grain purchase price and thereby relieved some of the budgetary pressure on the government associated with the bumper harvests of those years. Provincial data show that in 1985 the contractual purchase price of corn (*yumi*, 玉米) decreased by 4.4 per cent compared with state quota in 1984. The change in purchase pricing policies seriously affected individual farmers' incentives and led to the post-1985 slowdown in output growth. The grain system reform precipitated by fiscal pressures shows the significance of the fiscal budget as a determinant of China's agricultural policies. The central government's policies and actions in lowering grain prices were at the expense of grain output when output became a less important consideration than other factors. Figures show that the change in prices in 1984 led to something like a five per cent fall in state grain purchases in 1985, and fluctuations in 1986 and 1987.

The output maximisation imperative had driven China's food policy since the 1950s, and this was the first time that central rural policies reflected a deliberate choice not to maximise grain production—this being the main reason why output subsequently, until 1989, experienced a comparatively extended contraction.

3.3.2 Period 2: 1987–1989 and 1990–1992

In the late 1980s a dual-track pricing system was introduced in the industrial sector. With the market-oriented pricing system established in industry (agricultural input supplier) alongside the prevailing high inflation,

---

[13] State Council Central Document No. 1. 'Ten Policies of the Chinese Communist Central Committee and the State Council for Further Enlivening the Rural Economy' (*zhonggong zhongyang guowuyuan guanyu jinyibu huoyue nongcun jingji de shi xiang zhengce*, 中共中央国务院关于进一步活跃农村经济的十项政策). Beijing: Communist Party of China Central Committee, 1 January 1985.

72   J. Du

Table 3.1 Rural social labour force in China, 1985–1990 (million persons; per cent)

	Farming, forestry, animal			Industry[a]			Construction		
Year		Annual change	Growth rate (%)		Annual change	Growth rate (%)		Annual change	Growth rate (%)
1985	303.5	–	–	27.4	–	–	11.3	–	–
1986	304.7	1.2	0.4	31.4	4.0	14.5	13.1	1.8	15.8
1987	308.7	4.0	1.3	33.0	1.6	5.0	14.3	1.2	9.4
1988	314.6	5.9	1.9	34.1	1.2	3.5	15.3	0.9	6.6
1989	324.4	9.8	3.1	32.6	−1.6	−4.6	15.0	−0.2	−1.6
1990	333.4	9.0	2.8	32.3	−0.3	−0.8	15.2	0.2	1.4

Notes: [a]Industrial Labour force includes workers in factories at or below village level. Source: National Bureau of Statistics of China, Zhongguo Tongji Nianjian (China Statistical Yearbook). Beijing: Zhongguo tongji chubanshe. 1981–2009 Editions

the real grain price was now even more seriously affected. The real rice purchase price, as shown in Fig. 3.1, in 1989 was almost at the same level as in 1980. The continuous slow, at times negative, growth in grain output forced central government to lift its contractual purchasing price in 1987 and 1989 to stimulate farmers' incentives to produce. In 1987, a new policy, known as the 'three links' policy (*san guagou*, 三挂钩), was generated, with the state for the first time linking important agricultural inputs and grain purchase deposits to grain production. This policy was further endorsed in the State Council Document No. 1 (1988)—circular of the state council on improving grain contractual purchase via the "three links" (*guanyu wanshan liangshi hetong dinggou 'san guagou' zhengce de tongzhi*, 国务院关于完善粮食合同定购'三挂钩'政策的通知), in which the contractual grain purchase was linked to the provision of chemical fertilisers, diesel oil and the deposit paid for grain purchase to the farmer.[14] Meanwhile, post-1989 economic depression associated with urban sector contraction deterred rural labour from leaving agriculture and forced 'rural migrant labourers' (*nongmin gong*, 农民工) to leave industry and

---

[14] The 'three links' policy is easily understood: contractual grain purchase was directly linked to three issues, namely the provision of chemical fertilisers at fixed prices, the provision of diesel oil at fixed prices and the deposit paid for the state contractual grain purchase. The chemical fertiliser and diesel oil that was to be offered to farmers at fixed prices was specially supplied to the rural department at less than market price. To link grain production with important inputs at better prices was a major incentive that encouraged farmers to increase production.

return to agricultural production. As shown in Table 3.1, in 1989 the rural labour force working in industry and its subsequent construction sector contracted by 4.61 per cent and 1.55 per cent, respectively. The 1989 economic depression in the urban sector caused rural labour to flow back into agricultural production for the first time since 1979.

Thanks to output-enhancing policies and with labour flowing back to rural areas, grain production recovered from the post-1985 slowdown. From 1987 to 1989 the government effectively stimulated agricultural production, and in 1989 grain production reached its highest level since 1949.

As mentioned above, the 1984 bumper grain harvest led policymakers to believe that China was no longer in danger of suffering from grain shortages on the scale that could cause widespread famine. Hence the shift in central government policy became towards support for industrialisation. From 1985, however, grain output stagnated for four years, once more highlighting a contradiction between grain demand and supply. With a grain shortage looming, the market price of grain increased greatly, although the state's contractual purchase price hardly changed. This widening gap had two effects: first, it enabled the grain bureau to profit from grain circulation work; second, it dampened farmers' incentive to sell grain to the government. As the state's contractual price always stayed below the market price, farmers were no longer willing to sign grain contracts with the state. This was the background against which, in 1990, the state abolished contractual purchases and again established annual fixed quotas of grain by enacting a new grain policy by 'state procurement' (*guojia dinggou*, 国家定购). This order made it clear that quota sale of grain to the state was once more an unavoidable obligation for farmers. Unlike contractual purchase, the state procurement forced farmers to sell to the government stipulated amounts of grain at a fixed price below the market level. This policy change from contractual purchase to state procurement was a retrograde step back towards the former system whereby the state had monopoly control of grain purchasing. However, since farmers were still lawfully permitted to trade their excess grain, the new policy effectively established a formal dual-track grain pricing system in rural China.

The combined effect of the state purchase and the lower grain purchase price together was to lower the real grain purchase price.[15] And due to the high inflation of the late 1980s and early 1990s, the real rice purchase price in 1990 dropped by around 16 per cent from the peak level in 1989 and declined by a further seven per cent in 1991. This rapid fall in the real price of rice quickly resulted in output contraction: from 1990 to 1993 rice output fell from 189 million to 178 million tonnes and to 176 million tonnes in 1994. But thanks to the downturn in the economy, labour flowed back to the countryside and, despite the decline in production, total output still compared favourably with that of most of the post-1979 period. The economic depression and prevailing inflationary pressures partly offset the negative impact of the grain policy change. In short, during this period Chinese farmers continued to generate grain harvests that were historically still very high.

Years of bumper harvest relieved the state from fears of grain shortages. However, at the beginning of the 1990s the fiscal deficit once more emerged as a serious problem. According to Liu et al. (2004), during 1986–1991 the state distributed 136.3 billion yuan in subsidies to the urban sector, mainly in grain, cotton and oil. By the end of 1991, the year's grain circulation work had generated a 54.5 billion yuan state deficit, of which 48.6 billion yuan stemmed directly from grain purchases in 1991.[16] Facing this emerging large fiscal deficit in the grain sector, from 1990 to 1992 various price adjustments were made to relieve the pressure caused by the deficit: first through the establishment of dual-track pricing in the grain system (1990); and later, when the state increased the grain rationing price (*tongxiao jia*, 统销价) in the urban sector (1991). However, when these measures had no significant effect on the deficit, in 1992 the state finally put into place a new guideline for grain: namely, the notion of 'purchase and sales at the same price' (*gouxiao tongjia*, 购销同价).

The establishment of the rural dual-track pricing system and 'purchase and sale of grain at the same price' were mandatory policies designed to relieve the central government of pressures arising from the rapidly

---

[15] Excludes the current year's consumer price index (CPI) value.

[16] Liu, Bin, Zhaogang Zhang, and Gong Huo. *Zhongguo Sannong Wenti Baogao* (China Farming Countryside and Peasantry Issues Report). Beijing: China Development Publishing Ltd, 2004, Chap. 8.

expanding grain deficit in the grain bureau and the high level of urban subsidies. In a significant policy change, the central government's abrogation of the price difference between a high grain selling price and low purchase price marked a critically important political and economic shift in the 1990s. In addition to its reform of grain circulation, for the first time the state showed its readiness to reform the urban subsidy system through the decision to replace direct subsidies with allowance to urban citizens[17]; also, for the first time since 1979, in the face of the financial problems it faced, the state signalled its intention to relinquish its control rights over grain. In effect, the state now embraced the simultaneous possibility of cutting urban subsidies and introducing market forces into the grain system to lighten its fiscal burden. The 1992–1998 grain reform was indeed the first comprehensive reform of China's grain system. Under financial pressure, the state abandoned the previous direct financial support it had given to industry and the urban sector.

From the late 1980s the application of the dual-track pricing system speeded up the process of marketisation in the industrial sector and helped accelerate China's overall economic transition. But as marketisation expanded, the state was no longer able to control the grain bureau's running costs as had been possible under central planning. Indeed, the running costs (administrative costs) too were subject to marketisation. In addition to increasing the grain bureau's administrative costs, the high inflation rate in the early 1990s also raised the commodity prices in the urban sector by a considerable margin so that the state was forced to increase its budget for food subsidies to protect urban living standards. However, official Chinese statistics show that between 1984 and 1992, the urban CPI doubled, the total state subsidies, including grain, cotton and oil, paid to the urban sector only increased by 12 per cent. Apparently, central finance was now overwhelmed. Because of high inflation and economic depression, the state faced enormous fiscal pressure as a result of its incomplete market reforms in agriculture.

---

[17] In form of financial subsidies distributed to urban citizens through their work units (*gongzuo danwei*, 工作单位).

The dual-track pricing system of 1990 gave the grain bureau more opportunities to extract rent in grain circulation from the price difference between the rationing price and the real selling price. However, compared with what happened after the 1998 Grain Reform, this rent-seeking behaviour, was still small-scale and individually-based,[18] normally in the form of misrepresenting the grain stock level after rationing or misrepresenting the grain purchasing cost. The central government attempted to control such leakages through the introduction of mandatory policies (for instance, see Central Document No. 15 (1992)),[19] but without success.

In addition to adjusting the grain sales and purchase price, the government also took important decisions to set up 'the state special grain reserve system' (*guojia zhuanxiang liangshi chubei*, 国家专项粮食储备) (1990),[20] and a 'state grain risk fund' (*guojia liangshi fengxian jijin*, 国家粮食风险基金) (1994).[21] In the urban sector, 'allowances' replaced the food subsidies, which had previously been distributed to urban workers,[22]

---

[18] Before 1998, rent-seeking by the grain bureau may be regarded as 'individual behaviour' as the rent-seeking was conducted by some individual branches of the grain bureau. Rent-seeking normally took place at the level of a local grain bureau (branch), by (for example) misrepresenting the grain stock level and purchasing cost. Compared with leakages that occurred after the 1998 grain reform, this kind of 'leaking' behaviour was on a small scale. Later, the position of the grain bureau gradually changed from a governmental organisation to a sole holder of commercial monopoly power over the grain market. Consequently, the small-scale rent-seeking by an individual 'agent' was transformed into more systemic profit-making behaviour.

[19] The State Council Document No. 15 (1992) mainly sought to raise the state grain rationing price in the urban sector. In its appendix, the State Council however made it clear that the purchasing cost attributable to the grain bureau should be the same as the state order price for farmers. Central Committee Document No. 15. 'Decisions on Increasing the State Monopoly Selling Price of Grain' (*guowuyuan guanyu tigao liangshi tongxiao jiage de jueding*, 国务院关于提高粮食统销价格的决定). Beijing: State Council, 6 March 1992.

[20] On 11 Sept. 1990, the State determined to set up the 'state special grain reserve system': i.e., to stabilise grain supplies, the state designated the creation of a special fund to purchase excess grain output over and above the fulfilment of government orders from local farmers, with a protection price built in.

[21] The grain risk fund was mainly used to pay the price difference, interest and all relevant costs arising from government action in stabilising grain supply.

[22] In article two of the State Council Document No. 15 (1992), following increases in the urban grain rationing price, the state distributed allowances to urban workers to reduce living costs. Allowances were distributed along with monthly salaries. The allowance standard for workers in state organs, enterprises (i.e., SOEs) and government institutions was five yuan per person per month.

with the real grain rationing price increased by policy for the first time since the Mao period.[23] All these signals indicated clearly that the central planning system in grain distribution was to be abolished.

To summarise: grain output growth rate during 1987–1993 was much slower than in the early 1980s. Rice output in 1984 was 27.41 per cent above the 1980 level, whereas in 1993 it was a mere 1.83 per cent above that of 1987. Apart from the sluggish grain production, marketisation in the urban sector caused the fiscal deficit problem to worsen considerably in the early 1990s. Under this fiscal pressure, the central government realised that the cost of the annual subsidy issued via the grain bureau was no longer affordable, which is why it sought to replace the covert subsidy with an open monetary allowance to urban workers. The policy initiatives were evidence of the government's efforts to escape the growing fiscal burden it faced because of the price inversion—i.e., a high grain rationing price and low procurement price.

3.3.3 Period 3: 1993–1994

From 1990, the state began to relax its regulations and rules about the grain market (and the market for some other agricultural products), especially rice. After State Council Document No. 60 (1991) ('Circular of the State Council of how to further improve the circulation of agricultural products', *guowuyuan 'guanyu jinyibu gaohuo nongchanpin liutong' de tongzhi*, 国务院关于进一步搞活农产品流通的通知),[24] the central government attempted step-by-step to abandon the dual-track pricing system in both grain purchasing and marketing. After Deng Xiaoping (邓小平) made his 'inspection tour to the south' (*nan*

---

[23] The grain rationing price firstly increased during 1988–1989, however this increase was caused by high currency inflation happened at the end of 1980s and early 1990s. The second round of grain rationing price increase happened during 1993–1995, caused by the abolishing of grain coupons (*liangpiao*, 粮票), and was regarded the first time of real grain rationing price increase in the urban sector from Mao's era.

[24] Through this directive, the state lawfully abandoned control of all major grain types. Notably, the document No. 60 cancelled the grain bureau's exclusive rights over rice purchasing, and instead, the state opened the rice purchasing market to all other economic units. For all agricultural products cited in this directive, other governmental departments and local government were forbidden to intervene, unless authorised by the state council.

xun, 南巡) at the beginning of 1992, with support and permission of the central government, Guangdong (广东) sanctioned free market purchases and sales of provincial grain in April 1992. Thereafter, the reform of agricultural product circulation rapidly spread to cover almost the whole of China: more than 98 per cent of cities and counties had opened grain markets by the end of 1993.

With Central Document No. 9 (1993) ('Circular of the State Council on speeding up reform of the grain circulation system', *guowuyuan guanyu jiakuai liangshi liutong tizhi gaige de tongzhi*, 国务院关于加快粮食流通体制改革的通知), China finally abolished the dual-track grain pricing system.[25] Very shortly afterwards, the free trading principle in the agriculture product market was given legal endorsement in the new 'Agricultural Law of the People's Republic of China',[26] published on 2 July 1993.

Meanwhile, Central Document No. 40 (1993) stated that 'Since the 1980s, per capita grain output in China has reached 400 kilograms and the long-standing food shortage in our country has been eliminated'.[27] Because the central government considered that China no longer faced a food shortage problem, the CCP took the important decision to permit non-state-owned traders to participate in grain circulation and in China's huge grain market. In 1993, the grain rationing registration system was abolished in China after more than 40 years. Thereafter, changes in grain prices were determined by market forces.

The 1993 grain reform removed most barriers in China's grain market. Private grain traders were now allowed to directly purchase grain from individual farmers. The government's role reverted to that of gatekeeper of the grain market, using only the 'grain purchase protection price' as a mechanism for intervening in the market in order to prevent destabilisation of the national grain supply (State Council Central Document No.

---

[25] The State Council's Document 'No. 9' (1993) signalled its intention to open grain pricing and marketing in the next two to three years.

[26] Please refer to the Chap. 4 'Agriculture Product Circulation' in the Agriculture Law of the People's Republic of China (1993) (*zhonghua renmin gongheguo nongye fa*, 中华人民共和国农业法).

[27] Central Committee Document No. 40. 'China Dietary Pattern Reform and Development Program in the 1990s' (*guowuyuan guanyu yinfa jiushi niandai zhongguo shiwu jiegou gaige yu fazhan gangyao de tongzhi*, 国务院关于印发九十年代中国食物结构改革与发展纲要的通知). Beijing: State Council, 27 May 1993.

12 (1993)).[28] The 1998 Grain Reform signalled that 40 years of state monopoly of grain purchases and marketing had ended, and that henceforth grain circulation would be market-oriented.

With a high inflation rate shown by a CPI of 14.7 per cent, in early 1993 a 4.7 per cent decline in grain output by caused the grain price to increase sharply. To maintain social stability, the state announced that it would bring the inflation rate back to below 10 per cent in 1994. Accordingly, the emphasis of its work shifted back to grain and was characterised by the introduction of tight grain policies.

In March 1994, in Central Document No. 32 (1994) ('Circular of the state council on the further reform of grain purchase and selling system', *guowuyuan guanyu shenhua liangshi gouxiao tizhi gaige de tongzhi*, 国务院关于深化粮食购销体制改革的通知), provincial governors were appointed by the central government to take charge of local grain circulation, including both state purchases and sales—an initiative known as the grain provincial governor's responsibility system (*liangshi shengzhang fuze zhi*, 粮食省长负责制). Under this responsibility system, provincial governors assumed full responsibility for the 'rice bag' (*mi dai zi*, 米袋子),[29] as the state sought to achieve nationwide grain supply balance by devolving the task to provincial governments. Second, State Council Central Document No. 32 (1994) also emphasised that state-owned grain enterprises must take tight control of 70–80 per cent of circulating grain (around 90 million tonnes, based on 1993 output). Third, the new grain purchase regulations again forbade firms and individuals from directly purchasing grain from farmers. State Council Central Document No. 32 (1994) was explicit in stating that only authorised state-owned grain enterprises were lawfully and exclusively permitted to purchase grain. Fourth, in the same document the state undertook to purchase farmers'

---

[28] State Council Document No. 12 (1993), 'Circular of the state council on establishing grain purchase protection price system (*guowuyuan guanyu jianli liangshi shougou baohu jiage zhidu de tongzhi*, 国务院关于建立粮食收购保护价格制度的通知)', was essentially intended to establish a state guiding protection price to prevent grain purchases from fluctuation, especially when the market purchase price was falling. The central government set the grain protection price by covering grain-producing cost with an extra small amount of profit. Local governments could set the local grain protection price at a level no lower than the central guiding protection price. Besides the principle of setting the grain protection price, Document No. 12 (1993) also published 1993 central protection prices for major grain crops.

[29] Here 'rice bag' means grain supply.

80   J. Du

excess grain at a 'negotiated price' (*xieyi jia*, 协议价), which was much higher than the state procurement price. In this way, grain at 'negotiated price' entered the grain market.

From June 1994, the state considerably increased the state grain purchases, and transferred all grain trading back to the grain bureau. In the urban sector, a grain ceiling price was again set to maintain urban and industrial stability. In effect, the 1994 Document 32 brought the dual-tracking pricing system back to the grain economy.

In 1995, the CCP declared that grain issues would assume 'special importance' in the Ninth Five Year Plan (1996–2000), introduced in 1996. The changes in grain policies that now took place all underlined the return to tight grain regulation. In 1994, the trend towards grain marketisation was halted. Normally, the state's contracted purchases had been maintained at 50 million tonnes per year, but with the 1994 State Council Central Document No. 32 state-owned grain enterprises were ordered to generate an additional 40 million tonnes (see above).[30] This additional 40 million tonnes was expected to be achieved by the grain provincial governor's responsibility system, which meant that the cost of generating the extra grain would be borne by provincial governments, even though the requisitions would be handled by the state-owned grain enterprises, consisting of the grain bureau and the grain stock department.[31] However, if local governments were unable to provide the necessary fiscal budget, they usually took out loans with the Agricultural Development Bank of China (*zhongguo nongye fazhan yinhang*, 中国农业发展银行, hereafter the ADBC) or the Agricultural Bank of China. When it eventually acknowledged the financial embarrassment of local governments, the central government gave granary provinces and economically-underdeveloped provinces 'policy-based discounted interest rate loans' (*zhengcexing tiexi daikuan*, 政策性贴息贷款) that were 100 per cent interest free. For non-granary provinces and the provinces with better economic conditions, the state offered a 50 per cent interest

---

[30] As mentioned above in the total of 90 million tonnes, 70–80 per cent grain in circulation.

[31] The 1993 grain reform, the state established the central and local grain reserves—two-layer reserve—to maintain stable grain supplies. Thus, to distinguish from the function of the grain bureau in grain circulation, state-owned grain enterprises includes both grain circulation and above two-layer reserves.

deduction. The interest-free period was from 1 October 1994 to 31 December 1999, as set out in State Council Document No. 62 (1994).[32]

Again, private firms, including unauthorised grain SOEs without entry permits, were strictly prohibited from purchasing and marketing grain. All grain traders without a permit were compelled to operate through the wholesale market or buy from officially-authorised grain enterprises. The wholesale grain markets were established under guidelines set out in State Council Document No. 46 (1990), in which local governments and grain bureaus were given monitoring powers over grain circulation. In effect, grain circulation was back to where it had been before the 1993 reform, with government control over production and sales of the major grains. Grain circulation reverted from being market-oriented to becoming once again state-oriented.

The re-establishment of the state monopoly over grain was at the expense of further deterioration in state-owned grain enterprises' financial burdens. It was unlikely that the introduction of a five-year interest-free period would resolve the large fiscal deficit, and realisation of this forced the central government to intervene. Its intervention took the form of decomposing accountancy in state-owned grain enterprises into two parts—commercial business and policy-oriented business—in an attempt to bring about more effective control of the scale of emerging fiscal deficits (State Council Document No. 12 (1995)).[33] Where commercial transactions resulted in financial losses, the grain enterprises took full responsibility. But this strategy still faced difficulties: since the state-owned grain enterprises were not economically independent of the state, it was impossible to toughen the soft budget constraints. In fact, all deficits in grain enterprises were eventually paid out of the central budget.

---

[32] State Council Document No. 62 (1994) focused on interest-free loan policy. Central Committee Document No. 62. 'Circular of the State Council on the Report of the Ministry of Finance and Other Departments on Withholding Accounts and Suspending Interests in Accordance with the Grain Policy' (*guowuyuan pizhuan caizhengbu deng bumen guanyu liangshi zhengce xing caiwu gua zhang tingxi baogao de tongzhi*, 国务院批转财政部等部门关于粮食政策性财务挂帐停息报告的通知). Beijing: State Council, 29 November 1994.

[33] State Council Document No. 12 (1995). *Guowuyuan pizhuan zhongguo renmin yinhang deng liu bumen guanyu jiaqiang liang mian you zhengce xing shougou zijin guanli yijian de tongzhi* (Circular of the State Council on the Proposal of the Chinese People's Bank and Five Other Departments on Strengthening the Management of Funds for the Purchase of Grain, Cotton and Oil within the Framework of State Policies, 国务院批转中国人民银行等六部门关于加强粮棉油政策性收购资金等理意见的通知). Beijing: State Council, 30 May 1995.

3.3.4 Period 4: 1995–1997 and 1998–2003

Because the grain policies of 1994–1995 once again increased the state purchase price, in the next three years from 1995 to 1997, grain output started to rise. Following the introduction of the 1995 grain policy, in 1996 the rice harvest was the largest since 1949 at more than 195.1 million tonnes. This figure increased by a further 2.9 per cent in 1997, with rice output reaching 200.73 million tonnes. Because of these bumper harvests, the deficit in the grain system (including grain reserve system) grew dramatically from 5 billion to 100 billion yuan between 1996 and 1998.

In State Council Document No. 15 (1998), 'Decision of the State Council on Further Reform over the Grain Circulation System' (*guowuyuan guanyu jinyibu shenhua liangshi liutong tizhi gaige de jueding*, 国务院关于进一步深化粮食流通体制改革的决定), the state clearly indicated that the grain system deficit could no longer be covered by central government because it had gone far beyond government's expectations and its financial capacity. Under fiscal pressure, Chinese government for the first time asked the grain enterprises, including those at county level, to shift to independent accounting. Accordingly, the main purpose of the 1997–1998 Grain Reform was to set up a system, which, it was hoped, would provide a permanent solution to the financial problems of the grain enterprises.

As early as 1996, central government tried to tighten grain SOEs' soft budget constraints by setting up an external grain system monitor—namely, the ADBC. Following the rules of grain fund management set up in 1996, the special funds for grain procurement purposes (*gouliang zhuankuan*, 购粮专款) must be managed under joint monitoring by ADBC and the State Ministry of Finance. In the event, however, the joint monitoring system failed to have the expected effect because of the doubling in size of the state grain system in 1997.[34] In addition to this attempt to monitor grain fund usage, in 1998 the state published State Council

---

[34] Here refers to the administrative size of the grain system.

Decree No. 249 (1998),[35] designed to further restrict grain fund operations. Having failed in its previous effort to control the deficit of grain enterprises, through this latest Directive the State Council imposed closed operation of grain funds on all grain enterprises, and, in order to further control grain fund usage, it sought to regulate grain enterprises by appointing the ADBC as the only bank authorised to deal with grain funds (i.e., all funds were to be operated under an ADBC account).

With increasing financial pressure from the grain bureau, the core thrust of the 1998 Grain Reform was to help central government escape the large deficit by reforming the entire grain bureau system. Against this background, the 1998 reform comprised a bundle of important policies.

To reduce (ideally, eliminate) the grain deficit, the state abandoned the allowances distributed via the SOEs. In Central Document No. 27 (1997) 'Circular of the state council on unlimited purchase of negotiated-price grain at protective prices' (*guowuyuan guanyu an baohujia changkai shougou yigouliang de tongzhi*, 国务院关于按保护价敞开收购议购粮的通知), the state announced a basic principle to guide the grain bureau's work, known as 'cost plus thin profit' (*baoben weili*, 保本微利). The original purpose of this guiding principle was to financially disaffiliate the grain bureau system from central finance and enable the grain bureau to assume sole responsibility for its own losses and profits. However, this principle signalled to the state-owned grain system that the urban grain-selling price should not only cover costs but be profitable. Further in the same document, for the first time the state gave local governments the right to the lower the grain protection price by up to five per cent. Soon afterwards, in State Council Document No. 15 (1998), all grain pricing rights were given to provincial level government, including decisions relating to purchase price, ceiling price and protection price.

State Council Decree No. 244 (1998) 'Regulations on Grain Purchase' (*liangshi shougou tiaoli*, 粮食收购条例) summarised the new principles of grain pricing under two basic rules: to guide grain purchase pricing through 'grain pricing based on quality' (*anzhi lunjia*, 按质论价); and to

---

[35] Decree No. 249 of the State council of the People's Republic of China. Measures on Punishing Illegal Activities in Grain Purchasing and Marketing (*liangshi gouxiao weifa xingwei chufa banfa*, 粮食购销违法行为处罚办法). Beijing: State Council, 31 July 1998.

84   J. Du

guide grain sales in urban areas through 'selling grain at a favourable price' (*liangshi shunjia xiaoshou*, 粮食顺价销售) to cover all grain purchase costs. These principles were further elaborated in State Council Document No. 35 (1998) 'Circular of the State Council on Issuing the Proposals on Promoting the Reform of the Grain Circulation System under Current Circumstances' (*guowuyuan guanyu yinfa dangqian tuijin liangshi liutong tizhi gaige yijian de tongzhi*, 国务院关于印发当前推进粮食流通体制改革意见的通知), which gave complete rights to state owned grain enterprises to set both purchasing and market selling prices.

As well as being given complete grain pricing rights, state-owned grain enterprises also gained financial independence. In 1998, the State Council in its document No. 15 separated state-owned grain purchase and reserve firms from the grain bureau, making the grain enterprises independent corporations. Since the grain system was now financially independent from central government, its deficit no longer had to be made up from the annual fiscal budget. Meanwhile, with financial independence achieved, the grain system lost the right to claim subsidies and administrative costs from the state budget. With the separation of the grain purchase and reserve firms from the grain bureau,[36] the link between the grain bureaus and the treasury was cut and the grain bureau assumed responsibility for its costs, and profits and losses.

The 1998 reform further strengthened the grain enterprises' monopoly over grain purchasing and marketing. In several State Council Decrees and Directives, central government banned individual farmers from all forms of direct purchase activities. All buyers had to trade in state authorised wholesale markets and purchase from state-owned grain enterprises. This monopoly was confirmed and strengthened step-by-step in State Council Documents No. 38 (1997) 'Circular of the General Office of the State Council on Doing the Autumn Grain purchase work well' (*guowuyuan bangong ting guanyu zuo hao qiuliang shougou*

---

[36] The largest financial drain arose from grain storage and purchases. The grain bureau claimed that grain storage loss was one of the biggest parts of the state fiscal budget. According to Liu et al. (2004), from 1992 April to 1998 May the total deficit in the grain bureau had reached 120 billion yuan. This figure indicates that from April 1992, the grain bureau system generated a monthly deficit of 2.97 billion yuan, or almost 100 million yuan per day. During this period the grain bureau had 40 thousand employees dealing with grain, so that the average per capita deficit was 23 million yuan per day.

gongzuo de tongzhi, 国务院办公厅关于做好秋粮收购工作的通知), and Documents No. 35 (1998) and compulsory Decree No. 244 in 1998. Unlike some previous decrees and directives, the 1998 reform policies were not a simple copy of the 1994 act: rather, the state began to use policy force and the courts to punish insubordinate individual traders on the market, a legal decision written into State Council Decree No. 244 and Document No. 20 (1999) 'Supplementary Circular of the State Council on Policies and Measures for Further Improving Grain Circulation System Reform' (*guowuyuan guanyu jinyibu wanshan liangshi liutong tizhi gaige zhengce cuoshi de buchong tongzhi*, 国务院关于进一步完善粮食流通体制改革政策措施的补充通知). Under this framework, in every county and town there was one state-owned authorised grain enterprise that purchased directly from farmers. The 1998 Grain Purchase Act also prescribed that state-owned grain enterprises must not operate beyond their prescribed limits and/or purchase across borders. This reform emphasised the complete monopoly status of grain SOEs and their rights. In effect, the national grain market had been administratively divided into small pieces, each with a unique small monopolist over grain work.

The 1997–1998 reform fundamentally changed basic elements of China's grain circulation system—the most important such change being related to the channel and scale of state subsidy distribution. By the terms of the 1998 Grain Purchase Act, the government ceased the transfer of direct subsidies to the urban class made available by the difference between purchase price and selling price on the market through the grain system. Instead, central government only paid national grain storage costs, direct control of which was now assumed by the China Grain Reserves Corporation, Sinograin (*zhong liang chu*, 中粮储).

The rapid reduction of the state subsidy took effect through two appended regulations. First, to guarantee urban grain supplies within an affordable price range, the state retained the right to determine the grain ceiling price, as well as giving an undertaking that the wholesale price would never exceed this ceiling. Second, the monopoly of state-owned grain purchase and storage enterprises was strengthened, since they became the only traders who could purchase local farmers' products.

The 1998 grain framework provided state-owned grain purchase and storage enterprises with strong bargaining power in purchasing operations. The 1998 Grain Reform in fact raised the power of the grain bureau system over all grain work, including giving it pricing power which had previously been held centrally. At the end of the 1998 Grain Reform, central government successfully escaped the grain system deficit. However, the effect of the 1998 reform was to change the state monopoly into a grain bureau monopoly over grain purchasing and marketing.

The four years 1996–1999 were years of bumper harvests. Against the background of abundant grain supplies, central government announced in State Council Document No. 11 (1999) 'Circular of the State Council on Policies and Measures for Further Improving Grain Circulation System Reform' (*guowuyuan guanyu jinyibu wanshan liangshi liutong tizhi gaige zhengce cuoshi de tongzhi*, 国务院关于进一步完善粮食流通体制改革政策措施的通知), and Document No. 20 (1999) 'Supplementary Circular of the State Council on Policies and Measures for Further Improving Grain Circulation System Reform' (*guowuyuan guanyu jinyibu wanshan liangshi liutong tizhi gaige zhengce cuoshi de buchong tongzhi*, 国务院关于进一步完善粮食流通体制改革政策措施的补充通知) that food supply in China had moved from historical long-term shortage to an overall balance with temporary over-supply. In addition, some grains were removed from the list of varieties to which ceiling protection prices were attached (State Council Document No. 11 (1999)). As already mentioned, the temporary excess supply of food characterised conditions in 1999, and provincial governments in non-granary areas were given the right to exit the grain protection programme in State Council Document No. 20 (1999). Thus, it released some provincial governments from the fiscal deficit since the 1998 reform.

In fact, the 1998 Grain Reform provided an opportunity for local state-owned grain enterprises (operating with the connivance of local government) to sharply reduce the grain purchase price to narrow the fiscal gap.[37] Together with a further decrease in the protection price in 1999, the average real purchase price of grain in 2000 fell to its lowest

---

[37] Local state-owned grain enterprises were the major grain agencies to participate in local grain circulation.

point since 1979. As the fall in the real rice purchase price continued, by 2003 total rice output had declined to the level of 1982 (see Fig. 3.2), and was only 80 per cent of that of 1997, meanwhile, the total wheat output also dropped to the 1984 level, which was 70 per cent of the 1997 output level. In 2003, the Chinese government faced a grain supply crisis for the first time since 1979, eventually forcing the central government, under the terms of State Council Document No. 1 (2004) 'Opinions of the Central Committee of the CCP and the State Council on Several Policies for Promoting the Increase of Farmers' Income' (*zhonggong zhongyang guowuyuan guanyu cujin nongmin zengjia shouru ruogan zhengce de yijian*, 中共中央国务院关于促进农民增加收入若干政策的意见), to fully open-up the grain buying and selling market, and re-build the state subsidy mechanism. In the following Document No. 17 (2004) 'Opinions of the State Council on Further Deepening the Reform to the Grain Distribution System' (*guowuyuan guanyu jinyibu shenhua liangshi liutong tizhi gaige de yijian*, 国务院关于进一步深化粮食流通体制改革的意见), the State Council adjusted protection prices for major crops in the main producing regions. The China Grain Reserves Corporation once again assumed full responsibility for maintaining the purchase price at above-protection level. Meanwhile, the state started to grant direct subsidies to grain-planting farmers and households via village-level local governments.

State Council Document No. 1 (2004) established a competitive grain market. Thereafter, the Decree No. 407 of the State Council (2004) 'Regulations on Administration of Grain Distribution' (*liangshi liutong guanli tiaoli*, 粮食流通管理条例) confirmed that traders under various ownership forms would have the right to participate in the grain market, and that grain prices should be decided by market supply and demand. This marked the formal abolition of the 1998 Grain Purchase Act and re-affirmed the first version of the 1993 Agricultural Law. China's grain policy in 1998 reverted to a market-oriented direction. But unlike in 1993, the final decision of central government to re-open the grain market was made when the conflict between the fiscal deficit and food security became incompatible within the state's fiscal capacity. Following several failed attempts to reform the grain bureau, the state finally chose to release its control over the food supply and opened the grain market.

The core aim of the 1998 Grain Reform was to eliminate the bad debt in the grain bureau and to encourage it by allowing additional profit from grain. To achieve this goal, the state again used its power to enable grain enterprises to monopolise the grain purchase market. Although the grain enterprises were financially separated from the grain bureau system, in administrative terms local grain enterprises continued to work under the grain bureau's guidance and monitoring. The revised approach succeeded in reforming state owned grain enterprises, but also conferred on the grain bureau system much stronger bargaining power—something that contained the potential to impede the further development of the grain market.

When grain supplies fell to the low level of 2003 (430.7 million tonnes),[38] threatening to undermine China's food security, central government had no choice but to completely abandon its control over grain. The irreconcilable conflict—between the grain bureau's bad debts and the dictates of grain production—transcended the state's control capacity. Accordingly, the state eventually left the conflict to be resolved by the market. After 2003, the agricultural reform once more returned to the path of market-oriented.

3.4 Summary

The success of China's post-1979 agricultural reform is widely accepted in academic circles. Although the market may explain the periodic growth after the failure of centrally planning system, if it is used as the only factor to trace the long-term agricultural growth it cannot explain the output decline shown at the end of the different stages of the reform. Using the clue of real grain purchase price to chronologically trace the evolution of China's post-1979 agricultural policies, two policy goals, food self-sufficiency and fiscal constraint are observed to interact throughout the reform. Whenever grain costs and losses exceeded the state's fiscal ability, policy priority shifted towards preserving state control over grain work

---

[38] Total grain output in 2003 was 430.7 million tonnes—the lowest level since 1987 (403 million tonnes).

by depressing grain prices and limiting output. Out of these shifting and mutually-conflicting objectives emerged inconsistent agricultural policies. In short, the government faced an impossible balancing act between seeking to control the market and allowing reforms in the grain sector to follow a market-oriented path.

For the state, it was a question of whether to use the market as the major tool to orient reform or to retain tight government control over the market. The cost of enforcing state control of the grain market would rise considerably when the state kept the grain bureau in the grain market. But a return to a state monopoly in agricultural economy implied the loss of both farmers' welfare and production incentive. An ideal reform path was to provide the economy with an increasingly liberalised market environment. The implication was that the state should gradually give up its control over the market and offer *market guidance* in a new institutional framework.

As indicated at the beginning of this chapter, the main purpose is to review the failures and successes of China's agricultural policies, therefore to understand the rural market institution (including market structure and market environment) under which agricultural transition and technology change undertook.

China's agricultural reform has veered between different goals, creating the complex market institutions and a cyclical growth pattern in Chinese agriculture, with price an unbiased indicator of it all. This may explain why, when the observation period is extended to the long term, these periodic growth determinants (e.g., application of new seed varieties and chemical fertiliser) no longer explain the overall pattern of Chinese agricultural transition. Meanwhile, the state's passive response to food insecurity shows no sign of a continuous active process towards a market-oriented agricultural transition. Thus, China's agricultural transition is not a market-oriented but rather a state-oriented agricultural transition by means of a pricing system reform.

Return to the standard neoclassical theory of technology change. Technology change relies on the existence of a set of critical hypotheses as well as pre-condition in neoclassical IIC theory. But in most developing countries agricultural technology transitions are always accompanied by industrial transition and social transformation. Therefore, the hypothesis of an ideal market institution could hardly be satisfied in East Asian's agricultural transition, especially China. The market institution under which Chinese agricultural technology transition take is comparatively complex mainly resulted from the frequently-changing agricultural policies. In other word, the frequent changes of market institution formed by policy changes have intermittently activated agricultural growth and technology change.

The study of China's failures and successes in agricultural growth can facilitate our further analysis on the different features of agricultural transition among regions within China as well as the comparison between China and other East Asian economies. The next chapter will investigate China's grain output changes and technology transitions under complex market institutions after 1979.

References

Ash, Robert. 'The Peasant and the State Source.' *The China Quarterly* 127 (1991): 493–526.

———. 'Economic Aspects of Land Reform in Kiangsu, 1949–52 (Part 1).' *The China Quarterly* 66 (1976a): 261–292.

———. 'Economic Aspects of Land Reform in Kiangsu, 1949–52 (Part 2).' *The China Quarterly* 67 (1976b): 519–545.

Central Committee Document No. 9 [1993]. *Guowuyuan Guanyu Jiakuai Liangshi Liutong Tizhi Gaige De Tongzhi* (Circular of the State Council on Speeding up Reform of the Grain Circulation System, 国发[1993]9号《国务院关于加快粮食流通体制改革的通知》). Beijing: State Council, 15 February 1993.

Central Committee Document No. 11 [1999]. *Guowuyuan Guanyu Jinyibu Wanshan Liangshi Liutong Tizhi Gaige Zhengce Cuoshi De Tongzhi* (Circular of the State Council on Policies and Measures for Further Improving Grain Circulation System Reform, 国发[1999]11号《国务院关于进一步完善粮食流通体制改革政策措施的通知》). Beijing: State Council, 30 May 1999.

Central Committee Document No. 12 [1993]. *Guowuyuan Guanyu Jianli Liangshi Shougou Baohu Jiage Zhidu De Tongzhi* (Circular of the State Council on Establishing Grain Purchase Protection Price System, 国发[1993]12号《国务院关于建立粮食收购保护价格制度的通知》). Beijing: State Council, 20 February 1993.

Central Committee Document No. 12 [1995]. *Guowuyuan Pizhuan Zhongguo Renmin Yinhang Deng Liu Bumen Guanyu Jiaqiang Liang Mian You Zhengce Xing Shougou Zijin Guanli Yijian De Tongzhi* (Circular of the State Council on the Proposal of the Chinese People's Bank and Five Other Departments on Strengthening the Management of Funds for the Purchase of Grain, Cotton and Oil Within the Framework of State Policies, 国发[1995]12号《国务院批转中国人民银行等六部门关于加强粮棉油政策性收购资金管理意见的通知》). Beijing: State Council, 30 May 1995.

Central Committee Document No. 15 [1992]. *Guowuyuan Guanyu Tigao Liangshi Tongxiao Jiage De Jueding* (Decisions on Increasing the State Monopoly Selling Price of Grain, 国发[1992]15号《国务院关于提高粮食统销价格的决定》). Beijing: State Council, 6 March 1992.

Central Committee Document No. 15 [1998]. *Guowuyuan Guanyu Jinyibu Shenhua Liangshi Liutong Tizhi Gaige De Jueding* (Decision of the State Council on Further Reform over the Grain Circulation System, 国发[1998]15号《国务院关于进一步深化粮食流通体制改革的决定》). Beijing: State Council, 10 May 1998.

Central Committee Document No. 17 [2004]. *Guowuyuan Guanyu Jinyibu Shenhua Liangshi Liutong Tizhi Gaige De Yijian* (Opinions of the State Council on Further Deepening the Reform to the Grain Distribution System, 国发[2004]17号《国务院关于进一步深化粮食流通体制改革的意见》). Beijing: State Council, 23 May 2004.

Central Committee Document No. 20 [1998]. *Guowuyuan Guanyu Jinyibu Wanshan Liangshi Liutong TIzhi Gaige Zhengce Cuoshi De Buchong Tongzhi* (Supplementary Circular of the State Council on Policies and Measures for Further Improving Grain Circulation System Reform, 国发[1999]20号《国务院关于进一步完善粮食流通体制改革政策措施的补充通知》). Beijing: State Council, 11 October 1999.

Central Committee Document No. 32 [1994], *Guowuyuan Guanyu Shenhua Liangshi Gouxiao Tizhi Gaige De Tongzhi* (Circular of the State Council on the Further Reform of Grain Purchase and Selling System, 国发[1994]32号《国务院关于深化粮食购销体制改革的通知》). Beijing: State Council, 9 May 1994.

Central Committee Document No. 35 [1998]. *Guowuyuan Guanyu Yinfa Dangqian Tuijin Liangshi Liutong Tizhi Gaige Yijian De Tongzhi* (Circular of the State Council on Issuing the Proposals on Promoting the Reform of the Grain Circulation System under Current Circumstances, 国发[1998]35号《国务院关于印发当前推进粮食流通体制改革意见的通知》). Beijing: State Council, 7 November 1998.

Central Committee Document No. 40 [1993]. *Guowuyuan Guanyu Yinfa 'Jiushi Niandai Zhongguo Shiwu Jiegou Gaige Yu Fazhan Gangyao' De Tongzhi* (China Dietary Pattern Reform and Development Program in the 1990s, 国发 [1993]40号《国务院关于印发<九十年代中国食物结构改革与发展纲要>的通知》). Beijing: State Council, 27 May 1993.

Central Committee Document No. 60 [1991]. *Guowuyuan 'Guanyu Jinyibu Gaohuo Nongchanpin Liutong' De Tongzhi* (Circular of the State Council of How to Further Improve the Circulation of Agricultural Products, 国发 [1991]60号《国务院关于进一步搞活农产品流通的通知》). Beijing: State Council, 28 October 1991.

Central Committee Document No. 62 [1994]. *Guowuyuan Pizhuan Caizhengbu Deng Bumen Guanyu Liangshi Zhengce Xing Caiwu Gua Zhang Tingxi Baogao De Tongzhi* (Circular of the State Council on the Report of the Ministry of Finance and Other Departments on Withholding Accounts and Suspending Interests in Accordance with the Grain Policy, 国发[1994]62 号《国务院批转财政部等部门关于粮食政策性财务挂帐停息报告的通知》). Beijing: State Council, 29 November 1994.

Central Committee Document No. 137 [1982]. *Guowuyuan Guanyu Renzhen Zuohao Liangshi Gongzuo De Tongzhi* (Circular on the Diligent Execution of All Operations Affecting Grain, 国发[1982]137号《国务院关于认真做好粮食工作的通知》). Beijing: State Council, 28 November 1982.

Central Document No. 1 [1983]. *Zhonggong Zhongyang Guanyu Yinfa 'Dangqian Nongcun Jingji Zhengce De Ruogan Wenti' De Tongzhi* (Some Issues of Contemporary Rural Economic Policies, 中发[1983]1号《中共中央关于印发<当前农村经济政策的若干问题>的通知》). Beijing: Communist Party of China, Central Committee, 2 January 1983.

Central Document No. 1 [1984]. *Guanyu 1984 Nian Nongcun Gongzuo De Tongzhi* (The Notice of CPC Central Committee About the Rural Area Work in 1984, 中发[1984]1号《中共中央关于1984年农村工作的通知》). Beijing: Communist Party of China Central Committee, 1 January 1984.

Central Document No. 1 [1985]. *Zhonggong Zhongyang Guowuyuan 'Guanyu Jinyibu Huoyue Nongcun Jingji De Shi Xiang Zhengce* (Ten Policies of the Chinese Communist Central Committee and the State Council for Further Enlivening the Rural Economy, 中发[1985]1号《中共中央、国务院<关于进一步活跃农村经济的十项政策>》). Beijing: Communist Party of China Central Committee, 1 January 1985.

Central Document No. 1 [1988]. *Guanyu Wanshan Liangshi Hetong Dinggou 'San Guagou' Zhengce De Tongzhi* (Notice on Improving Grain Contractual Purchase via the "Three Links"', 中发[1988]1号《国务院关于完善粮食

合同定购"三挂钩"政策的通知》). Beijing: Communist Party of China Central Committee, 3 January 1988.

Central Document No. 1 [2004]. *Zhonggong Zhongyang Guowuyuan Guanyu Cujin Nongmin Zengjia Shouru Ruogan Zhengce De Yijian* (Opinions of the Central Committee of the CPC and the State Council on Several Policies for Promoting the Increase of Farmers' Income, 中发[2004]1号《中共中央国务院关于促进农民增加收入若干政策的意见》). Beijing: Communist Party of China Central Committee, 31 December 2003.

Central Document No. 75 [1980]. (Circular on Several Problems in Further Strengthening and Improving the Responsibility System in Agricultural Production, 中发[1980]75号《中共中央关于进一步加强和完善农业生产责任制的几个问题》). Beijing: Communist Party of China Central Committee, 27 September 1980.

Dawson, L. Owen. *Communist China's Agriculture: Its Development and Future Potential*. New York: Praeger, 1970.

Decree No. 244 of the State Council of the People's Republic of China. *Liangshi Shougou TIaoli* (Regulations on Grain Purchase, 中华人民共和国国务院令第244号《粮食收购条例》). Beijing: State Council, 6 June 1998.

Decree No. 249 of the State Council of the People's Republic of China. *Liangshi Gouxiao Weifa Xingwei Chufa Banfa* (Measures on Punishing Illegal Activities in Grain Purchasing and Marketing, 中华人民共和国国务院令第249号《粮食购销违法行为处罚办法》). Beijing: State Council, 31 July 1998.

Dikotter, Frank. *Mao's Great Famine: The History of China's Most Devastating Catastrophe, 1958–62*. New York: Walker & Company, 2010.

Du, Jane, and Cheng King. 'Unrevealing China's Food Security Puzzle, 1979–2008.' EAI Working Paper Series No. 167. National University of Singapore, Published in December 2016.

General Office of the State Council No. 38 [1997]. *Guowuyuan Bangong Ting Guanyu Zuo Hao Qiuliang Shougou Gongzuo De Tongzhi* (Circular of the General Office of the State Council on Doing the Autumn Grain Purchase Work Well, 国办发明电[1997]38号《国务院办公厅关于做好秋粮收购工作的通知》). Beijing: General Office of the State Council, 2 October 1997.

Huang, Jikun, and Scott Rozelle. 'Market Development and Food Demand in Rural China.' *China Economic Review* 9, no. 1 (1998): 25–45.

Ishikawa, Shigeru. 'Resource Flow Between Agriculture and Industry—The Chinese Experience.' *The Developing Economies* 5, no. 1 (1967): 3–49.

Kuo, Leslie Tse-Chiu. 1972. *The Technical Transformation of Agriculture in Communist China*. New York: Praeger Press.

Lin, J.Y. Collectivization and China's Agricultural Crisis in 1959–61. *Journal of Political Economy* 98, no. 6 (1990): 1228–1252.

Liu, Jung-Chao. *China's Fertilizer Economy*. Chicago: Aldine, 1970.

Liu, Bin, Zhaogang Zhang, and Gong Huo. *Zhongguo Sannong Wenti Baogao* (China Farming Countryside and Peasantry Issues Report). Beijing: China Development Publishing Ltd, 2004.

National Agricultural Statistics Services. United States Department of Agriculture (USDA). *National Agricultural Statistics Services*. 15 May 2013. http://www.nass.usda.gov.

National Bureau of Statistics of China. *Zhongguo Tongji Nianjian* (China Statistical Yearbook). Beijing: China Statistics Press, 1981–Present.

Perkins, Dwight H., ed. *China's Modern Economy in Historical Perspective*. Stanford: Stanford University Press, 1975.

Qian, Xuesen. 'Liangshi Muchan Liang Huiyou Duoshao' ('How Much Grain Yield per Mu?'). *Zhongguo Qingnian Bao* (China Youth Daily), 16 June 1958.

Sen, Amartya. *Development as Freedom*. Oxford: Oxford University Press, 1999.

Stavis, Benedict. *Making Green Revolution: The Politics of Agricultural Development in China*. Ithaca: Cornell University, 1974. Rural Development Committee, Monograph No. 1, 274.

———. *The Politics of Agricultural Mechanization in China*. Ithaca: Cornell University Press, 1978.

Vermeer, Eduard B. *Water Conservancy and Irrigation in China: Social, Economic and Agrotechnical Aspects*. Leiden: Leiden University Press, 1977.

Walker, Kenneth R. 'Organization for Agricultural Production.' In *Economic Trends in Communist China*, edited by Alexander Eckstein, Walter Galenson, and Ta-chung Liu. Chicago: Aldine Press, 1968.

Wong, John. *Land Reform in the People's Republic of China*. New York: Praeger, 1973.

Xinhua She (Xinhua News Agency). 'Henan Suiping Xian Weixing Nongye She Xiaomai Muchan 2105 Jin' ('Wheat Yiled from Weixing Agricultural Producer's Cooperative in Suiping County Henan Province Achieved 2,015 Jin per Mu'). *Renmin Ribao* (The People's Daily), 8 June 1958.

———. 'Macheng Jianguo Yi She Chuxian Tianxia Diyi Tian: Zaodao Muchan Sanwan Liuqian Jiubai Duo Jin' ('Macheng Jianguo No. 1 Corporative Shows the Ever Best Farm After Foundation: Early Rice Yield per Mu Reached More Than 36,900 Jin'). *Renmin Ribao* (The People's Daily), 13 August 1958.

Yang, Jisheng. *Tombstone: The Untold Story of Mao's Great Famine*. Trans. Stacy Mosher and Jian Guo. London: Allen Lane, 2012.

Zhao, Deyu, and Haiying Gu. 'Regional Differences in Direct Subsidization to Grain Producers in China and the Reasons.' *Chinese Rural Economy* 8 (2004): 58–64.

Zweig, David. *Agrarian Radicalism in China, 1968–1981*. Cambridge, MA and London: Harvard University Press, 1989.

4

Trends in China's Grain Production

4.1 Introduction

A major feature of East Asian irrigated paddy field rice planting technique is a demand of intensive factor inputs, especially labour. However most East Asian economies' agricultural transition has taken place simultaneously with overall economic take-off and industrial transition, and inter-sectoral competition for factors has made agricultural transition alternate with factor accumulation throughout the transitional era. Thus, the complete factor accumulation is difficult to satisfy the precondition of adequate factor accumulation in East Asian economies—especially China. Economic history shows that the involutionary growth pattern in East Asian rice economies (representative by China) was caused by the absence of adequate factor accumulation to support rapid agricultural technology change. But different examples from involutionary growth options of agricultural technologies in the industrial era are plentiful. Therefore, the prolonged use of a single agricultural technology was unlikely to happen in modern Chinese agriculture.

© The Author(s) 2018
J. Du, *Agricultural Transition in China*, Palgrave Studies in Economic History,
https://doi.org/10.1007/978-3-319-76905-9_4

97

From China's historical experience, induced technology change is a special case of agricultural technological transition. That is, when technology transition starts, the factor accumulation within agriculture can satisfy both critical criteria: the 'absolute level of factor accumulation' and 'factor ratio'. So, when either internal or external (non-agriculture) sectoral factor accumulation fails to provide agriculture with the minimum requirement of factor accumulation, agricultural technology transition could possibly deviate from standard IIC path.

Thus, in addition to the existing level of factor accumulation in the agriculture sector, the main factor affecting whether agriculture can obtain 'available' factors is the inter-sectoral institutional arrangement. How institutional factors promote or restrict factor re-allocation during the transitional era will determine the direction of agricultural technology change, as well as the national economic structure. When agricultural factor accumulation is inadequate throughout the economy, meanwhile institutional arrangements can affect inter-sectional and inter-regional factor flow not based on relative factor price changes, the institutional factors determining the short-term factor flow will be the most significant determinant to the agricultural technology transition. With these points in mind, when studying the technology change in China's agricultural transition, the inter-sectoral competition of factor between agricultural and industrial sector becomes the best angle from which to observe regional agricultural technology change.

Through an empirical study of inter-sectoral and inter-regional factor flow—especially that of labour—this chapter will illustrate the different features of regional agricultural technology variations in Chinese agriculture under complex market institutions and structure.

The next section (Sect. 4.2) shows trends in grain production and highlights the correlation between resource flow and grain output fluctuations. Sections 4.3, 4.4, and 4.5 look at geographical sources of regional production differences, using Northeast China and coastal area as case studies. Section 4.6 uses previous empirical studies to examine the major determinants of China's agricultural transition. Finally, there is a short conclusion in Sect. 4.7.

4.2 Trends in Grain Production in Chinese Agriculture

4.2.1 Salient Features of China's Grain Production

Compared with the reform era, it is easy to interpret China's agricultural production before 1979. Since all economic behaviour—including agricultural production—was incorporated into the CCP's policies, agricultural production under central planning shows a high correlation with major policy initiatives. For example, when the policy of communisation of agriculture failed and the economy faced chaos (political, as well as economic) during and after the 1958 GLF, there was a corresponding and very clear drop in China's agricultural production. By contrast, after 1979 tracking agricultural production is a good deal more complex.

As mentioned above, market-oriented and central planning factors coexisted in China's post-1979 agriculture sector, where, for example, the operations of the grain bureau, in effect, facilitated direct government control over monitoring the grain market.[1] Although the grain bureau's—and therefore state's—monopoly on grain purchasing and marketing ended in 1992, the state's control of the circulation of the main grain crops—especially rice and wheat—did not in fact cease. Indeed, following the less-than-successful reform initiatives of the mid-1990s (see Chap. 3), the state strengthened its control and monitoring of grain circulation, especially rice, wheat and cotton. This tight control lasted until grain shortages began to emerge in 2003 and 2004.

As a result, from the 1990s, the state began to adjust its control of grain circulation, and circulation policies for different grains started to diverge: grains were gradually allowed to respond to market forces; but rice and wheat remained under the tight control of the state. The new grain policy, which got under way in the mid-1990s, was focused on the circulation of rice and wheat: this was the state's so-called food security strategy. The new initiative was reflected in the behaviour of grain production. Because the purchasing policy only embraced specified

---

[1] The grain bureau, a remnant of the central planning economy, was the organ in charge of state control of grain purchasing and marketing. See Chap. 3 for details.

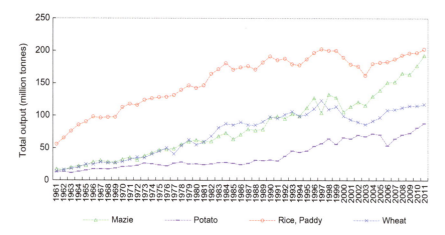

Fig. 4.1 Output of four major grain crops in China from 1961 to 2011 (unit: million tonnes). Source: FAOSTAT. *Food and Agriculture Organization of the United Nations Database*. 27 May 2013 http://faostat3.fao.org/home/index.html/

agricultural products, it was only these controlled products where output showed a strong correlation with changes in purchasing price. Market-oriented agricultural products meanwhile displayed quite different output trends. Nevertheless, as shown in Fig. 4.1, yields of all major grain crops increased greatly after 1979.

4.2.2 Resource Flow Trends and the Manifestation of Regional Divisions in Grain Production

The second challenge that China's agriculture faced, following the collapse of central planning after 1979, was the blurring of the boundary between the rural and urban sectors.

Before 1979, resources in both the rural and the urban sectors were tightly constrained by the central planning system. Labour was prevented from leaving the rural sector and entering the urban sector under the dual constraints of central planning and China's household registration system—*Hukou* (户口). However, the boom in non-state-owned enterprises in some of China's eastern coastal provinces after 1979 became a major source of labour demand and encouragement the movement of labour out of agriculture into the urban, non-agriculture sector. Until the mid-1990s, jobs for university graduates were still being allocated by Chinese government, whilst most of the labour needed by non-state-owned enterprises was filled by migrants from rural areas. In short, from 1979 the agriculture and non-agriculture sectors started to compete for labour resources.

Therefore, after 1979, Chinese agriculture faced a new challenge of rural labour out-migration—an outflow that changed the marginal product of farm labour (shown in Fig. 4.2). In fact, from the early 1960s the urban share of total population remained at about 17 per cent for nearly two decades, although from 1979 it steadily rose to reach 51 per cent in 2011. From the point of view of the flow of *labour*, we may suppose that the rural outflow rate was even higher than such figures suggest. This is because (a) those who left for the urban sector mainly comprised young and middle-aged rural labourers, leaving behind children and elderly people who did not have the same capacity for work; and (b) in southern coastal areas a large number of enterprises were set up in rural areas (i.e., Township and Village Enterprises—TVEs), the employees of which were counted as rural residents even though they were *de facto* workers in the

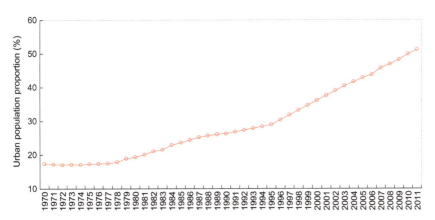

Fig. 4.2 Urban population proportion changes in China from 1970 to 2011 (unit: per cent). Source: *Zhongguo Tongji Nianjian* (China Statistical Yearbook). National Bureau of Statistics of China. Beijing: China Statistics Press, 1981–2013 editions. Note: The military personnel of Chinese People's Liberation Army is classified as urban population in the item of population by residence

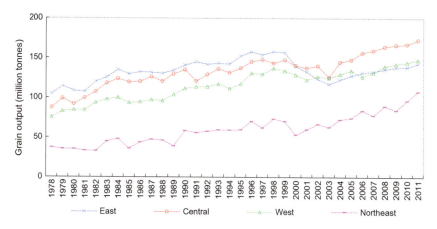

Fig. 4.3 Trend in grain production in four major areas in China from 1978 to 2011[2] (unit: million tonnes). Source: *Zhongguo Tongji Nianjian* (China Statistical Yearbook). National Bureau of Statistics of China. Beijing: China Statistics Press, 1981–2013 editions

industrial sector. For such reasons, the rate of rural labour outflow from agriculture to non-agriculture was higher than the 27 per cent increase in the urban population share suggested.

Significantly, however, despite this large-scale outflow of labour, agricultural production did not fall. On the contrary, the unit area yield of all major grain products[3] increased steadily after reform (see Fig. 4.3). Most notably of all, the rate of increase of post-1979 grain production was significantly higher than in the pre-reform era. Given the decrease in labour input, technical change seems the most likely source of sustained output growth.

But although technical change may be able to explain the output increase from 1979 at a national level, it is more difficult to cite this as the main reason for regional yield differences under the impact of a similar trend in technology change.

If we group China's provinces into four major geographical groups—namely, the Eastern (coastal), Central, Western and Northeastern

---

[2] Grain production in four major areas is calculated from annual China Statistical Yearbook.
[3] Expect potatoes.

regions[4]—we find that grain production in the Eastern region fell to a quarter of the national total output, after the failure of reform of the grain circulation system in 1997–1998 (Fig. 4.3). From 1978 to 2007, while production in Eastern China only rose by about 30 per cent, the corresponding increase in Central, Western and Northeastern regions was much higher—up to 82 per cent, 74 per cent and 107 per cent respectively.

Thus, China's most important regional structural change in its grain production was the decreasing contribution of the eastern provinces. After the failure of grain circulation reform in the 1990s, the contribution of eastern China to national output fell from one third to a quarter.

4.3 Characteristics of Regional Grain Production Difference

Overall, after 1979 total grain output showed an increasing trend. However, the rate of increase and the range of annual fluctuations varied across provinces areas (as shown in Figs. 4.4 and 4.5).

First, in addition to Beijing (北京) and Shanghai municipalities, Zhejiang and Guangdong provinces saw large declines in grain production. This was principally attributable to the substantial shrinkage of arable land in both provinces: total arable area contracted by two thirds in Zhejiang, and by half in Guangdong compared with the pre-reform era.

Second, areas along the middle and lower reaches of the Yangtze River (Jiangsu, Zhejiang, Shanghai, Anhui, Jiangxi, Hubei and Hunan 湖南 Provinces) were traditionally the major grain producing areas of China, and an important transitional region for Indica rice (*xianmi*, 籼米) and

---

[4] Geographically, we group China into Eastern, Central, Western and Northeastern regions following *China Statistical Yearbook*. The eastern region comprises Beijing, Tianjin (天津), Hebei (河北), Shanghai, Jiangsu, Zhejiang, Fujian (福建), Shandong (山东), Guangdong and Hainan; the central region includes Shanxi (山西), Anhui, Jiangxi, Henan, Hubei and Hunan; the west includes Neimenggu (*Inner Mongolia*, 内蒙古), Guangxi, Chongqing (重庆), Sichuan (四川), Yunnan (云南), Guizhou (贵州), Xizang (西藏), Shaanxi (陕西), Gansu (甘肃), Qinghai, Ningxia (宁夏) and Xinjiang (新疆); and the Northeastern region comprises Liaoning (辽宁), Jilin (吉林) and Heilongjiang (黑龙江).

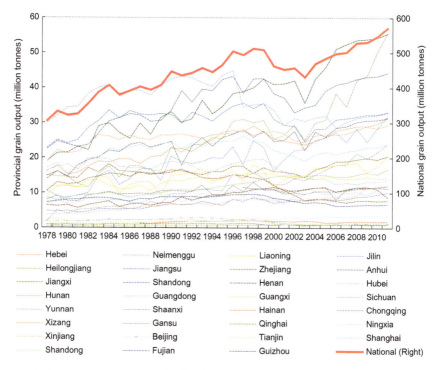

Fig. 4.4 Provincial grain production from 1978 to 2011 (including minority areas and municipality) (unit: million tonnes). Source: *Zhongguo Tongji Nianjian* (China Statistical Yearbook). National Bureau of Statistics of China. Beijing: China Statistics Press, 1981–2013 editions

Japonica rice (*jingmi*, 粳米) varieties. On the eve of the reform era, grain production in this area accounted for a third of total national grain output, and as late as 2007 it was still 27 per cent. In contrast, land alongside the middle and upper reaches of Yellow River (*huanghe*, 黄河), including the Hetao area (河套地区),[5] and in Northeastern China (Liaoning, Heilongjiang and Jilin provinces) each contributed an increasing share of national grain output: from 12 per cent in 1978 to 15.5 per cent, and from 20 to 28 per cent in 2007, respectively. This geographical change in grain production resulted in a change in the production status of the region along the middle and lower reaches of the Yangtze River—

---

[5] The Hetao area includes Henan, Hebei, Shanxi, Neimengu, Shaanxi, Gansu, Qinghai, Ningxia and Xinjiang.

Trends in China's Grain Production   105

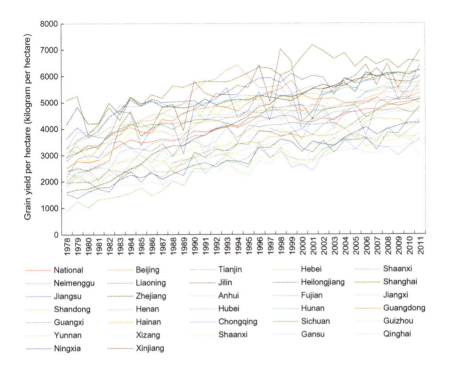

Fig. 4.5 Provincial per hectare grain yield from 1978 to 2011 (including minority areas and municipality) (unit: kilogram per hectare). Source: *Zhongguo Tongji Nianjian* (China Statistical Yearbook). National Bureau of Statistics of China. Beijing: China Statistics Press, 1981–2013 editions

including Hunan and Hubei—from a grain net exporting region to a net grain importer. Implied in this shift was increasing difficulty in maintaining self-sufficiency in grain production in this region.

Unit area yields of grain varied widely across China and these regional gaps have been unaffected by major yield increases that have taken place in the wake of technological progress. In 1978, for example, the highest unit area yield of grain was 5098 kg per hectare in Shanghai,[6] and the lowest 889 kg per hectare in Neimenggu, the difference being around 4200 kg per hectare. But in 2007, 30 years later, the difference between Shanghai and Neimenggu was still almost 3000 kg per hectare, despite significant technological progress having meanwhile taken place in

---

[6] Next to Shanghai, Zhejiang's yield was 4164 kg in 1978, ranking the second highest in China.

106　J. Du

China's agriculture. Interestingly, by 2007 Jilin province in the Northeast had the highest grain yield in China at 7025 kg per hectare, and the gap between the provinces with the lowest and highest yields had widened to almost 3900 kg.

This grain output gap mainly reflects different regional cropping techniques. In the case of rice, for example, due to geographical and climatic reasons the Japonica rice variety grown in northern China normally produces one harvest a year; however, on land in the south China (for example, Hainan 海南), rice planting techniques have changed to double or even triple cropping (producing two or three harvests every year). This caused North China's sown area yield significantly higher than in the south, but arable areas yield still lower than in the south.

4.4　Regional Rice Yields Fluctuations

Leaving aside its provinces located in the subtropical zone, China can be geographically divided into three major yield areas, based on different tillage management systems.

The first area comprises the provinces along the middle and lower reaches of the Yangtze River (including Jiangsu, Zhejiang, Anhui, Hunan and Hubei). Normally, unit area grain yields in this area have been higher than the national average, and in most years the Lower Yangtze Delta region has traditionally generated the highest rice yields in the country (see Fig. 4.6). The second region is northern China with its newly developed agricultural provinces Jilin, Heilongjiang and Liaoning (see Fig. 4.7). Per unit yield here normally stays around the national average, but in Heilongjiang it is slightly lower due to its climate conditions. The third area is along the middle and upper reaches of the Yellow River (including Hebei, Henan, Shanxi, Shaanxi, Gansu, Neimenggu, Qinghai, Ningxia and Xinjiang) and most provinces in this area produce less than the national average (see Fig. 4.8).

If we look at the fluctuation in output in the above three areas, they show different features.

The area of the middle and lower reaches of the Yangtze River shows a slow increase in total grain output after 1979 (see Fig. 4.6), which has slowed since 1985. Although the increase is not as significant as those

Trends in China's Grain Production   107

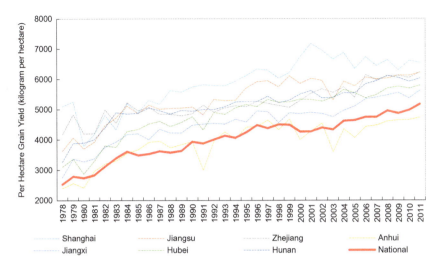

Fig. 4.6 Per hectare grain yield change in Lower Yangtze Delta region from 1978 to 2011 (unit: kilogram per hectare). Source: *Zhongguo Tongji Nianjian* (China Statistical Yearbook). National Bureau of Statistics of China. Beijing: China Statistics Press, 1981–2013 editions

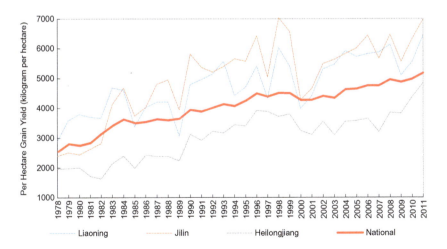

Fig. 4.7 Per hectare grain yield change in Northeast China from 1978 to 2011 (unit: kilogram per hectare). Source: *Zhongguo Tongji Nianjian* (China Statistical Yearbook). National Bureau of Statistics of China. Beijing: China Statistics Press, 1981–2013 editions

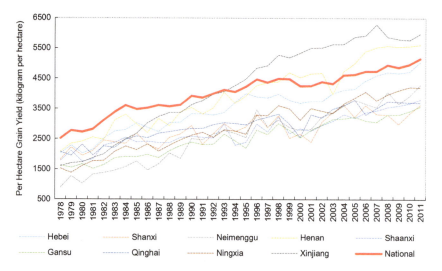

Fig. 4.8 Per hectare grain yield change in the middle and upper reaches of the Yellow River from 1978 to 2011 (unit: kilogram per hectare). Source: *Zhongguo Tongji Nianjian* (China Statistical Yearbook). National Bureau of Statistics of China. Beijing: China Statistics Press, 1981–2013 editions

in other areas, grain total output in this area was steady and per unit grain yield fluctuated little under the grain circulation reform. In the northern region the increase in yield has been substantial and much higher than the national average, although the fluctuation range in per unit yield has also been higher than average (see Fig. 4.7). The third area—along the middle and upper reaches of the Yellow River—the rate of growth of grain yields in this region has been the same as the national average and its fluctuations have only mirrored those in the country. The exception has been Henan province, which, thanks to a sharp increase in total grain output, contributed ten per cent of national grain output from 2005, the exception (see Fig. 4.8).

4.5 Theories and Practice

From a macroscopic perspective, the regional differences in China's grain production can be explained by differences in geography and climate, as mentioned above. In the South China—basically Dongting Lake area

(洞庭湖区) and Yangtze Delta, where tillage conditions allow double cropping, unit land annual production is normally above the national average (see Hunan and Hubei in Fig. 4.6), and much higher than in northern China where climatic conditions dictate a single cropping pattern—although Northeastern China provinces also have very high rice yields. Natural factors may determine regional yield capacity, but they do not explain the wide variations in yields and total grain output that can occur in the same region. For example, substantial output variations in the short-term or fluctuations in the same watershed areas can hardly be explained by natural factors alone.

After examining the regional differences in total output and per unit yields, in the following section we narrow the research to inter-regional analysis and try to identify the factors influencing regional agricultural transition by examining the trends in inter-regional grain output growth.

Here we begin by looking at grain output fluctuations in Northeast China.

4.5.1 Northeast China: Grain Production and the Land–Labour Ratio

Output fluctuations in the Northeast—in both total output and unit area yields of grain—since middle 1980s have been greater than anywhere else in China (Fig. 4.7). Interestingly, if we calculate the land–labour ratio, this figure also fluctuates more widely than the national average, and the fluctuations mirror the changes in grain purchasing price and era (Figs. 4.9 and 4.10),[7] especially since early 1990s. On one hand, the population has changed little in Northeast China since 1979 (Table 4.1).

From the viewpoint of labour inputs, Northeast China experienced no significant change in labour stock: the natural growth rate—especially since the 1990s—in Northeast is almost the lowest in China due to its low birth rate. And Northeast China also did not contribute a lot to low-skill labour flows—rural migrant labourers—from the rural sector to eastern coastal industrialising areas. Thus, without either large scale

---

[7] Here we use arable area to define the land–labour ratio. This research regards the total sown area or grain sown area as flexible inputs.

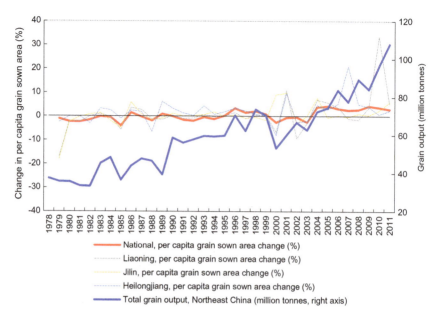

Fig. 4.9 Grain production change and provincial per capita grain sown area change in Northeast China from 1979 to 2011 (unit: per cent (*left*); million tonnes (*right*)). Source: *Zhongguo Tongji Nianjian* (China Statistical Yearbook). National Bureau of Statistics of China. Beijing: China Statistics Press, 1981–2013 editions; *Liaoning Sheng 2010 Nian Diliu Ci Quanguo Renkou Pucha Zhuyao Shuju Gongbao* (The 2010 Provincial Data Bulletin of the Sixth National Population Census of Liaoning). The Liaoning Provincial People's Government, The Central People's Government of the People's Republic of China, accessed 27 May 2013, http://www.gov.cn/gzdt/2011-05/13/content_1863235.htm. *Heilongjiang Tongji Nianjian* (Heilongjiang Statistical Yearbook). Heilongjiang Provincial Bureau of Statistics, and the State Statistics Bureau Heilongjiang Investigation Team. Beijing: China Statistics Press, 1987–2013 editions; *Liaoning Tongji Nianjian* (Liaoning Statistical Yearbook). Liaoning Provincial Bureau of Statistics. Beijing: China Statistics Press, 1983–2013 editions; *Jilin Tongji Nianjian* (Jilin Statistical Yearbook). Jilin Provincial Bureau of Statistics, and the State Statistics Bureau Jilin Investigation Team. Beijing: China Statistics Press, 1984–2013 editions. Note: Provincial rural population data are collected from corresponding provincial statistical yearbooks; Liaoning's 2010 rural population is calculated by the percentage from '2010 Liaoning Population Census'; 2011 data are from China Statistics Yearbook of 2012

labour outflow or the rapid local population growth, the population of Northeast China remained relatively stable during the reform era. This may be said to have conferred on the agricultural transition in Northeast China an advantage in rural labour supply.

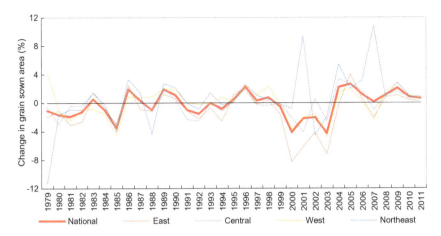

Fig. 4.10 Link relative ratio of grain sown area of China from 1979 to 2011 (unit: per cent). Source: *Zhongguo Tongji Nianjian* (China Statistical Yearbook). National Bureau of Statistics of China. Beijing: China Statistics Press, 1981–2013 editions

Table 4.1 Population change in Northeast China after reform (million persons)

Year	1978	1985	1990	1995	2000	2005	2011
Population	86.73	93.41	99.01	102.86	105.70	106.79	108.16

Source: *Heilongjiang Tongji Nianjian* (Heilongjiang Statistical Yearbook). Heilongjiang Provincial Bureau of Statistics, and the State Statistics Bureau Heilongjiang Investigation Team. Beijing: China Statistics Press, 1987–2013 editions; *Liaoning Tongji Nianjian* (Liaoning Statistical Yearbook). Liaoning Provincial Bureau of Statistics. Beijing: China Statistics Press, 1983–2013 editions; *Jilin Tongji Nianjian* (Jilin Statistical Yearbook). Jilin Provincial Bureau of Statistics, and the State Statistics Bureau Jilin Investigation Team. Beijing: China Statistics Press, 1984–2013 editions

Based on slowly growing labour stock and nearly constant labour supply, it seems that agriculture in Northeast China followed a non-standard growth path in terms of agricultural transition, compared with those regions with large scale labour inflows and outflows (e.g., eastern coastal provinces).

First, area of sown land in the Northeast fluctuates from year to year (Figs. 4.9 and 4.10), showing that it is sensitive to external conditions such as the changes in grain purchase price. This means that farmers usually make decisions on (a) whether to grow grain products or non-grain crops;

and (b) the quantity of their labour and capital invested to produce grain subject to the changing external conditions. The implication is that the labour capital ratio in Northeast China's grain production could easily be adjusted according to the change in grain prices. In other words, Northeast's grain supply has greater elasticity than other areas. Grain is regarded as a cash crop or a semi-cash crop: this is a different pattern from other main grain production area. However, the supply elasticity, and therefore elasticity in labour and capital input does not apply cross-sectional: even when the grain price dropped greatly between 1998 and 2003, which led the decline of the whole agriculture sector's income level, no obvious labour outflow from agriculture was observed in Northeast China.

Northeast China's own distinctive characteristics in grain productions are obvious. First, labour force has been geographically locked in the Northeast area. However, such a lock-in effect has a different technological foundation from the traditional paddy rice production.

The traditional paddy rice area, middle and lower reaches of the Yangtze River, was known as the 'paddy field' area. The 'paddy-field' is the traditional paddy rice fields, which needs to be maintained by long-term, continuous, intensive labour inputs. The maintenance work of such paddy fields is a non-stop process, once interrupted, most work processes (such as soil improvement, field irrigation, etc.) would be lost as a large part of these works need to be done continuously. Based on the inherent features of paddy rice production technology, when arable land has been converted to paddy rice field, rice production can hardly be stopped as this would cause land devaluation.

However, the Northeast's labour lock-in is not caused by such technological constraint. Historically, Northeast China's agriculture was not developed until the late nineteenth and early twentieth centuries, when the Han majority immigrated into the area under Qing dynasty's ethnic policies. The agricultural history of Northeast China is therefore much shorter than that of other regions of the country, and—partly in consequence—it has enjoyed superior conditions in terms of its arable area, soil quality and man–land ratio (e.g., per capita arable land availability), compared with the rest of China. As is shown in Fig. 4.11, the total sown area in Northeast China shows an obviously increasing trend compared

Trends in China's Grain Production 113

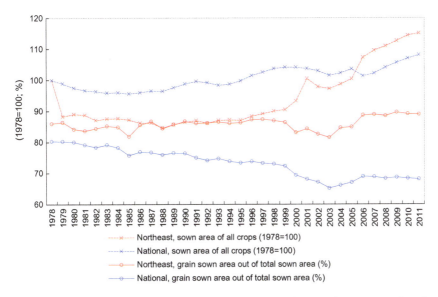

Fig. 4.11 Comparison of total and grain sown area changes between national level and the Northeast China from 1978 to 2011 (constant = 1978; unit: per cent). Source: *Zhongguo Tongji Nianjian* (China Statistical Yearbook). National Bureau of Statistics of China. Beijing: China Statistics Press, 1981–2013 editions

with a decrease in national level. This had comparatively increased the peasant's income in the Northeast. And based on the weather condition—most of this area is sub-arctic—this area has never developed paddy-field based rice plating technology.

In the first ten years after the 1979 reform the Northeast was still the most important industrial area of China, and therefore commanded a higher labour price than most eastern coastal provinces. For example, by the year 1989, Liaoning province's gross domestic product (GDP) per capita is still 14 per cent higher than that of Guangdong. In the early stages of post-1979 reform, benefitting from the planning system that was still operational, the Northeast had a better level of social welfare than other areas in China, and which pushed up the Northeast's labour price. Consequently, the higher labour price discouraged rural labour from leaving this region, especially to provinces on the east coast, on a large scale (as was happening in Central China at the same time).

4.5.2 Eastern Coastal and Inland Areas: The Flow of Labour

In contrast to the Northeast, agricultural workers in eastern coastal provinces were an important source of labour flowing into the industrial sector.

In the southern provinces there was a continuous decrease in grain output from the 1990s, first in Guangdong, then the east coast along the area of middle and lower reaches of the Yangtze River. Under the impact of rapid income growth in industrial sector, and the urbanisation in these regions, we may suppose that the decline reflected a contraction in both the arable land base and the supply of farm labour. However, as China's total arable land declined 6.4 per cent from 1996 to 2008, the ratio of reduction in arable land is much less than the reduction in agricultural labour. By way of illustration, according to Jiangsu statistics, the rural population accounted for 53 per cent of the total provincial population in 2003, and rapidly dropped to 47 per cent in 2007—which means 11 per cent of rural population became urban citizen within just a four-year period. Furthermore, in the Yangtze Delta region many small towns were located very close together (often only four to five kilometres apart), so that a large part of non-agricultural workers was still accommodated in rural area.

In short, the labour outflow from the coast provinces' agriculture sectors after the mid-1980s caused a sharp decrease in labour available for grain production in Guangdong, later the Yangtze Delta region. Taking the decreasing proportion of labour input in grain production into consideration, it is inappropriate to evaluate the southeast coastal area's agricultural performance simply by its total output.

An examination of grain production in the eastern coastal region, especially the Yangtze Delta, shows that up until now per unit area yields were remained in the top group in China, despite the slow pace of increase in yield. In other words, although the large number of factors (including both land and labour) outflow to the non-agriculture sector decreased the labour input in this area, the improvement in land productivity (yields per hectare) offset the negative impact of the continuous outflow of production factors, enabling overall agricultural production to increase in the Yangtze Delta and south-eastern coastal areas.

4.6 Grain Production: Two Patterns in Short-Term and Long-Term

In the simplified dual typology above, we sort major Chinese agriculture areas—especially grain production—as two patterns during the transition. The first pattern in a geographical schema is grain production in resource abundant areas (such as the Northeast). In those areas, thanks to their natural endowments and other historical reasons, during the reform era they have enjoyed higher marginal revenue in terms of both human capital and physical capital. Because of higher marginal revenue, returns from the agriculture sector are maintained at a relatively high level. The second pattern comprises inland China ('central' provinces) and the eastern coastal regions, where marginal output of the non-agriculture sector is far higher—usually for labour—than the agriculture sector, and this forces labour (mostly the young adult labour force) moving out of agriculture to the non-agriculture sector on a massive scale in pursuit of higher wages.

In each pattern of a geographical scheme, we can observe two different trends/patterns in agriculture growth,[8] factor intensification and technology change: (a) factor intensification process means current technology allows more factor inputs with greater marginal output; oppositely, (b) technical and institutional change converts current technology to another form, with different marginal output schedule, which usually equivalents different scale economy. As we have mentioned briefly in previous chapters (e.g., Chap. 2), it is easy to see, the main characteristics of China's major agriculture geographical schemas are composed of the degree of each growth pattern, their timing and the interactions between these two trends.

In the short term, we may separate factor intensification from factor-saving institutional and technology changes. Taking the reforms in the Chinese grain circulation system (as in Chap. 3), for instance, the degree of factor intensification in agricultural production changed instantaneously when grain purchasing prices were adjusted under the impact of

---

[8] By definition, agriculture growth can be identified as increase in per capita output.

reform policy. In such circumstances, the method of factor intensification was constrained by existing technological and institutional conditions, so the peasants' remaining choices were simply to increase or reduce the quantity of inputs.

In the long-term, as standard micro-economic theory predicts, factor intensification and factor-saving institutional and technology changes would generate different patterns of agricultural growth. However, this does not mean we can easily separate these two patterns. There are two reasons.

First, empirically, transitional economies always experienced rapid technological improvements, as well as booming in available resources—usually capital goods come from the rapidly developed industrial sector—that mix the actual factor-saving technical change and factor intensification together in agriculture sector. This could make the usual economic measurement, for example, Total Factor Productivity (TFP), less sensitive to changes in production technology. Again, taking the reforms in the Chinese agriculture sector as an example, during the 1980s (as well as early 1990s till 1998), we can observe general TFP increasing, and we surely know this is a result of two facts, (a) increase in the degree of factor intensification in agricultural production caused by increase in grain purchasing prices, and (b) improvements in fundamental agriculture technologies brought by industrial technologies such as the use of new seed varieties and chemical fertiliser. However, the separation of (a) and (b) in agricultural data is almost impossible. Thus, when applying the TFP-based method, in most cases it will overestimate the contribution of one certain fact but lower estimate in the other.

Second, most importantly, factor-saving technical and institutional changes would be incorporated into factor intensification and vice versa. On one hand, as mentioned previously, liberalisation in the 1980s pushed nationwide agricultural technology progress in the use of new seeds, pesticide and chemical fertiliser, and this progress has further enabled increases in long-term and short-term production potential—especially in the Northeast. The popularisation of water-saving irrigation in the 1990s, and mini-tractors in the 2000s also produced similar results. Such technological progress increased the possible level of factor intensification in the long-term. On the other hand, not only historical data—such as the establishment of paddy-field rice production—but also very recent experience like the agriculture mechanisation (greatly benefitted from output increase) in rural area shows that factor intensification is a necessary step for technological progress.

The dual typology in Chinese agriculture production, is in actual a result of multiple alternant technical and institutional changes. In our observations, the most obvious change is the labour flow, and thereafter the coming changes in labour productivity.

First, reference to labour migration in the coastal and central regions does not necessarily imply a flow of labour from the agriculture to the non-agriculture sector—but wherever the destination of labour flow, the originating region's agriculture productivity was improved. Labour migration may simply reflect a difference in the price of labour in alternative uses, causing peasants to leave local agriculture to seek higher returns elsewhere. However, the migrants' destination may also be another rural area where the agriculture sector provides a better reward to labour: in such cases, the flow of labour is kept within the agriculture sector but takes place between different regions. A typical case of this kind of labour flow occurs in central and west provinces (e.g., Henan and Sichua), where peasants are the main source of seasonal agriculture workers: Xinjiang and Neimenggu's agriculture sector attract huge numbers of seasonal agricultural workers every year. The fast labour outflow is one of the most important reasons of agriculture productivity improvement, especially in those labour abundant provinces.

Second, besides the short-term factor price-based labour flow, in the long-term the labour outflow from the agriculture sector reflects the technical and institutional changes. For example, along the middle and lower reaches of the Yangtze River, sowing and harvesting have traditionally been highly physical labour-intensive activities, as some heavy works need to be carried out by large numbers of young adult labourers. After 1949, the Chinese government even allowed workers with rural relatives to have several day holidays at peak seasons of the farming calendar, known as 'busy farming holiday' (*nong mang jia*, 农忙假),[9] to help sowing, transplanting and harvesting in rural area. However, in the past one to two

---

[9] The 'busy farming holiday' refers to industry labour participation in farm work during the busy sowing and harvesting farming seasons.

decades in southern and eastern coastal regions the intensity of the physical labour required for sowing has been greatly reduced and labourers have been replaced by small agricultural machinery. The background of such changes is technological improvement: before the 1990s the Chinese farming machine industry basically only produces copies of US- or Soviet Union-style large units, such as the combine harvester—but these machines are not only expensive—which most farmers cannot afford—but also maladjusted units to Chinese small-scale paddy-field planting.

Since large reaper and/or harvester units were not suitable for use on land along the middle and lower reaches of the Yangtze River, China started to import farming machinery from Japan, whose small-scale cropping units,[10] intense labour input and improved local grain varieties were like those of the Yangtze Delta. Since China adopted Japanese technology in agricultural machinery, made some key improvements and successfully lowered machinery prices, demand for agricultural labour has dropped with the application of new machinery, making it possible to replace young adult agricultural labourers with the elderly and children. Therefore, the technical change significantly lowered the opportunity cost of young adult agricultural labour, creating conditions that would facilitate a major rural labour outflow in this region. Therefore, the rural labour outflow to other areas and local flow to the non-agriculture sector (happening in many provinces), are a part of agriculture technological and institutional transition. Comparative static analysis would suggest that if there is a loss of a factor of production, output will tend to decline, but in several rapidly industrialising provinces (which also means fast labour outflow from agriculture sector) in China—for example, Guangdong, Zhejiang and Jiangsu—the decrease in grain output was brought about by the considerable shrinkage in arable land, not per capita or per unit land output reduction. One might infer that this buoyant

---

[10] China's paddy rice cultivation techniques are similar to those of Japan. Thus, in contrast to US- or Soviet Union-style large agricultural machines, Japanese-style paddy rice machinery is more suitable for China's rice economy, especially in the middle and lower reaches of Yangzi River. With the post-war economic and technological development in Japan, paddy rice machinery also improved during Japan's green revolution. The introduction of Japan's small agricultural machinery to the middle and lower reaches of the Yangzi River has been an important ingredient in agricultural technology change in this region since the 1990s.

yield performance reflected factor adjustment—for example, the use of elderly persons for agricultural production purposes. But perhaps the more likely explanation lay in the introduction of new agricultural technologies, which facilitated further improvements in farm productivity.

4.7   Summary

Through the empirical analysis of regional changes in agricultural factor accumulation, this chapter finds two distinct paths of agricultural technology change. Northeast China has a comparatively higher level of land accumulation with stable rural population change. And due to some historical reasons, agricultural and non-agricultural factors in Northeast China have a higher marginal return than other areas in China. This high marginal return to factors creates little inter-sectoral and inter-regional factor flow observed in Northeast China. Therefore, the agricultural output increase in Northeast China is mainly achieved by changing the use amount of factor inputs in agricultural production. Different from Northeast China, in Central and East China return to factor input in the non-agriculture sector is usually higher than in agriculture, especially the return to labour. As a result, based on the inter-sectoral and inter-regional relative price difference, a rural factor (labour) largely flows out of agriculture to the local and neighbouring industrial sector. Together with arable land shrinkage, the only reason to explain both total and per hectare output increase must be the adoption of factor-saving technology.

Thus, there are two basic patterns of agricultural output growth—factor intensification-based and factor-saving technology-based. Factor intensification and technology innovation both can generate growth. In the short run, factor intensification-based and technology-based agricultural growth paths are easy to distinguish. For example, when real grain purchase price increased in grain circulation system reform, we can observe an apparent increase in factor in agricultural production. And the short-run output increase is highly correlated with the level of factor intensification. But this level of factor intensification is still subject to the constraints of existing technology and institution. Different from factor intensification, technology innovation could fundamentally change the existing technical constraint on the production potentials.

In the Northeast land intensification has been much lower than in the rest of China. As a result, the grain output performance in this region reflects fluctuations in grain purchasing prices during the transition. Thanks also to the low man–land ratio, Northeastern China has not experienced any large-scale inter-sectoral or inter-regional labour flow during the reform era. With arable land available in sufficient quantities to accommodate agricultural inputs, agricultural growth in the Northeast was achieved by factor intensification production, and Northeast China did not obviously make use of factor-saving technology during the post-1979 agricultural transition. Until post 1998 grain reform, there was no significant structural change in agricultural technology in the Northeast China.

By contrast, the Yangtze Delta, as the representative of east and southeast coastal regions of China, experienced a significant labour outflow from the very beginning of the post-1979 reform. Southeast China is a traditional agriculture area with high level of factor intensification (see Chap. 2), and the large-scale labour outflow lowered the man–land ratio here. Even so, rice (as the main agriculture products of this area) yields per hectare in this region have remained among the highest in China, showing a slow but gradual increase. Rising unit area yields alongside declining labour input suggests that labour-saving technological progress must have taken place. Thus, in the southeast coastal provinces and the middle and lower reaches of Yangtze River, an increasing factor substitution rate arising from factor-saving technology change offsets those negative impacts on grain production from labour and arable land outflow, especially bearing in mind that Japanese small agricultural machines substituted for part of the labour input in grain production in this area.

Market structures vary among different regions in China, and such differences have significantly influenced the nature of regional agricultural transition. These differences in regional agricultural transitions highlight the importance of factor inputs in shaping the transition process. This conclusion may be an extension of mainstream agricultural economics IIC theory in the explanation of the technological transition in contemporary Chinese agriculture.

Back to the beginning. Given the exogenously set initial technology, technology change depends on the level and ratio of factor accumulation. Technology generation gap usually happens between different countries, in other word, differences in the basic institutional frameworks eventually determine the technology generation gap between countries. Under the same basic institutional framework and given the same technology set to choose from, differences in specific institutional arrangements may determine the regional technology variations. In the case of China, such differences are summed up in the market structure. When we relax those critical hypotheses in neoclassical economics, empirical studies in China show us different paths of agricultural technology changes from the standard IIC path. China's agriculture is a good example to interpret the possible technology deviation under complex market institutions. For example, with a large labour price difference between central and east coastal areas in China, this relative factor (labour) price difference induces neither different technology changes, nor different patterns of agricultural transition. But if those missing but critical hypotheses in neoclassical economics could be partially introduced or compensated for by some compensatory conditions, such as the grain policy changes discussed in Chap. 3 and regional market structure bias in this chapter, technology change in agriculture would likely happen earlier.

References

FAOSTAT. *Food and Agriculture Organization of the United Nations Database.* Accessed 27 May 2013. http://faostat3.fao.org/home/index.html.

Heilongjiang Tongji Nianjian (Heilongjiang Statistical Yearbook). Heilongjiang Provincial Bureau of Statistics, and the State Statistics Bureau Heilongjiang Investigation Team. Beijing: China Statistics Press, 1987–2013 Editions.

Jilin Tongji Nianjian (Jilin Statistical Yearbook). Jilin Provincial Bureau of Statistics, and the State Statistics Bureau Jilin Investigation Team. Beijing: China Statistics Press, 1984–2013 Editions.

Liaoning Sheng 2010 Nian Diliu Ci Quanguo Renkou Pucha Zhuyao Shuju Gongbao (The 2010 Provincial Data Bulletin of the Sixth National Population

Census of Liaoning). The Liaoning Provincial People's Government, The Central People's Government of the People's Republic of China. Accessed 27 May 2013. http://www.gov.cn/gzdt/2011-05/13/content_1863235.htm.

Liaoning Tongji Nianjian (Liaoning Statistical Yearbook). Liaoning Provincial Bureau of Statistics. Beijing: China Statistics Press, 1983–2013 Editions.

Zhongguo Tongji Nianjian (China Statistical Yearbook). National Bureau of Statistics of China. Beijing: China Statistics Press, 1981–2013 Editions.

5

Agricultural Transition in Taiwan: Towards a Comparative Study with Mainland China

5.1 Introduction

After the empirical analysis of Chinese agriculture in Chaps. 3 and 4, this chapter focuses mainly on the consequential outcomes of policies leading to agricultural transition in mainland China and Taiwan, with a particular focus on differences in factor returns.

The framework used here follows neoclassical theory. Assuming an ideal pattern of production in which the relationship between the agriculture and the non-agriculture sectors reflects the existence of an ideal market institution without any non-market forces to distort product price signals (product market) or factor returns (input market). The factor price equalisation theorem (Samuelson 1948, 1953) ensures that prices of all the factors of production in agriculture will be equalised to those in non-agriculture sectors as a result of trade in commodities and factors, such as physical input products, labour and capital. The application of factor price equalisation (FPE) theory to agricultural reform and transition generates the following principle: if agricultural reform is market-oriented and successful, then in the long-term factor prices in the agriculture sector will be equalised to those in other sectors. However,

© The Author(s) 2018   123
J. Du, *Agricultural Transition in China*, Palgrave Studies in Economic History,
https://doi.org/10.1007/978-3-319-76905-9_5

there is a potential complication. Even if individual workers in the agriculture sector have higher incomes than that in other sectors, the part of income that does not directly reflect production activities (e.g., government subsidies) should not be included in the calculation of factor return. Quite simply, factor return should reflect that part of return, or income, accounted for by production only.

The economies selected for investigation in this chapter are mainland China and Taiwan. In addition to having the same Chinese cultural background, agricultural production in both areas has traditionally been based on small-scale household production. Both were trying to embark on modern economic growth and structural change after WW2, starting with agriculture, which included programmes for accelerated rural development featuring land reform in the early 1950s in both areas and the HRS from the early 1980s in mainland China. Both agricultural transitions were designed to promote rapid and sustained agricultural growth and programmed to increase rural income.

Before reform, incomes in the rural sectors of mainland China and Taiwan were low: Taiwan's agriculture was mostly damaged by WW2; and in China's case, the GLF and Cultural Revolution seriously damaged the agricultural productivity and took the greatest toll on the agriculture sector. In both cases—in Taiwan in the 1950s, and in China in the 1980s—the agricultural reforms were successful in achieving an output increase. During the first few years of the agricultural transition an obvious output increase and gradual income increase could be detected, and the transition quickly spread from agriculture to the non-agriculture sectors.

The above similar aspects provide a research base from which to compare the transition experiences in mainland China and Taiwan as a distinctive social science research topic. However, three factors differentiate the two areas, bringing difficulties with the comparison of these two examples of agricultural transition. The first and most obvious is the land size and geographic features of the two areas.

Taiwan's climate corresponds only to that of Southeastern China (even more specifically, of southern Fujian and Hainan Provinces), where abundant summer monsoons and warm temperatures allow two or more crops per year. This contrasts with northern China, where less rainfall and lower temperatures allow a much shorter planting season. As a result, cropping patterns differ significantly, causing major difficulties in making comparisons at a national level. When output comparison is not convincing, this chapter considers using factor return to see the efficiency of agricultural production across the strait.

In addition, the agricultural transition in East Asia is always accompanied by political intervention, directly impacting on agricultural production. However, as mentioned, economic transition and the effects of policy on agriculture were not evaluated by farm output expansion or decline. Successful agricultural transition is normally reflected in a strengthened rural sector, with increased returns to factor inputs. If neoclassical theory holds, successful transition of the economy shows a convergence of labour and capital return between agriculture and non-agriculture. This is the main signifier used to evaluate the success of agricultural transition in this chapter. However, successful policy or reform is not the same as successful agricultural transition. In the case of reform, if the policy or reform itself fulfils its original purpose, it should be considered successful. If labour and capital return during the transition shows a divergence, then it means that market institutions prevent factor return from equalising.

Based on these criteria, in what follows this chapter reviews Taiwan and mainland China's agricultural reform process and tries to compare their different features in agricultural transition. In so doing, it seeks to show the transition path of agriculture and its convergence with non-agriculture, or to the contrary, demonstrate the influences derived from policies that cause agriculture to deviate from standard neoclassical trajectory.

5.2 A Brief Historical Retrospect

Before transition began, Taiwan had been under Japanese occupation between 1895 and 1945, during which period it was transformed into an agricultural base, serving Japan, and with a focus on the production of rice and sugar. Nearly 60 per cent of its arable land was well-irrigated whereas less than half of China's arable land was irrigated.[1] In the late

---

[1] For example, in the year of 1937, the irrigated area in Taiwan has been 511,000 hectares, out of arable land of 857,000 hectares, around 60 per cent.

1930s (1935–1939), 48.2 per cent of total rice output was exported, of which 99 per cent went to Japan, the corresponding figures for sugar were 93 per cent and 94 per cent respectively. Before WW2, Japanese emphasised agriculture much more than industry—the aim was, after all, to turn Taiwan into an agriculture base for Japan. The agricultural production declined after 1937 since investment in agriculture was diverted to the war.

In its own pre-reform period mainland China suffered from various disasters during the Sino-Japanese War (1937–1945) and the Chinese Civil War (1945–1949). Having recovered from WW2 and civil war, China's agriculture began to grow, accompanied by early land reform and the further development of irrigation facilities. Although many of the government's irrigation systems were left unused, the considerable state investment in irrigation stimulated individual peasant's incentives to do small-scale production investment, indirectly affecting agricultural production. Later in the 1950s, the emphasis quickly was moved from agricultural production to the industrial sector as the PRC government turned to the Soviet economic model. The GLF brought intensive industry production to a climax while agriculture grew at a low or even negative rate with an increased population. With an emphasis moved to accelerate industrial development, during the GLF: (a) rural industry absorbed much time and effort of investment; meanwhile, (b) millions of farmers were recruited for work in support to industrial production; (c) with a statistical reporting system for agriculture collapses; and (d) grain procurements were excessive in agriculture, the agricultural productivity and signalling mechanism was distorted in Chinese agriculture, precipitating famine. Then the Three Years of the Great Famine almost destroyed agricultural production in mainland China.

A second pre-condition was investment in developing agriculture of the areas under analysis. Under Japanese occupation, Taiwan was transformed from a traditional society to a semi-modern economy. Japan invested in irrigation, transportation and communications, developed modern business institutions and thus generally provided a more effective infrastructure for economic development.

As mentioned above, during 1935–1939, around 60 per cent of cultivated land in Taiwan was well-irrigated and cropping patterns were improved by introducing new varieties, especially paddy rice, in which the key breakthrough was the introduction of the Ponlai rice (japonica rice, 蓬莱稻) variety of early-ripening japonica rice. This affected Taiwan's agricultural pattern significantly. Hitherto, agriculture in Taiwan was not merely subsistence orientated, but had become, under Japanese tutelage, quite strongly export-orientated; in China, some regions were also quite strongly trade-orientated, but others were subsistence-based. In any case, the grain supply orientation of farm production in mainland China was very apparent. In Taiwan during the 1950s and first half of the 1960s the USA contributed US$1.47 billion in economic aid to Taiwan, and 60 per cent of the funds went towards developing agriculture and its supporting infrastructure. After 1949, mainland China invested a considerable sum in the irrigation system as mentioned above. However, many of these irrigation investment projects were inefficient or left unused, for example, some large-scale dams built in the 1950s and 1960s were even the source of serious disasters.[2] In addition, the Soviet Union stopped its financial and technological industrial assistance at the time of the GLF, and thus all of China's concentration and devotion was put into its industrial development. The 'agriculture first' emphasis was fairly short-lived.

5.2.1 Taiwan: The Sino-American Joint Commission on Rural Reconstruction (JCRR)

Governments played a particularly important role in agricultural transition, although their impact and the way in which they shaped development differed between Taiwan and mainland China.

After WW2 the Kuomintang (KMT) was the dominant force in Taiwan. From 1949, JCRR became the main source of foreign economic assistance to Taiwanese agriculture.[3] Between 1951 and 1965, the USA provided US$1.47 billion in total to Taiwan in economic aid, a significant part of which was used to strengthen infrastructure and used for direct

---

[2] For example, in 1962 a leak in the Sanmenxia Dam (三门峡大坝) caused serious destruction of local arable land, and again in 1975 the same dam caused the Banqiao reservoir (板桥水库) to collapse killing thousands of people in Henan in the consequent flood.

[3] In the 1950s and 1960s JCRR accounted for the rapid agricultural growth in Taiwan, and correspondingly for Taiwan's overall economic growth. The JCRR programme contributed significantly to developing crop and irrigation and created the solid basis of agricultural economy that supported Taiwan's economic take-off since the 1970s.

investment in the farm sector. Compared with local industry, in the 1950s and early 1960s, agricultural investment came mainly from the government budget, whereas industrial development was more reliant on private sector resources. Many scholars, such as Bruce Cumings (1984), consider the use of US economic assistance in agriculture, and later, industrial development, a good example of efficient institutional arrangements.

The JCRR worked with all levels of government. It was a highly efficient agriculture-support programme: by minimising bureaucratic expenses, it ensured that most of the funding available under the programme could go directly into agricultural production. In addition, its hands-on approach made it possible for JCRR officers to work side-by-side with individual Taiwanese farmers. In contrast to mainland China—and to transition experiences in other Asian economies—under the JCRR programme, planners were empowered to identify objectives in specific projects at local level, generally without political interference from higher or central levels of government. With local farmers involved in the agricultural development plan, production and other related targets were more readily fulfilled.

From 1949 onwards, Taiwan's annual production was adjusted in every four-year plan to accommodate changes in local market conditions. Normally, a country's agricultural plans were established by local-level agricultural organisations, normally with the involvement of farmers as heads and representatives. This was very different from the centralised approach followed in mainland China and certainly facilitated increased production efficiency and the fulfilment of output targets. In its role as 'agent', the JCRR programme maximised the efficiency of available funds in Taiwan's agricultural transition. It made decisions in conjunction with local farmer organisations about the amount of funding, and the kinds of economic and technological help needed for local agricultural production. This programme helped determine the direction followed by agricultural policy-makers and directly promoted new technologies and management systems adopted by agricultural producers. As well as undertaking direct investment in agricultural production, JCRR also contributed to agriculture-related research and education. With its strong, well-organised farmers' associations, this support programme combined specific agricultural production planning and education with research implementation. Perhaps the most important benefits that derived from its existence were the creation of a self-enforcing local agricultural production association and the provision of mutual help practised among local agricultural organisations.[4]

5.2.2 Taiwan: Land Reform

After WW2 the rural population made up more than half of the total population of Taiwan, but landowner-operators constituted 40 per cent of all farmers and outright tenants, 41 per cent. Tenant farmers had to give up a certain percentage of their annual output as land rent, and this was regarded by KMT as a source of potential social instability in Taiwan. Obviously, the higher percentage of their output that farmers had to release, the smaller the surplus that was left for maintenance and production in the following year, thus the rental element generated a serious disincentive effect. Consequently, KMT wanted to maintain social stability in Taiwan, since it had itself had added a heavy economic burden to the state, with more than two million government staff, KMT army and their families migrating to Taiwan during 1948–1952 to make up almost one fourth of Taiwan's 1952 population.[5] One of the solutions chosen was land reform.[6]

The land reform in 1949 was the beginning of Taiwan's agricultural transition—indeed, of its whole economic transition—and was the first step carried out by the KMT government in terms of promoting rural

---

[4] At a local level, the most important agricultural association in Taiwan was the Taiwan Joint Irrigation Association (TJIA), originally established in the Japanese colonial period in 1922 to popularise Water Conservancy Cooperatives and supervise community welfare and development. The organisation was extensive, with branches set up by municipal governments in most areas. After the defeat of Japan, the Taiwan Water Conservancy Cooperative Association was reconstituted as the 'Water Conservancy Association'. In 1948 the Water Conservancy Association was re-organised and became the 'Water Conservancy Commission'. In 1956, it became the 'Farming Water Conservancy Commission', and in 1957 was again renamed the 'Taiwan Farming and Water Conservancy Promotion Society', with the responsibility of handling relevant liaison and collaborative affairs. In 1985, the Society expanded to embrace both business and research work and was re-organised as the 'Taiwan Farming and Water Conservancy Association'. Finally, in 1999 it became the 'National Irrigation Association'.

[5] Taiwan's total population in 1952 was 8.13 million persons.

[6] Land reform in Taiwan had a social purpose, as much as an economic one.

130   J. Du

development. Land reform proceeded gradually through three steps, the first of which was the reduction of land rents. Rents were strictly fixed at 37.5 per cent of the yearly output of the major crop, with a lease contract of six years (with the option of being extended thereafter). This reduction from previous typical rental payments of more than 50 per cent was a very important initial step in Taiwan's agricultural transition. It stimulated farmers' motivation for production and encouraged investment in land, and as discussed later, Taiwan's post-war agricultural production significantly increased as a result.

Second, to ease the pressure of the large rural population the government sold part of its 'public land' (*gong tian*, 公田) to cultivators at a fixed price of 2.5 times the value of the per hectare yield of the main crop with an interest-free mortgage to be paid in 20 instalments over ten years.

The final step was the 'Land-to-the-Tiller' (*gengzhe you qitian*, 耕者有其田) programme. In this phase, every landlord owning a large estate was able to keep only around three hectares of medium-level paddy field or around six hectares of dry land. Areas of holdings beyond the criteria were purchased by the KMT government in the name of public land and later resold to tenant peasantry at the same price. However, only 70 per cent of the selling price was given to the landlord, the balance being handed over in the form of shares in state owned industries. This forced capital from rural areas into the hands of local industry and farmers. This was key to enabling farmers to make long-term investments and to adopt technological improvements in agriculture.

Yield per hectare in Taiwan has traditionally been very high but agricultural output per labour has been low. The constricted area of cultivated land and the large rural labour stock imply that Taiwan has tended to have a comparative advantage of 'low labour cost' in cultivating labour-intensive agricultural products, such as paddy rice, and a drawback in planting land-intensive varieties. From the theoretical perspective, this is a valid observation. Nevertheless, during its colonial rule of the island, Japan regarded rice as one of the two main crops (along with sugar). During the Qing dynasty too, Taiwan was primarily a rice-producing region. Even today, rice remains the principal grain crop, although its production has long been overtaken by that of fruits and other horticultural products. However, from the 1960s Taiwan's agriculture has become more diversified (i.e., rising incomes and changing patterns of demand) and gradually moved to non-grain crop varieties (especially fruits and economic crops, such as tea).

Taiwanese agricultural experience highlights the important role of rural infrastructure as a means of creating a stable production environment and reducing agricultural production risks. It also shows, perhaps more importantly, how improvements in infrastructure may speed up agricultural transition. In Asian-style, rice-based agricultural production, irrigation is a key factor. To a significant extent, such as in paddy rice production (particularly high-yielding varieties), where an abundant water supply is indispensable, it determines yield levels. Rural growth and development also depends upon road transportation links connecting rural areas to major highways, and on railways to carry agricultural inputs and output. The building-up of farm transportation was coordinated with the land consolidation programmes and the construction of irrigation system. Few villages in Taiwan are without paved roads despite some being in mountain regions.

5.2.3 Mainland China: Land Institution After 1979[7]

China's agriculture sector has traditionally been characterised by a scarcity of land, an abundance of labour and the practice of household-based production using limited mechanisation. Most agricultural production is carried out on small-scale farms of an average of 0.65 hectares in 2005. Mainland China's per hectare grain yield is comparatively higher than that of most other economies based on household farm production, per labour output is however relatively low. Its limited area of arable land and huge rural population determines that Mainland China has an advantage in labour-intensive rural production rather than in the land-intensive one, and its rural production has traditionally been largely determined by the price of rural labour, except during the Mao period when production was driven by targets and quotas.

---

[7] China's first land reform took place during 1949–1952. Here the land reform that this chapter mainly refers is the decollectivisation land reform taking place during the post 1979 economic reform.

After 1979, China's agriculture experienced unprecedented output growth. Beginning with the introduction of the HRS, farm land that had previously been collectively managed was allocated on an egalitarian basis for a fixed term to rural families.[8] Most studies, such as Lin (1992), believe that this institutional initiative had a major positive incentive impact, encouraging farmers to reduce costs, take risks and improve agricultural production skills. The new land tenure system was based on land contracts, which initially lasted for 30 years. Importantly, however, farmers enjoy only land use rights, but not ownership rights: arable land has remained under collective ownership. Thus, there is no scope for selling land, although recent years have seen increasing transfers of land leases. In early reforms, land policies were based on HRS, which generated many positive effects. Compared with the collective system, the HRS gave farmers closer links to their farmland and output, which enhanced growth in both agricultural output and rural income level. The egalitarian access to land use rights within villages it had avoided large numbers of rural landless workers at the expense of underemployment, avoided potential food shortage as happened during collectivisation and therefore enhanced social stability.

However even despite the quick poverty reduction in China, the intersectoral income gap was in fact widened alongside the reform progressed. In the mid-1980s, China's urban income per capita was 1.9 times as much as rural income per capita. However, in recent years, the statistical yearbook shows that per capita income gap ratio has been 3.12 in 2011.[9]

---

[8] HRS and land reform were controversial policies implemented at the beginning of economic reform. In September 1980, the state confirmed the new rural land contractual system, and on 1 January 1984, the Chinese central government announced that 'this term should be at least 15 years' to strengthen the implementation of HRS policy. In November 1993, the state announced a further extension of 15 years after the expiration of the previous land contract. The land contract term has since been extended gradually to 30 years in 'PRC Land Administration Law (Revised)' published on 29 August 1998.

[9] According to the 2012 statistical yearbook, per capita income in urban China in 2011 was 21,809.8 yuan, while 6977.3 yuan in rural China (National Bureau of Statistics of China 2012).

5.3 Taiwan's Agricultural Transition: With a Comparison of Mainland China

Efficiency can, after all, be measured in which case it is explicit in economic research. Agricultural production efficiency, as in the industrial sector, reflects the way in which each unit of input is used. Improvements in agricultural production take place as production efficiency is enhanced. However, since the natural uncertainties in agricultural production are much greater than that of the industrial sector, thus if unsecured property rights of the main agricultural inputs[10] have significantly affected production incentives, the measurement of agriculture efficiency will be more difficult.

Labour and land are two main input factors that affect production efficiency in farming. In contrast to the non-agriculture sector, agricultural land has been farmed under different property right and tenure systems between mainland China and Taiwan during transition. In Taiwan farmland is privately owned by individuals and has a similar leasehold system to that of the English system. However, KMT initiatives after WW2 partly changed the ownership structure by adding more regulations on land ownership.[11] In mainland China most agricultural land is 'collectively owned' by local communities, and a small part is state-owned.[12] This variation in property rights and land ownership has led to differences in the paths that agricultural development has followed in mainland China and Taiwan. The property rights of farmland largely affected agricultural production efficiency: production incentive is a well-taken viewpoint that property rights have prior impact on production. There is abundant evidence too to suggest that stable property rights to farmland encourage farmers to undertake the long-term investment needed to raise production efficiency. The land tenure system in Taiwan and mainland China's post-1979 land system based on collective ownership and the factor of land as a main agricultural input have not received the attention they

---

[10] For example, land, irrigation systems and other natural endowment-based means of agricultural inputs.

[11] For example, 37.5 per cent tax reform and 'Land-to-the-Tiller' policy.

[12] Collectively, ownership in China could be regarded as a kind of state-ownership.

deserve, except in the work of Steven Cheung (1969, 1989). According to Cheung (1969), Taiwan's land reform policies brought higher expectations of agricultural returns, leading to intensive input investment, which caused dramatic temporary increases in agricultural output: in other words, at an early stage of Taiwan's land reform, intensive use of inputs led to increases in output.

Labour-intensive production is a common characteristic of Asian agriculture, especially in East Asia. Like land, labour plays a key role in determining the level of agricultural output, and in most cases increased labour input will relieve the pressure arising from land scarcity and reduce production uncertainties from natural conditions. Taiwan has a better climate for cropping compared with mainland China, however, labour is still the key input for paddy rice production regardless of better natural endowment. If controls on rural–urban migration could be observed during transition, in most cases, the price of rural labour would have been depressed by inter-sectoral migration limitation. Thus, using an underestimated price of rural labour as measurement of labour input cost would increase the returns on labour input. For example, mainland China restricted the rural labour flow to urban areas after 1960s: a controlled labour flow is bound to cause a biased price for rural labour, which will also cause an illusion of higher factor return due to underestimated cost of input.

The ratio of factor return is thus chosen in this chapter as the indicator of agricultural production efficiency based on which to evaluate the agriculture performance in transition of both Taiwan and mainland China. The agricultural transition of both economies sought to improve production efficiency and generate increased national wealth. As mentioned earlier, under perfect market conditions, labour and capital flow freely between the agriculture and non-agriculture sectors. Thus, any enhancement of production efficiency will increase the relevant sector's return on factor and attract inflows of labour and capital until the inter-sectoral gap between factor returns is eliminated. In perfect market conditions the factor return is equalised between sectors without any transition cost associated with labour and capital flows. The logic is quite clear: *ceteris paribus* (i.e., assuming no change in market conditions), then if the difference in terms of factor return between the agriculture and non-agriculture sectors is reduced in the aftermath of the implementation of policies, we may conclude that the policy is effective. Moreover, the extent to which the gap is reduced can be regarded as an indication—a measure—of the economic impact of policies. A widening of the inter-sectoral gap points to a failure in terms of economic policies in implementing agricultural reform or transition, even if transition or reform has been accompanied by an output increase.[13] This is why an increase in total output is a biased estimator of agricultural growth in developing economies.

Another advantage in using the difference in factor return as an indicator of agricultural production efficiency is that it overcomes difficulties in comparative studies of agricultural transition arising from differences in location and time where and when the reforms took place. Bearing in mind the difficulties of making comparisons because of differences between resource endowments and in technological conditions in different sectors, to make different reforms comparable and generate convincing results, we first compare returns to agricultural capital with that in local non-agriculture sectors. Eliminating the influences of timing and location on agricultural production is probably impossible, comparisons of factor returns in agriculture non-agriculture in the same location and in the same period helps overcome such constraints.

Unlike estimates of output–input ratios, the main difference in calculating factor return lies in the treatment of labour cost and fixed asset investment. Early in China's post-1979 reforms labour flows were largely restricted to rural areas, thereby ensuring adequate provision of agricultural labour for the finite arable land area; while controls over current capital investment prevented the rural wage from increasing. The sharp increase in the urban non-agricultural labour wage opened a wide gap

---

[13] Intension of transition or reform policies does not equal the result. During China's post-1979 agricultural reform, although some policies brought agriculture a short-term rapid output increase, they still failed to re-allocate factor and resource to efficient use in agricultural production. Thus, though agricultural transition or reform has usually been accompanied with output increase, this increase may not bring any improvement to the agricultural economy, because those factor-intensification-based output increases may cause a long-term deterioration in technology selection. Although technology and factor-intensification-based output increases both show an increasing trend in total output, they differ in the value of factor return. This chapter uses factor return as an indicator to distinguish those output increases brought about by technological changes from those factor-intensification-based, to detect possible technology changes in agriculture in Taiwan and China.

between agricultural and rural non-agricultural wages, but thanks to the regulatory impact of the *Hukou* system, there was insufficient movement of labour to compensate for the difference.[14] Using the rural labour wage to calculate the output–input ratio would therefore bias the result by exaggerating industrial profit. In this chapter, the opportunity cost of rural labour is used as the proxy cost of labour throughout the economy in mainland China. This price may reflect the market price of rural labour, otherwise rural capital return would be exaggerated by the distorted cost of labour in the agriculture sector.

A further issue used in previous output–input ratio research is adjusted here: namely, the cost of land. During the transition period, both mainland China and Taiwan imposed politically inspired policies to control the market trading of cultivated land, so that the price of land was less than what its market price would have been in the absence of such land regulation. As mentioned above, the reduced cost of land and labour will increase the returns of current inputs and give the illusion of a higher payoff other agricultural inputs, which is known as an increased shadow cost of agricultural inputs. In the short-term this will attract factor flow into agricultural production and lead to a short-term factor-intensification-based agricultural growth (and thereby a rise in agricultural output). However, in the long-term, if the difference of factor returns, rather than output–input ratio, is enlarged, other sectors (especially industry) will be affected by an increased shadow cost of factor inputs, generating higher returns and fluctuations in farm output. Moreover, the restriction in farm size, at least in China, during much of the reform period, has deterred certain kinds of high-return investments from being undertaken in agriculture. If investments are scale sensitive and only profitable for large-scale farming, small-scale farmers will not be able to fund investment which can generate new technology and increase marginal returns (both physical and human) from agricultural production. Controlled land

---

[14] Guangdong's coastal areas, especially Shenzhen and nearby towns in the Pearl River Delta (*zhu-jiang sanjiao zhou*, 珠江三角洲) region such as Dongguan, had fewer *Hukou* restrictions. This area experienced China's first wave of cross-province labour migration in the 1980s and early 1990s.

prices will cause capital to be excluded in certain key forms of investment in agricultural production, such as fixed assets and human capital. Further, this may distort agricultural production and make agriculture more labour intensive due to a lower price of labour relative to other inputs. We may infer that land control policies are significant in agricultural transition and influence agricultural production in the long-term.

5.3.1 Descriptive Statistics and Data Summary

Agricultural returns are calculated in this chapter by multiplying local farmgate purchase prices by annual gross agricultural production. The use of farmgate purchase prices will ensure that calculations of agricultural factor returns are not influenced by urban–rural price difference and exportation. Taiwan's agricultural statistics have been mainly sourced from Taiwan Agricultural Statistics 1901–1965 (1966) and the Taiwan Agricultural Yearbook (*taiwan nongye nianbo,* 台湾农业年报). Some missing data in the above two series are estimated from relevant indices to maintain the accuracy of annual agricultural capital return.

The Taiwan Agricultural Yearbook groups agricultural production into four main categories: crop production; livestock or livestock products; fishery; and forestry. This chapter only calculates returns for the first two groups, crop production and livestock or livestock products, since fishery and forestry were little affected by the agricultural reform. The most important crop products have been selected, accounting for around four-fifths of annual total value of output: the *ponlai* and *Chailai* (Indica rice, 在来稻) varieties of paddy rice; sweet potato; wheat; soybeans; peanuts; cassava; sugar; tea; tobacco and jute. Of the above crops, wheat and cassava production gradually declined over time, and from 1991 wheat constituted a small share of total agricultural production (in value terms). Cassava is not included in the main crop statistics where its farmgate purchase price is not available. Consequently, from 1991 agricultural returns do not include wheat and cassava. Taiwan has produced a great variety of fruits, from which bananas and pineapples have been chosen, since these have been ranked first and second (in terms of production) in most years from

1951 to 2000. Livestock is also a source of return and one of increasing importance for farmers. This chapter counts only those slaughtered livestock because only this part is included in the annual return.[15] Livestock feeding costs are not separated into those for slaughter and those not slaughtered in case the investment was based on that year's expectation of returns of feeding livestock. Since a farmer's investment expectation is based on the previous year's production conditions, there will be a one-year lag of the real return to investment. But for trend of factor return, a one-year lag is still not biased.

Prices of selected items will use farmgate purchase prices, not including trading and resale market prices, to ensure that the analysis reflects actual gross agricultural return. Prices of crops and livestock are taken from *Taiwan Agricultural Statistics*. For the period 1960–1965 the data sometimes differ; to maintain data coherence, this chapter follows the estimates given in the most recently published sources.

Land, in terms of importance, is the most substantial input. In this chapter land is measured in terms of the annual market price of total arable land. Early in Taiwan's agricultural reform (i.e., during land reform), rents were reduced to 37.5 per cent of the total annual output per land unit, and re-sales and trading of land in rural areas were severely restricted; later, cultivated land was sold in accordance with 'land to the tiller' policies. Normally, land rent[16] and market price reflects land productivity in agricultural production, but under the Taiwan Rent Reduction programme the land rent paid by tenants no longer represented the market price for arable land. Farm rent to a landlord could not exceed 37.5 per cent of the total annual output of land, nor could the percentage be increased if land quality and productivity improved. Thus, land rent fixed at 37.5 per cent was not a reflection of real market demand and supply, and therefore not to be used as an estimator factor return. Under KMT's land reform, reduction in rents was, to an extent, arbitrary which further greatly

---

[15] The remaining part of livestock will be calculated in later years' slaughtered livestock or annual assets formation.

[16] Besides the reflection of market price, land rent may also reflect what the landlord can squeeze from the tenant.

increased farmer's current revenue and household income. However, a biased land value obscures actual agricultural input costs where land occupies the largest share. A low land price might push farmers to invest more in labour and other inputs, significantly increasing output. This is the main argument proposed by Cheung (1969) to explain the rapid increase in agricultural output in Taiwan in post-war years,[17] and may indeed explain at least part of mainland's increased grain output early on in its transition—an intensive-input-based output increase.[18] However, when the reduced land price increased output, the marginal product based on shadow costs was also reduced.

Numerous conclusions can be drawn from the preceding analysis. First, if there is no restriction on inter-sectoral labour flows, in the long run more labour will be trapped in the agriculture sector, since cheap farmland input makes labour and other non-farmland inputs more profitable, as Cheung argues, therefore distort agricultural production incentives and the structure of economy. Second, when the flow of capital into the agriculture sector was restricted due to the absence of a free-land market, underestimated capital factors would flow out of agriculture into other sectors. The 'trapped' labour and other non-capital factor inputs will push intensive-inputs-based output increase. However, such an input-based output increase cannot raise the agriculture sector's factor return in the long-term. When the emphasis of Taiwan's economic policies shifted towards the industrial sector in the 1960s arable land started to be traded on the market, and its market price is available for this research. The market price of land before that time is estimated according to land prices in the industrial sector as its shadow price. After arable land was released to the market, land with underestimated return was re-sold to farm households that enjoyed higher returns to land or flowed out of agriculture. Under the impact of these adjustments, the opportunity cost of land eliminated production units with low capital returns, while raising capital returns for

---

[17] Cheung, Steven. *A Theory of Share Tenancy: with Special Application to Asia*. Chicago: University of Chicago Press, 1969.

[18] Besides, a significant part of the agricultural output rise reflected recovery from depressed levels of production caused by wartime dislocation. In 1949, output levels were still well below the 1937 peak.

agriculture. In this study, we will use the opportunity cost of land as the indicator of the shadow cost of arable land input.

Labour is the other input of major significance in household-based agricultural production. The annual cost of labour input in Taiwan is calculated here simply by multiplying the annual rural labour wage by the amount of labour employed in the agriculture sector. The method of estimating labour cost in production in the annual *Taiwan Agricultural Yearbook* is the primary production cost, and embodies direct costs, indirect costs (excluding land rent) and capital interest. Unlike the land input, labour flowed freely in Taiwan throughout agricultural transition. The price of rural labour was shaped over the long run by upward pressure exerted from the non-agriculture sector, as rural labour was attracted out of the farm sector from the late 1960s.

Thus, controlled land trading and reduced land rents at a constant level can also be viewed as a restriction to capital flow in the agriculture sector. It retains the total capital amount in the agriculture sector but has little effect in terms of influencing capital returns in the agriculture sector.

Plotting mainland China's agricultural return follows the same approach as that for Taiwan, but due to the different agricultural policies, farmland and labour costs are estimated during the whole reforming period to achieve an unbiased capital return ratio of mainland China's agriculture sector during its transition.

In contrast to Taiwan, the price of mainland China's agricultural output embraces several prices: namely, quota price, above quota price and negotiated purchase price (*yigou jia*, 议购价). Given various grain price, calculation of agricultural return will use the weighted average purchase price of major crop varieties,[19] similar to that for the livestock. The main sources of statistics are *China Statistical Yearbook* (*zhongguo tongji nianjian*, 中国统计年鉴), the *China Agriculture Yearbook* (*zhongguo nongye nianjian*, 中国农业年鉴), and most importantly, the *Cost Benefit Statistical Compendium of China's Major Agricultural Products 1953–1997* (*jianguo yilai quanguo*

---

[19] For example, the weight of quota price is the percentage of the traded quantity at this price over the total quantity. The weighted average purchase price of agricultural product will give us an unbiased return on agricultural production.

zhuyao nongchanping chengben shouyi huibian, 建国以来全国主要农产品成本收益资料汇编). The values of land and rural labour are estimated from the same-year data in the industrial sector to avoid inflated estimates.

Mainland China's agricultural production is grouped into farming, fishery and forestry categories. According to the Cost Benefit Statistical Compendium of China's Major Agricultural Products 1953–1997, China's major agricultural products are wheat, rice, soybean, corn, oil bearing crops (peanuts and rapeseed), cotton, flue-cured tobacco, sugarcane, beetroot, mulberry silkworm cocoons and, as a proxy for livestock products, pork. Due to data limitations, fruits and other agricultural products have not been included. The above bundle of 12 products accounts for most of mainland China's annual agricultural output and revenue and will give almost unbiased output data.

Land has been tightly controlled as non-private property since the early 1950s. China has no private rural land market, and there is therefore no market price of land. The HRS re-distributed farmland to individual rural households and helped enhanced agricultural production efficiency. However, under the early HRS contract a certain quantity of agricultural products had to be sold to the grain bureau at a fixed price in exchange for usage rights to cultivated land. Under this household-state sales contract, the value of land is an invisible cost of annual agricultural production which should be reflected in the cost of products. Lack of price data for China's cultivated land poses the biggest problem in plotting the factor return of the agriculture sector. This chapter uses the land price in the non-agriculture sector in the rural, where land transfer and market activities still exist.

As with land, flow of rural labour is also restricted in China until recent rural outmigration has taken place. Under the *Hukou* system, the flow of labour from agriculture to the non-agriculture sectors was traditionally limited, even the regional inter-sectoral flow. If we use the underestimated return to rural labour under the *Hukou* system, it may generate an agricultural production cost that is too low and an output-input ratio that is too high, giving an illusion of high payoffs in China's agriculture

142 J. Du

sector. The low mobility of rural labour makes it difficult to estimate a rural market labour wage, and instead we use here the wage level of workers in state-owned agricultural farms[20] and in rural industries in the late 1980s (known as TVEs) to estimate the shadow cost of mainland China's agriculture labour.[21]

5.3.2 Analytical Framework

The numerator of the agriculture sector's factor return, is the same year net income from total farm output. This, in turn, is the difference between annual gross agricultural profit and production costs (direct and indirect) in the same year. Gross agricultural profit is simply measured by multiplying output by relevant purchase prices. Annual agricultural production costs are divided into two categories: direct costs and indirect costs. Direct costs consist of current factor inputs needed to sustain production, such as the cost of seeds, fertiliser, labour input, chemicals and herbicides, irrigation and land rent, and so on. Indirect costs are calculated as depreciation of farm machinery and tools, and agricultural taxes and fees. Different from direct cost in production, indirect cost will only calculate the current incurred production cost—therefore, for land only rent and for tools and machinery only the depreciation costs of that year are taken into consideration.

The denominator is calculated in terms of the total input or gross capital formation at the end of the year. Normally, total input is the value of rural land, of rural labour input and of other fixed assets (e.g., machinery and farming tools). The denominator should seek to calculate the true value of all investments rather than their current price (since current prices may be distorted). The agricultural policy in Taiwan, post-1949, sought to reduce tenants' rents, meanwhile China's post-1979 agricultural policies re-distributed arable land to households, which fixed farmer's production incentives of land use rights. Early in Taiwan's reform a rent

---

[20] Before the 1990s, numbers of state-owned agricultural farms located throughout China decreased as a rural economy developed after post-1979 reform. Nowadays, most state-owned agricultural farms are located in Northeast of China, such as Heilongjiang and Hainan.

[21] Because of the absence of a rural labour market, to avoid underestimate of wage of farmers, here we use the opportunity cost of the wage of farmers by using a weighted wage calculated from rural workers in TVEs and the state-owned farm workers.

reduction to 37.5 per cent was considered an effective policy incentive to increase agricultural production, while in China the HRS distributed arable land to household on condition that a certain amount of the output of their major crop was sold to the government at a fixed price. The fixed land rent in Taiwan[22] and fixed state purchase price in China may be viewed as the contract price of the land use rights; however, this price was not formed in the private rental market but determined by government. It follows that using the fixed price to evaluate the largest part of investment in agricultural production will lead to biased results. Thus, the value of arable land is derived from its market price, or, where this is not available, from the use market price of industrial land in rural areas. Valuing labour presents the same problem. Taiwan imposed no restriction on labour flows from the agriculture sector, which means that the labour wage stated in the annual *Taiwan Agricultural Yearbook* was the market price of rural human capital. For household-supplied labour, we use the rural labour wage, as the opportunity cost, to replace to calculate the true value of labour investment for a given year's agricultural production. Unlike Taiwan, before 1990s, China's rural labour is strictly controlled and prohibited from flowing into the urban sector under the *Hukou* System, which prohibited the free flow of labour from the agriculture to the industrial sector until the emergence of TVEs and later relaxation of rural labour movements. In the denominator we use the labour price as the opportunity cost of rural labour and estimate those years where data for the actual price of rural labour are missing by using as proxy the wage in TVEs or peasant labour in urban construction. Other inputs measured are agricultural production gross capital formation, data for which are available in *China Agriculture Yearbook*. These contain the value of current capital investment in machines and farming tools after depreciation.

An estimator of industrial factor return is easier to obtain. Industrial factor return is industry net profit divided by the sum of industrial sector fixed assets, total wages and liquid assets for the relevant year. All these data are available in the statistical yearbooks of both Taiwan and China mentioned above. As in the explanation of the agriculture sector above, net income measures return from the industrial sector, and fixed assets are

---

[22] The policy of fixed rent of land at 37.5 per cent was carried out in Taiwan from 1949.

long-term investment in industrial production, including machinery, tools and land. The wage rate is the price of labour in industrial production. In contrast to agriculture, industrial labour prices both in China and Taiwan are available. Other assets measured are all current inputs used in annual production, including the costs of raw materials.

5.3.3 Factor-Return Analysis

Estimates of output and returns from 1950 to 2000 in Taiwan and the rate of return on agricultural factor reveal the main effect of Taiwan's agricultural policies. Obviously, the implications from the results of factor return are greatly different from the agricultural output per capita.

Figure 5.1 plots Taiwan's annual total agricultural value output and production expenses (excluding the cost of arable land). It shows a steady increase in returns to the agriculture sector return from 1950 to 2000 in Taiwan with a sharp increase in 1963, 1973 and 1991, and a sharp downturn in the mid-1990s. In Taiwan, rural income per capita increased by 19.4 per cent per year during the post-war recovery from 1955 to 1966, but by only 14.7 per cent in the non-agriculture sector. The sectoral factor

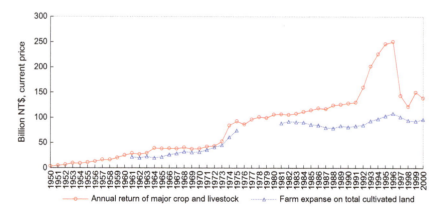

Fig. 5.1 Annual gross return and expenses of Taiwan agricultural production. Sources: *Taiwan Nongye Nianbao* (Taiwan Agricultural Yearbook). Department of Agriculture and Forestry, Provincial Government of Taiwan. Taiwan: Department of Agriculture and Forestry, 1947–2013 Editions; FAOSTAT. *Food and Agriculture Organization of the United Nations Database*, 27 May 2013, http://faostat3.fao.org/home/index.html

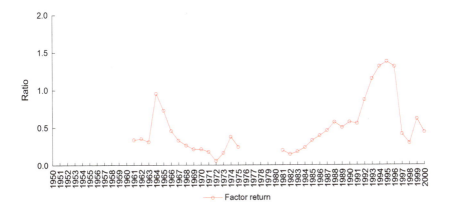

Fig. 5.2 Factor return in Taiwan agricultural production. Sources: *Taiwan Nongye Nianbao* (Taiwan Agricultural Yearbook). Department of Agriculture and Forestry, Provincial Government of Taiwan. Taiwan: Department of Agriculture and Forestry, 1947–2013 Editions; FAOSTAT. *Food and Agriculture Organization of the United Nations Database*, 27 May 2013, http://faostat3.fao.org/home/index.html

return difference attracted inflow of new capital into agriculture, thus the increasing rate of output growth was sustained, with a high return to agricultural investment (Fig. 5.2).

Figure 5.3 shows revenue accruing from China's major agricultural crops. Both cost and revenue increase continuously and gradually until a sharp increase in the early 1990s. From 1993 to 1996, the difference between cost and revenue increases, giving a dramatic increase rate in net income from China's agricultural production. However, after this period it starts to fluctuate with a slight decreasing trend.

The return ratio of agricultural production in mainland China (not including the price of land) shows a different increasing trend to that of revenue and net profit in Fig. 5.4. After 1978, the factor return ratio increases rapidly up to 1985. From 1985 to 1989 both output ratio and factor return ratio fluctuate and decrease a little. But as in Taiwan, around 1994 this ratio rises but then decreases sharply in the following three to four years.

Reform began in the agriculture sector in China, and a significant increase in agricultural efficiency indicated by the revenue ratio is observable up to 1985, showing the impact of those early reforms. But after 1985, the first HRS contract period ended, and new pricing policies,

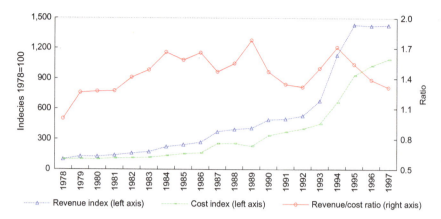

Fig. 5.3 Revenue-cost ratio of mainland China's major type of agricultural production. Sources: *Zhongguo Nongye Nianjian* (China Agriculture Yearbook). The Editorial Committee of China Agricultural Statistical Yearbook. Beijing: China Agriculture Press, 1980–2013 Editions; FAOSTAT. *Food and Agriculture Organization of the United Nations Database*, 27 May 2013, http://faostat3.fao.org/home/index.html

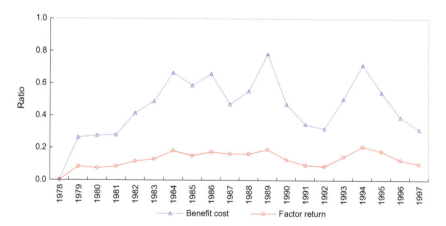

Fig. 5.4 Factor return in China's major type of agricultural production. Sources: *Zhongguo Nongye Nianjian* (China Agriculture Yearbook). The Editorial Committee of China Agricultural Statistical Yearbook. Beijing: China Agriculture Press, 1980–2013 Editions; FAOSTAT. *Food and Agriculture Organization of the United Nations Database*, 27 May 2013, http://faostat3.fao.org/home/index.html

with the new approach signalled in Document No. 1 in January 1985,[23] led to a slowdown in the second half of the 1980s. In 1989, after several years' slowdown, the government extended the period of cultivated land usage rights and this stimulated the ratio to return to the pre-1985 level.

Agricultural product circulation in China was strictly regulated before the 1979 reform. Even after 1979, the main trading bodies in the wholesale market—those certified companies with the right to purchase grain directly from peasants—were still controlled by the government. The level of agricultural revenue during the reform era reflects the degree of marketisation: if the market can clear out sufficiently quickly, and if factor prices are overestimated—or underestimated, the revenue ratio will be stable; but this did not happen. If factor return (price) in the agriculture sector shows a long-term divergence trend comparing with that in non-agriculture sectors, there must be some disturbance blocking intersectoral factor flows—possibly the long term institutional issues.

Mainland China's agricultural production pattern contrasts with that of Taiwan. Without the calculation of land value, mainland's agriculture factor return ratio mainly changed within the frame from 0.3 to 0.8. It changed less rapidly mainly because mainland's agricultural production was less affected by market influences except during the 1993 grain reform. From 1993 until the late 1990s China was reforming its agricultural market system. The task of sales price and purchase price regulation was gradually devolved to local government, and even the free market trade of major agricultural products was sanctioned. This is the main reason why, from 1993, a sharp increase in revenue, net profit and return to factor was driven by a sudden increase in the selling price of major agricultural products. After 1995, the government re-centralised power to address the huge fiscal deficits in the state's grain purchase system and in the name of national food security (e.g., the 1998 reform).

---

[23] Central Committee Document No. 1. 'Ten Policies of the Chinese Communist Central Committee and the State Council for Further Enlivening the Rural Economy' (*zhonggong zhongyang guowuyuan guanyu jinyibu huoyue nongcun jingji de shi xiang zhengce*, 中共中央国务院关于进一步活跃农村经济的十项政策). Beijing: Communist Party of China Central Committee, 1 January 1985.

5.4 Summary

In the comparable periods of Taiwan's and China's agricultural transitions, both areas experienced non-market intervention from the political institutional framework. By observing factor return in agricultural production under complex market institution, this chapter aims to detect the occurrence of technical change in agricultural transition, as well as the general trend of technical change. Although the method of factor return cannot verify which specific technologies are selected from the existing technology set during agricultural technological transition, this method will facilitate our further analysis of technical change and help to explore the conditions that affect China's, as well as other East Asian economies', agricultural transition, in the following chapter. On the other hand, since Taiwan's agricultural techniques were mainly diffused from Japan during colonialism, the next chapter will move onto a comparison between China and Japan. To compare it with IIC framework, empirical studies in the next chapter also touch some selected Southeast and East Asian economies.

Although Japan has a relatively easier economic and political institution compared to other East Asian economies, it still did not induce obvious agricultural technology changes during the 1960s when green revolution spread throughout South and Southeast Asian economies. As another important rice economy in East Asia, green revolution technologies in China were not introduced to agriculture until its opening in the 1980s. Therefore, the absence of technology change in the 1960s' Chinese agriculture was more likely an interception process that blocked new technology from diffusing to Chinese agriculture. And obviously this technology interception was caused for political reasons. But in post-war Japan, political and economic institution were both closer to an ideal institution which contributed a lot to the economic take-off. So, what caused or distorted the agricultural technology change in Japan after the 1960s? And what prevented Japanese agriculture to introduce technology changes? The following chapter will answer these questions and interpret possible technology distortions under different market institutions in selected Asian economies.

References

Central Document No. 1 [1985]. *Zhonggong Zhongyang Guowuyuan 'Guanyu Jinyibu Huoyue Nongcun Jingji De Shi Xiang Zhengce* (Ten Policies of the Chinese Communist Central Committee and the State Council for Further Enlivening the Rural Economy, 中发[1985]1号《中共中央、国务院<关于进一步活跃农村经济的十项政策>》). Beijing: Communist Party of China Central Committee, 1 January 1985.

Cheung, Steven. 'Privatization vs. Special Interests: The Experience of China's Economic Reforms.' *Cato Journal* 8, no. 3 (1989): 585–596.

———. *A Theory of Share Tenancy: With Special Application to Asia*. Chicago: University of Chicago Press, 1969.

Cumings, Bruce. 'The Origins and Development of the Northeast Asian Political Economy: Industrial Sectors, Product Cycles, and Political Consequences.' *International Organization* 38, no. 1 (1984): 1–40.

FAOSTAT. *Food and Agriculture Organization of the United Nations Database*. 27 May 2013. http://faostat3.fao.org/home/index.html.

Jianguo Yilai Quanguo Zhuyao Nongchanping Chengben Shouyi Ziliao Huibian 1953–1997 (Cost Benefit Statistical Compendium of China's Major Agricultural Products 1953–1997). Department of Prices, National Development and Reform Commission. Beijing: China Prices Press, 2003.

Land Administration Law of the People's Republic of China. National People's Congress of People's Republic of China. The Tenth Session of the Ninth National People's Congress. Beijing, 29 August 1998.

Lin, Justin. 'Rural Reforms and Agricultural Growth in China.' *American Economic Review* 82, no 1 (1992): 34–51.

National Bureau of Statistics of China. *Zhongguo Tongji Nianjian* (China Statistical Yearbook). Beijing: China Statistics Press, 1981–2013 Editions.

Samuelson, Paul. 'International Trade and the Equalisation of Factor Prices.' *The Economic Journal* 58 (June 1948): 163–184.

———. 'Prices of Factors and Good in General Equilibrium.' *Review of Economic Studies* 21 (1953): 1–21.

Taiwan Agricultural Statistics, 1901–1965. Joint Commission on Rural Reconstruction (JCRR), Rural Economics Division. Taiwan: Chinese-American Commission on Rural Reconstruction, 1966.

Taiwan Agricultural Statistics, 1961–1975. Joint Commission on Rural Reconstruction (JCRR), Rural Economics Division. Taiwan: Chinese-American Commission on Rural Reconstruction, 1977.

Taiwan Nongye Nianbao (Taiwan Agricultural Yearbook). Department of Agriculture and Forestry, Provincial Government of Taiwan. Taiwan: Department of Agriculture and Forestry, 1947–2013 Editions.

Zhongguo Nongye Nianjian (China Agriculture Yearbook). The Editorial Committee of China Agricultural Statistical Yearbook. Beijing: China Agriculture Press, 1980–2013 Editions.

6

Agricultural Transition in Selected Asian Economies

6.1 Introduction

This chapter will observe the agricultural technology changes in selected Asian economies. In Asian agricultural development, especially in the first phase of the green revolution, technical change was mainly represented by improvements in the inputs, such as seeds. These improved inputs may be regarded as imported technology, made available through their diffusion from developed countries. In this case, improvements in the means of production were not the product of domestic efforts, indicating that technical change in the early phase of the green revolution was unrelated to Asia's domestic technological externalities.

Following this first phase of technological diffusion, technical change in Asian economies, including that of China, began to reflect the process of technology localisation. This process may be regarded as defining the second phase of Asia's green revolution. Along with the externality diffused from America, this same externality however sparked different technology transitions among Asian economies. Thus, the unique features of 'diversification' and 'imbalance' in Asian agriculture imply that there are still other important factors determining the agricultural technology transition in Asia in addition to the technology diffusion from America.

© The Author(s) 2018   **151**
J. Du, *Agricultural Transition in China*, Palgrave Studies in Economic History,
https://doi.org/10.1007/978-3-319-76905-9_6

Hayami is one of the economists who observed the particularities in Asian agricultural and technological transition. His 'induced innovation' theory, based on the empirical studies of the Philippine rice economy, emphasises the role of the agricultural institution in determining the agricultural growth and technology change in Asia (Hayami 1969; Hayami and Ruttan 1970a, b, 1985, 1995). However, as mentioned earlier, IIC theory is a paradigm under the neoclassical economic framework. IIC theory about technology change is strongly dependent on some key hypotheses on market institution from neoclassical economics. This is partly because IIC theory was deduced from Southeast Asia's empirical studies. Although Southeast Asia's economic level was below the Asian average, its institutional framework was easier during the green revolution, with little government interventions over agricultural transition. Therefore, Southeast Asian's agricultural empirical facts can objectively satisfy the requirement of key market institution hypothesis from IIC theory. Put simply, the empirical studies based on Southeast Asia's agricultural technology transition cannot highlight the constraint of key institution to shape the technology 'diversification' and 'imbalance' in Asian agricultural transition.

However, in Asia the concentrated area of rice planting is East Asia, especially the East Asian irrigated rice planting area. When we observe agricultural technology changes, the features of technology 'diversification' and 'imbalance' are even more obvious in East Asia, such as the timing and duration of technology change and the choice of technology varieties. Japan, the Korean peninsula and Taiwan's agricultural technology change started before the WW2, however mainland China's agricultural transition started after the end of the 1970s. Given the initial technology exogenous (diffused from the same technology origin), above differences could not be explained by relative factor price difference among East Asian economies. Therefore, empirical studies of East Asia indicate that IIC theory based on relative factor price difference was and is not a powerful explanation for the East Asia's technology change and agricultural transition. On the other hand, China's inter-regional rural income level differs greatly, but this inter-regional rural income difference does not induce any technology generation gap within China. Thus, these phenomena in agricultural technology change in East Asia imply that some other key institutional factors, different from those in IIC theory, influenced on East Asia's agricultural technology change significantly.

6.1.1 Transition Patterns and Regional Difference

Economic development in China and some other Asian economies, for example Malaysia, has typically been characterised, during the transition process, by unbalanced development across regions. This has generally had two outcomes: first, it has generated inter-regional resource flows; second, it has generated wide differences in labour–capital–land ratios. Theoretically, following the standard Heckscher–Ohlin factor endowment theory (Heckscher and Ohlin 1991; Samuelson 1953), product flows between regions will, through FPE, offset the above differences in regional labour–capital–land ratio. In the real economy, however, this regional equalisation path, facilitated by resource flows and product sales, has not been attained in agriculture, especially in developing countries. In China, for instance, differences in regional agricultural labour–capital–land ratio have not shown a convergence trend in the long run. Rather, resource and labour flows have tended to reinforce the existing differences and even cause inter-regional gaps in terms of technical and institutional difference—as different technology and institutions lead to different labour–capital–land ratio.

From the point of view of technological and institutional transition, path dependence between regions may evolve in various ways. The first path culminates in convergence. Although there may be regional specialisation, or labour–capital–land ratio difference caused by historical reasons, but when factor prices are equalised through the flow of resources and factors, the return to capital or labour converges between areas in the long run. Implied in this 'solution' is the role of the market as a facilitator of factors flows between regions and, further, as a vehicle for FPE between regions.

The second potential evolutionary path states that specialisation between regions eventually enlarges inter-regional differences in capital availability per capita and widens inter-regional personal income gaps. The essential point here is that under certain institutions, the externality of factors (e.g., human capital and physical capital) may be 'locked' within a region so that capital accumulates at different speeds in different regions. Both above evolution paths are observable in Asian empirical studies.

6.1.2 Capital Accumulation and Technological Progress

Most research literature on agricultural transition, view technical change and capital accumulation as independent processes. Thus, factor accumulation based on some Asian empirical studies is viewed as a separate process from technological transition. However, in China, the Korean Peninsula and some other East Asian economies including Japan, the irrigation technique is inseparable from physical and human capital accumulation. This is an obvious core feature of agricultural development in China, where the irrigation system originated before the Song dynasty (tenth century) and thereafter continued to evolve in the Kiangnan area until it became well-developed in the late Ming dynasty (1368–1644). It took hundreds of years for the irrigation system to become universally adopted in Kiangnan, the most important reason for this being the slow speed of capital and labour accumulation in pre-industrial China as aforementioned in Chap. 2.

The history of the popularisation of irrigation systems in East Asia shows that it was, in fact, technological breakthroughs that were contingent on continued labour and capital accumulation. Such evidence from Asia challenges the standard transition pattern captured in IIC. Irrigation is an essential element to support agricultural technology change in East Asia's irrigated paddy rice planting region, in addition to seed and fertilisers. In this area irrigation technology was therefore well-developed, and more efficient than other aspects of rice planting technology. However, due to lack of sufficient labour and capital, irrigation technology could not push rice planting technology to be adopted during the first five hundred years when it has been introduced into Kiangnan.

From a micro-perspective, there are three types of technological transition in agriculture. In the first, with inputs unchanged, technological transition can raise total output. That is, resources (labour, capital and land) remain the same in the short term, and the main impetus for increased production comes from technical change. In the second type of technological transition, like the first type, productivity has been increased, but the improved technology allows more resources to flow into this sector. In other words, marginal productivity has been improved so that the new production in more 'intensive'. However, such kind of technical change requires resources flow into this sector with improved technology level to achieve better economic performance. The second case is essentially a variant of neoclassical sectorial growth; however, crucially, there must be a competitive market or appropriate market institutions to enable the sector in which technical change has taken place to obtain resources (capital, labour or other products) from other parts of the economy. Third, technical change may completely change the whole form of production, the previous mode of production has been omitted, and resources were re-organised. As recorded in some developing countries, existing techniques have been entirely replaced by better technologies imported from other countries. Under the specific transition conditions in Asia, the technological transition hypothesis is decomposed into the following questions: first, if we observe for Asia as a whole, after WW2, did rice production—in both irrigated and non-irrigated areas—show a converging or diverging trend? From the framework of neoclassical growth theory, the answer is that it is converging: the meaning of convergence in neoclassical growth embodies a factor equalisation process of per capita output caused convergence in per capita capital stock. However, we should point out that convergence in agriculture has different implications from convergence in industry. Basically, this difference arises from the properties of the form of production: agricultural production strongly depends on external conditions, such as the climate change, over which humans have no control. These factors thus dominate the technology that can be applied, which further determines the proper level of capital stock.

The second question addresses the relationship between the localisation of agricultural technological progress (as a part of technical change) and agricultural transition. The nature of this relationship is likely to vary when different hypotheses are applied. In neoclassical economics, technical change is regarded as neutral, so that it could spread instantaneously to every sector of the economy. This neoclassical view may can, however only be applied in the industrial sector. When there exists externality—say, an externality is shared within a certain sector—technological progress is in fact determined by the capital (physical/human) stock. Then, in the agriculture sector it is the economic size of the whole sector. Taken further, we argue that if in a specific area or country the agriculture sector lacks the proper necessary factor stock, its route to technological improvement may be blocked. This will result in an inefficient agriculture. This argument is also based on one condition: the agriculture sector relies on local resources more than other sectors. If so, we can say that agricultural technical change depends only on the local externalities of economic factors rather than those imported from outside.

Finally, we assume agriculture and non-agriculture compete for resources. If sectors are competitive and the industrial sector gains priority status, will adopted technical change in agriculture accommodate the reduction in resources to which it has access? In the IIC model, agricultural technology can accommodate the limited resources and change accordingly in the long-term. However, implicit in this IIC argument is that agricultural technology is free in the whole economy (or, say, the technology is given with zero information cost). If the IIC model holds in the long-term, we must be able to observe that agricultural technology has a convergence trend in areas with similar trends in non-agriculture sector development. We therefore take these questions to the following empirical studies on agricultural growth in selected Asian economies.

6.2 International Comparisons

Following the implementation of the green revolution in Asia, Asian rice output showed a stable and continuous growing trend. The technological origins of the green revolution in Asia were twofold. One dimension was the improved rice varieties and existing technology diffused from Japan—but this diffusion was limited in East Asia and mostly took place in Taiwan; the other reason was the application of post-war USA—European technology, if we consider China's agriculture development after 1979 as a continuation of Asia's green revolution, then the technology diffusion may also include the latest version of innovation such as in the genetic improvement in biological technology.

The narrowly defined green revolution in Asia started in South and Southeast Asia after WW2. Initially in the 1960s, it was a typical example of technology transfer involving the diffusion and adoption by Asian economies of new rice (and wheat) varieties. As natural conditions are important in adopting agricultural technology, the green revolution's diffusion path in later 1960s and 1970s also highlighted the technology localisation process. In Asia, at least part of the green revolution can be defined as factor-saving agricultural technology and the diffusion of related technologies from the originating country—Japan and the Philippines—to other Asian economies. The early green revolution by a broader definition, especially that part of it concerned with growing rice, followed the historical pattern of technology transfer during the early twentieth century, when Japanese rice planting technology was transferred from Japan to the Korean Peninsula and Taiwan. Through the adoption process, the core of the green revolution was the application of the new farm technology in different economies, with appropriate local variety development initiatives that accommodated different local natural endowments and environmental conditions. Therefore, the green revolution, in fact, consists of two aspects: (a) the transferral of existing technological processes; (b) the corresponding localisation process with innovative adoption and appropriate modification.

6.2.1 Three Features of Rice Production in Asian Economies After WW2

From the indicators of average yield per unit of land shown in Fig. 6.1, post-war rice output trends in Asian economies show three obvious features.

Despite differences among major rice planting economies in Asia, as rice production per hectare has increased more than doubled, the first characteristic of the post-war Asian rice output is the overall yields growth. Annual fluctuations in individual economies' yields might be caused by non-economic reasons, as in Indonesia the unstable political situation can always cause agriculture instability. Two observations suggest themselves (a) over the long run, the absolute level of rice yield increased greatly, since potential yield declines induced by institutional or other factors could be fully compensated by increased output generated by enhanced technology; (b) Asia as a whole, especially South and East Asia,

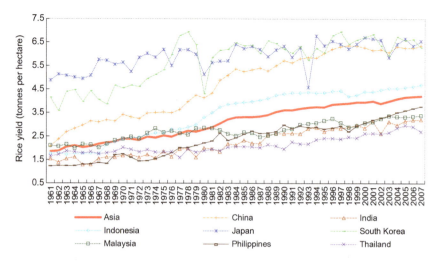

Fig. 6.1 Per hectare paddy rice yield in selected Asian economies, 1961–2007. Source: FAOSTAT, FAO, accessed 19 June 2013, http://faostat3.fao.org/home/index.html

saw an obvious increase in per hectare rice output despite annual fluctuations in individual economies (e.g., South Korea and Japan). Even allowing for technology and institution variations across economies, the green revolution generated increases in yields throughout the entire region. This steady growth was not coincidental.

The second factor is that Asia's average per hectare rice yield far exceeded the world average. Historical factors helped produce this outcome: Asia, especially South and East Asia, is the origin of rice and rice-planting technology. Asia's natural conditions are more suitable for rice cultivation than other parts of the world (Asia has the largest sown area of rice of all continents). Rice planting is only a small-scale agricultural activity outside Asia and its history is more recent. For example, rice was introduced to Spain by the Arabians in the middle ages, but never became popular in Europe.

The third feature of Asian rice production is the special importance in rice cultivation in East Asia (Japan, China, the Korean Peninsula and Taiwan). The average rice yield per hectare in East Asia economies has long been higher than in other Asian economies (see Fig. 6.1), although it is noteworthy that in irrigated areas the single-cropped rice yield per hectare may be less than

Agricultural Transition in Selected Asian Economies   **159**

in non-irrigated areas, but where are two or even three crops (usually one is wheat) are harvested each year, the average arable area yield in these areas has tended to be the highest in Asia. Japan, China, Korea and Taiwan's accumulation of skills over many centuries has given them special superiority in rice planting, which has translated into high yields, thanks especially to the development of double or even triple rice cropping.

6.2.2 Implications of Rice Production

The tradition of planting rice as a major crop gives Asia a higher average yield per unit of land. Rice production in Asia, especially East Asia, has been characterised by a significant feature 'involution', which implies that the increase in output is merely brought about by continuous increases in factor input.[1] From this perspective, rice cultivation in East Asia is often regarded as the embodiment of a special technology. This partly explains why Asia's rice yields always remains at high level, especially the East Asian economies.

For a long period, rice production in East Asian economies, not only in China, showed similar 'involutionary' characteristics. But in the late nineteenth and early twentieth centuries, the 'involutionary' process began to differentiate. Japan after Meiji Restoration (*Meiji Ishin*, 明治維新, 1868) was the first country in Asia to introduce modern institution. By the 1930s, Japan had also developed a completely new agricultural technology package, including the use of modern hybrid seeds and chemical fertilisers. During its colonial period, Taiwan benefited from Japan's earlier agricultural transition. In short, Japan and its colonies were the first group of economies in Asia to undertake an agricultural transition with new agricultural technologies diffused from Japan. We may therefore say that the modernisation of Asian's agriculture began before WW2. In Asia's experience, rice cultivation before WW2 relies on labour input more than machines, the green revolution in major Asia rice planting economies—from the early Japanese transition to China's post-1979 transition—involved the use of new seeds, chemicals

---

[1] Thanks to a sharp and continuous decline in the marginal product of labour, the involutionary process was characterised by high land output side by side with a low output-to-labour ratio.

(fertilisers and pesticides) and other non-mechanical agricultural technologies. However, the origins of such technologies are to be found in developments that took place before WW2, and from this viewpoint Asia's post-1960 green revolution should therefore be viewed as part of a longer-term agricultural transition in the region, rather than simply the result of post-1960 advances in agricultural technology.

To explain more fully the pattern and evolution of rice production in Asia, especially East Asia, various patterns of technological transition will be discussed below.

The first pattern of technological transition was the pattern which embodied early rice cultivation technology in East Asia. In pre-industrial times East Asian economies developed irrigated rice planting technology, which often evolved into a double cropping—rice–wheat or rice–rice—pattern of cultivation. This significantly reduced dependency on soil quality in East Asia and made non-fallow cropping possible throughout the year. However, constrained by some crucial natural conditions such as rainfall and water supply, irrigation cropping technology could only be carried out in certain parts of Asia. In the east coast of Asia, where most irrigated land is located, the diffusion of modern technology from Japan began.

The second type of technological transition involves technology import. Not only were the seed varieties in Asian economies underdeveloped, compared with those of Europe and North America; so too were pesticides and chemical fertilisers. Benefiting from the development of local chemical fertiliser and pesticide industries, and fast-growing international trade in the post-war era, many Asian economies were able to access modern fertilisers and pesticides more easily than ever before, to the benefit of local production. The widespread application of chemical fertilisers, pesticides and—much more recently—bio-technologies helped protect agricultural production against natural constraints. The imported technology also enabled rice cultivation to be extended to non-irrigated fields. In the north and some parts of Northwest China, new seeds, fertilisers and pesticides together with the application of water-saving irrigation technology (drip and spray irrigation) considerably raised yields on dry land.

The two technological origins form the background to Asia's green revolution. More broadly, such technological changing process lasted from the green revolution to China's post-1979 agricultural transition. Although in theory two types of technology transition patterns can easily be distinguished, in practice the boundary between the two is blurred. For instance, in India and some other Southeast Asia economies, the so-called 'Second Green Revolution' was in fact a local adaptation and consolidation of imported technologies. In East Asia these imported technologies accelerated the substitution effect whereby capital increasingly replaced labour, especially in terms of the introduction of irrigated cultivation. According to Hayami and Kikuchi (1985, 1999), increased rice output in East Asia followed a similar pattern—from expanding the arable area to increasing non-land capital factors (e.g., fertiliser, machinery, etc.).

However, inherent in this process are two different effects that translated into higher total production, which Hayami and Kikuchi fail to separate in their work. First, Japanese agricultural intensification started from the Tokugawa Shogunate (徳川幕府, 1600–1868),[2] but after the Meiji Restoration, with arable land having been exhausted in Hokkaido, Japan was forced to generate further increases in total output through higher per hectare yields. Thus, Japan's agricultural technology transition may be regarded as a self-enforced technology transition pattern carried over from the pre-industrial period. Second, the yield increases in the Philippines during the green revolution and thereafter initially relied on the diffusion of technology from other economies, although later the Philippines embarked on its own indigenous technology initiatives. Thus, the second type of technology transition came from technology imports that were then from further self-enforced innovation.

Based on empirical studies of Southeast Asian economies, the IIC theory embodies two logical arguments: the first of these is that local originated technological transition and imported technological transition are similar. This is obvious in the analysis of induced innovation in Southeast Asian agriculture. IIC is a theory of choosing technology from an existing set of technologies. In other words, when resources come under pressure, individuals can adjust technologies or institutions (their choice be constrained only by what technologies and institutions are

---

[2] This is also known as the Edo Bakufu (江戸幕府).

available). As those developing countries are not normally at the frontiers of technology so that they are reliant on technology imports from developed countries to advance their technologies, by contrast, technological progress in developed countries (frontier technologies) is still costly. And, even if, in the early phase of technology transfer, the technology to developing countries is free—no research and development cost. But when the market no longer has available and suitable technology to choose from, the technological transition in developing economies must involve with a certain level of research and development cost to meet their local demand.

Second, IIC implies the free flow of capital and labour between sectors during the technological transition. However, contrary to this assumption, in the Asian economies especially the East Asian economies, there existed a variety of barriers that prevented resources from flowing in this manner. In addition, neoclassical new growth theory also carries an implication that the level of innovation is a product of the externality: more externality, more innovations. However, externality is a product of scale economy. In other words, the size of the economy and the level of factor accumulation determines the level of the externality, therefore determines the innovation process.

From the preceding it emerges that the crucial difference between IIC theory and new growth theory may be expressed as follows: IIC assumes that an individual can react to the market directly with the ready-to-use technology and such technology adoption can be implemented with the absence of collective action. In new growth theory, innovation arises from the externality of capital, and such externalities—for example research and development process—are relatively dependent on existing market institutions.[3] Thus IIC and new growth theory complement one another: new growth theory focuses on how technologies are generated; IIC focuses on how technologies are introduced and applied to the production process.

---

[3] It is determined by the cost of: (a) collective action; (b) the level of incentive to generate innovation; and (c) the nature of the distribution of revenue between the innovator and other beneficiaries.

6.3 Japan and China

Return to rice production. After WW2 total rice output in Asia more than tripled; however, this increase was uneven across countries.

Nearly 55 per cent of the increase in output (1961–2007) occurred in China and India—and 33 per cent of incremental rice output was generated by China (shown in Fig. 6.2). Since rice total output in Japan declined by one third, it is clear that Asian developing economies were responsible for the entire increase in total output. In short, a salient feature of post-war rice production in Asia is that increases in production were first and foremost a phenomenon of developing economies.

6.3.1 Japan

East Asia, China and Japan have comparable basic agricultural environments for rice growing. Japan and China both have a long history of rice cultivation, both countries' agricultural economies were based on rice planting until comparative recently. Besides the rice planting history, their traditional varieties of paddy rice are also similar. For geographical and environmental reasons, rice cultivation in Taiwan and the

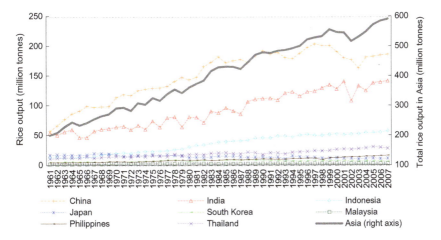

Fig. 6.2 Rice output in selected Asian economies, 1961–2007. Source: FAOSTAT. *Food and Agriculture Organization of the United Nations Database*, 27 May 2013, http://faostat3.fao.org/home/index.html

Korean Peninsula has however, to a greater or lesser extent, shown greater differences from that of China and Japan.

Post-war agricultural development in China and Japan has a special significance: prior to the 1970s, Japan was the only Asian country to have undergone modern industrialisation, and its agricultural transition had ended long before WW2. However, after the war, Japan's grain production, including rice, stagnated for a long time from 1970 and Japan became the largest grain importer in the world while its rice production declined year by year. It had had the highest per hectare rice yield after the war, but its land productivity was subsequently superseded by China and South Korea.

Japan's rice production during its post-war economic development did not match its industrial growth. Not only did the rice output decline from early 1970s, but also the Japanese agricultural GDP (shown in Fig. 6.3) fell into stagnation status and such stagnancy continued

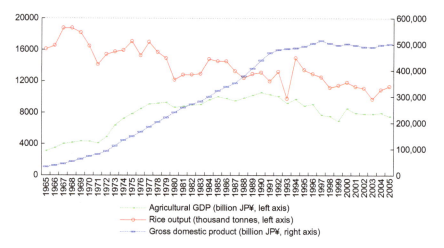

Fig. 6.3 National GDP, agricultural GDP and total rice output in Japan. Source: *Japan Statistical Yearbook*. Statistical Research and Training Institute, MIC. Statistics Bureau, Ministry of Internal Affairs and Communications of Japan. Tokyo: Japan Statistical Association, 1960–2013 Editions; World Rice Statistics. IRRI. *International Rice Research Institute World Rice Statistics Online Query Facility Database*, 15 May 2013, http://ricestat.irri.org:8080/wrs2/entrypoint.htm

throughout the 1980s, and, from the early 1990s, both total agricultural output and agricultural GDP began gradually to fall—previously the increase in agriculture product prices compensated the drop in output so agricultural GDP did not decline. Recourse to international economic theory would suggest that the reasons for this were that because relatively lower international agricultural prices, imported farm products increasingly replaced local products to meet domestic Japanese demand. One might infer from the Japanese example that Asian—or anyway East Asian—agriculture is essentially and inherently labour-intensive and cannot be shifted to a capital-intensive pattern of production. However, on empirical and theoretical grounds, this explanation, derived from international trade theory, is problematic.

First, Japan was the leading country in Asia's agriculture—especially rice farming—before WW2, and the price of labour in Japan and its colonies, including Taiwan and Korea, had always been the highest in East Asia in the half century before WW2. Before WW2, Japan and its colonies had a clear advantage in terms of the prices of their agricultural and semi-finished agricultural products. Further, and more importantly, if the earlier explanation holds, the implication would be that Japan was able neither to shift towards more capital-intensive forms of farm production nor to upgrade its technology to increase labour's marginal product. As a result, even in Japan (and its colonies) there existed the relatively higher price of labour and lower price of capital, induced innovation still would not have happened in the agriculture sector simply because comparative advantage is a 'primary' effect.

Empirical evidence shows that the post-war economic performance of Japan's agriculture sector is two-fold. Before 1970, rice output continued to grow after the post-war recovery era, and per capita agricultural GDP grew (although failed to match average national GDP growth). However, from 1970 the total rice output began to decline, this caused that in nominal terms, per capita agricultural GDP in Japan did not reach one million Japanese yen until 2006, by which time per capita national GDP was almost four million yen. In fact, agricultural GDP per capita was around half of the national average level in the 1950s; however, after years of continuous decline this figure reached its lowest level in 1989 at 16.7 per cent just before the Japanese economic bubble burst in the 1990s.

Here we raise a crucial question about Japan's agriculture: why did high-speed growth only happen in industry (or, put slightly differently, why did externality accumulation only happen in the industrial sector), and why was the *agriculture* sector not stimulated to grow more rapidly? Given comparatively easing economic institutions, what makes agriculture in Japan inferior to its industrial growth? And if agricultural technological change partly determined by the externality diffused from the local industrial sector, then what blocks the industrial-product-based agricultural technology from diffusing? In the context of the agricultural growth experience of most Asian economies, this question seems unique to Japan.

As already mentioned, unlike other Asian economies, before WW2 Japan was an exporter of agricultural technology (especially technology relating to rice varieties and planting methods)—indeed, exports from which other Asian economies benefited. But when such Asian economies embarked on a stable growth phase, Japan's agricultural technology began to stagnate. Japan's post-war economic boom reflected technological development in manufacturing, especially in Southeast Asia and Taiwan, but not in agricultural technology.

The ratio of the Japan's per capita agricultural output to per capita national GDP shows a declining trend throughout the 1960s–1980s (shown in Figs. 6.4 and 6.5), although following the economic bubble burst in the 1990s, it recovered to reach between 0.2 and 0.25. If we examine this in the neoclassical economic framework, some interesting implications seem to emerge. First, even in the absence of technological progress, low marginal product of agriculture should have forced production factors—especially labour—to flow out of agriculture, so raising the factor price in the agriculture sector via the equalisation effect. Second, considering Japan as an advanced economy, its industrial sector or research groups (e.g., research and development companies and universities) should have had the ability to powering technological or institutional change in agriculture sector. But neither of the above happened (Fig. 6.5).

Turning to empirical evidence again, if we compare rural household income from the late 1970s, Japan's agricultural household income was not significantly lower than national household income. Even taking agricultural costs into consideration, Japanese agricultural household income level was still closer to that of industry than any other Asian

Agricultural Transition in Selected Asian Economies 167

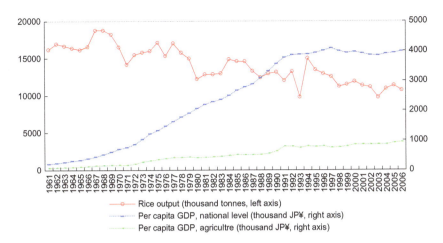

Fig. 6.4 National GDP/GNP per capita, agricultural GDP/GNP per capita and paddy rice production in Japan, 1951–2009. Source: *Japan Statistical Yearbook*. Statistical Research and Training Institute, MIC. Statistics Bureau, Ministry of Internal Affairs and Communications of Japan. Tokyo: Japan Statistical Association, 1960–2013 Editions

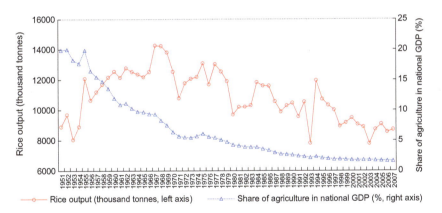

Fig. 6.5 Paddy rice production and agriculture share in national GDP from 1951 to 2009. Source: *Japan Statistical Yearbook*. Statistical Research and Training Institute, MIC. Statistics Bureau, Ministry of Internal Affairs and Communications of Japan. Tokyo: Japan Statistical Association, 1960–2013 Editions; World Rice Statistics. IRRI. *International Rice Research Institute World Rice Statistics Online Query Facility Database*, 15 May 2013, http://ricestat.irri.org:8080/wrs2/entrypoint.htm

country. After the post-war recovery, in 1960s Japan started to pay large subsidies to agriculture: for example, in 1995 the average government payment to agricultural households was about two million Japanese yen per household (almost US$25,000, calculated by the 1:80 exchange rate of 1995). Therefore, from this perspective, agricultural labourers' income in Japan was not low at all, even though a large part of the income was paid by Japanese government in the form of subsidies and only a small part came from productive farming activities. In 1985, for instance, after deducting agricultural production costs, Japan's rural household income was 5.5 million yen, of which only 1.07 million was from the sales of agricultural products (shown in Fig. 6.6).

Thus, in Japan's agriculture sector, labour commanded two prices. In the formal labour market, Japan's agricultural labour price was very high, and this raised the opportunity cost associated with leaving farming.[4]

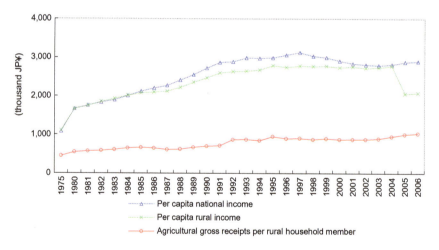

Fig. 6.6 National and agricultural income per capita and agricultural receipt per capita in Japan from 1975 to 2009. Note: Per capita income is shown in nominal terms. Source: *Japan Statistical Yearbook*. Statistical Research and Training Institute, MIC. Statistics Bureau, Ministry of Internal Affairs and Communications of Japan. Tokyo: Japan Statistical Association, 1960–2013 Editions

---

[4] This has caused the price of agricultural labour to equalise with the industrial sector's labour price, and thus no price difference between agriculture and industry labour markets. Consequently, the conditions leading to induced innovation type of institutional and technological change will no longer hold.

The second labour price is measured by marginal product—that is, the marginal product of Japanese agricultural labour, which is significantly lower than the national average for the entire economy. As a result, from the neoclassical economic view, per capita capital stock in the Japanese agriculture sector should be much lower than the national average, and this could explain why Japanese agriculture stagnated although the average household income in agriculture sector was kept in the line with national average level. The subsidies on the one hand increased Japanese farmer's average income level, but on the other hand offset the difference in the relative price of labour, which is the key determinant to induced technology change (IIC change) from the view of neoclassical economics. In other words, the agricultural subsidy system offset the engineer in IIC theory for Japan to induce the agricultural technology change diffused from America, just as South and Southeast Asian economies did during the green revolution.

6.3.2 China

In contrast with Japan, rice production in China increased by more than 200 per cent since 1960s (shown in Fig. 6.7).

From 1979, rice output quickly increased to above 150 million tonnes per year. Except for the first few years of the twenty-first century, from the 1990s China's annual rice output ranged from a low of 180 million tonnes to a high (1997) of 200 million tonnes (Fig. 6.7). Although the growth rate of agricultural GDP was much lower than that of national GDP—same as in Japan—there are some fundamental differences between China and Japan's agriculture sectors.

First, before 1979 China was dominated by agriculture. The total population in 1979 was 960 million (shown in Fig. 6.8), of whom 790 million—over 80 per cent of the total—lived in rural areas, whereas when Japan's population reached 100 million in 1967 its rural population was only 27.8 million. The structures of Japan and China's populations were also totally different. In China, beginning in the Mao Era, the government encouraged fertility to stimulate population growth. It gave financial subsidies to those with more children and used political incentives to

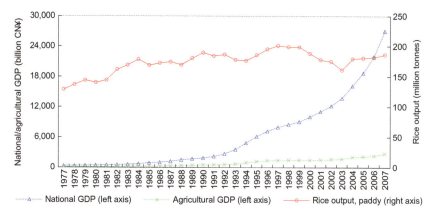

Fig. 6.7 National and agricultural GDP and rice production in China, 1977–2007. Source: *Zhongguo Tongji Nianjian* (China Statistical Yearbook). National Bureau of Statistics of China. Beijing: China Statistics Press, 1981–2013 Editions

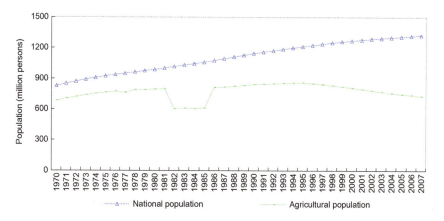

Fig. 6.8 National and agricultural population in China from 1970 to 2007. Source: *Zhongguo Tongji Nianjian* (China Statistical Yearbook). National Bureau of Statistics of China. Beijing: China Statistics Press, 1981–2013 Editions

encourage couples—especially rural couples—to *have* more children. As a result, China's population quickly rose from 400 million after the war to one billion in the early 1980s. On the other hand, China's industrial policy in Mao's era was copied from the Soviet model, which favoured the development of capital-intensive heavy industry. The rapidly increasing rural population could not be absorbed by the industrial sector. As a result, until the early 1980s, there was a large labour surplus trapped in the agriculture sector—evidence of the existence of widespread 'invisible unemployment' or under-employment. Consequently, China's industrial labour demand was mainly supplied by the rural sector. Thus, in the post-1979 China there is an observable outflow of labour from agriculture sector to industrial sector, but there is not such flow in Japan since late 1960s.

Further, until 2003 Chinese agriculture sector was highly-regulated as discussed in Chap. 3. The entire grain market remained under central control, with grain prices determined by the government. Because private traders were legally prohibited from purchasing grain and being party of the wholesale market, all buying was via the grain bureau. Thus, China's crop output performance indicated farmers' willingness to produce in a monopolistic purchase market. China's rice yield after 1979 was clearly affected by the government's purchase price. When the government lowered the rice purchase price or failed to adjust it in line with the inflation rate, rice production in China declined sharply in the following year (shown in Fig. 3.2).

6.3.3 China Versus Japan: Two Patterns

China and Japan embody two agricultural institutional patterns in Asia. Japan used direct payment transfers to raise farmers' income, which was a substantial subsidy for the rural population. China used its government monopoly over grain to stabilise the grain supply and price, thereby effecting a *de facto* transfer of farmers' welfare to the urban sector. Both institutional frameworks sought to adjust the distribution of welfare between the agricultural and urban sectors. The final outcomes were, however, totally different.

In Japan, as mentioned above, the payment transfer ensured that rural labourers achieved the market labour price and eliminated the price difference between sectors. According to IIC this type of relative price difference should have powered Japan's technical and institutional change. In China the welfare transfer occurred via invisible methods, in which only the government had the right to adjust the purchase price at any

172   J. Du

time, and, under the dual-track pricing policy, made the welfare transfer taken in a less visible way. The following two facts show the different results brought about by the above two types of welfare transfer under different agricultural institutional arrangements.

First, China's strongly upward trend in grain production indicates that the squeezing policy squeezes on farmers did not offset the growth potential in Chinese agriculture. Second, when the real grain purchase price (after the elimination of inflationary price increases) reached its historical peak, China's grain output also reached its highest level ever in recent years.[5] This output performance is strong evidence of Chinese farmers' reactions: when and only when the real grain purchase price increased then grain output increased, which means grain production had never been biased by distortions from welfare system and frequent institutional interventions. Although institutions in China repeatedly promote and depress a farmer's incentive to produce, in the long-term a farmer's effort level in production and technology selection is never distorted by this rural–urban welfare transfer.

Thus, the inter-sectoral relationship between agriculture and industry in China and Japan show different structures under different institutional arrangements, which have, in turn, generated different patterns of technology change. From the point of view of sectoral competition, Chinese agriculture and industry faced more severe competition for resources, because in contrast with post-war Japan, most labour came from rural China. Taking China's agricultural labour structure as a basic starting point, during the reform era Chinese agricultural labourers had to choose between staying in agriculture or entering non-agricultural employment markets. Therefore, the structure of Chinese agriculture was more flexible than in Japan since agricultural labourers faced different wages in different sectors. From this basic starting point—a hypothesis—Chinese agriculture might have been expected to develop a matching structure (or institution) to allow an inter-sectoral labour flow. And this is really the case inter-sectoral and inter-regional labour flows significantly determined technology variations within China as previously discussed in Chap. 4.

---

[5] The 2010 grain output reached 500 million tonnes.

6.4 Summary

Based on the comparison study of agricultural technology changes between China and Japan, this chapter finds that a technology generation gap inclines to happen between countries and economies. In other word, it is the basic institutional framework between economies that eventually determines the technology generation gap among major East Asian economies. And this basic institutional framework's decisive influence on agricultural technology transition explains on possibility of technology change given the absence of critical hypothesis of some key market institutions in the IIC theory. Or we say standard IIC technology change is only a special case of agricultural technology change in Asia.

References

FAOSTAT. *Food and Agriculture Organization of the United Nations Database*, 27 May 2013, http://faostat3.fao.org/home/index.html

Hayami, Yujiro. 'Sources of Agricultural Productivity Gap Among Selected Countries.' *American Journal of Agricultural Economics* 51 (1969): 564–575.

Hayami, Yujiro, and Masao Kikuchi. 'Agricultural Growth Against a Land Resource Constraint: A Comparative History of Japan, Taiwan, Korea and the Philippines.' *The Journal of Economic History* 33, no. 4 (1985): 839–864.

———. 'Technology, Market, and Community in Contract Choice: Rice Harvesting in the Philippines.' *Economic Development and Cultural Change* 47, no. 2 (1999): 371–386.

Hayami, Yujiro, and Vernon Ruttan. 'Agricultural Productivity Differences Among Countries.' *American Economic Review* 60 (1970a): 895–911.

———. 'Factor Prices and Technical Change in Agricultural Development: The United States and Japan, 1880–1960.' *Journal of Political Economy* 78, no. 5 (1970b): 1115–1141.

———. *Agricultural Development: An International Perspective*. Baltimore and London: Johns Hopkins University Press, 1985.

———. 'Induced Innovation Theory and Agricultural Development: A Personal Account.' In *Induced Innovation Theory and International Agricultural Development: A Reassessment*, edited by Bruce Koppel. Baltimore: The Johns Hopkins University Press, 1995.

174   J. Du

Heckscher, E., and B. Ohlin. *Heckscher-Ohlin Trade Theory.* Cambridge, MA: MIT Press, 1991.

Japan Statistical Yearbook, edited by Statistical Research and Training Institute, MIC. Statistics Bureau, Ministry of Internal Affairs and Communications of Japan. Tokyo: Japan Statistical Association, 1960–2013 Editions.

Samuelson, P. Prices of Factors and Good in General Equilibrium. *Review of Economic Studies* 21 (1953): 1–21.

World Rice Statistics. IRRI. *International Rice Research Institute World Rice Statistics Online Query Facility Database*, 15 May 2013, http://ricestat.irri.org:8080/wrs2/entrypoint.htm

Zhongguo Tongji Nianjian (China Statistical Yearbook). National Bureau of Statistics of China. Beijing: China Statistics Press, 1981–2013 Editions.

7

Conclusion

7.1 The Origin of the Research Questions

Among the earliest neoclassical studies of agricultural growth and technological transition were the pioneering work of Schultz (1964, 1978) and North and Thomas (1971, 1973). Based on the North–Thomas framework, Hayami and Ruttan developed the IIC theory, which has become a major paradigm of agricultural transition, emphasising the technical and institutional changes caused by changes in relative factor price (Hayami 1969; Hayami and Ruttan 1970a, b, 1985, 1995; Hayami and Kikuchi 1980). By introducing and endorsing the core role of relative factor price change in the progress of technological and institutional change, IIC theory integrates technological and institutional transition into the neoclassical economic framework and uses relative factor price to investigate the existence and evolution of institutional change.

Within the framework provided by IIC theory, research studies of agricultural transition are usually based on specific hypotheses relating to key market institutions and a critical pre-condition. This pre-condition is that the agriculture sector can, directly or indirectly, secure sufficient factors to satisfy the demands of agricultural transition in terms of both *absolute*

© The Author(s) 2018   **175**
J. Du, *Agricultural Transition in China*, Palgrave Studies in Economic History,
https://doi.org/10.1007/978-3-319-76905-9_7

level of, and the *ratio* between, relevant factor accumulations. In other words, this hypothesis states that, when technological or institutional transition starts in response to changes in relative factor prices, a set of (ideal) market institutions, which ensures that production factors are accessible from the agriculture sector, is assumed to already exist. However, this hypothesis may not be applied if certain conditions are missing from the real economy. For example, (scenario 1), when the stock of a specific factor in the whole economy is inadequate to meet the minimum factor accumulation requirements, will technological transition circumvent this scarce factor through recourse to the selection of other available technologies, or (scenario 2), will the technological transition process stagnate until factor accumulation requirements have been met? Furthermore (scenario 3), when factor accumulation takes a long time, will the technological transition become a correspondingly long-term process? And finally (scenario 4), in the short term, if institutional factors influence factor flows in a way that is contrary to the changes in relative factor prices, what will be the impact on the process of agricultural technological transition?

These are the questions that have inspired us to reconsider the empirical studies of agricultural transition in Asia. From the foundations of Hayami's IIC theory—developed in an empirical study of the Philippines—it is apparent that, although the level of economic development in some Southeast Asian economies was behind the average level of economies in East Asia, government control over the agriculture sector was much looser in these economies than in their East Asian counterparts. Therefore, theoretically speaking, the agriculture sector—and especially local agricultural markets—in the Philippines approximated much more closely to an unregulated market than those of other Asian (especially East Asian) economies. However, when we extend observations of agricultural transition to the entirety of Asia and make cross-country comparisons, we find that the nature, timing, and time span of agriculture technology transitions have varied considerably between different economies. This finding is very different from that of other studies, which argue that some South, Southeast and East Asian economies collectively undertook green revolution in the 1960s. In Japan and Taiwan, agriculture technological transition started very early; South and Southeast Asia began the process after WW2; but it was not until the 1980s that agricultural transition went under way in mainland China. Given the premise that the initial technology set is exogenous (deriving from developed countries' technology diffusion), the above differences cannot be explained by inter-regional (or cross-country) differences in relative factor prices (e.g., relative price of capital, land and labour). In short, under the impact of exogenous technology, change in relative factor prices is not a persuasive explanation for the major differences in agricultural technological transitions displayed by the history of Asian economies.

For instance, in East Asian economies, especially China, the IIC theory can explain some regional technological or institutional changes. But, in general, technical change in East Asia's agriculture was more strongly influenced by non-market factors than by the relative factor price changes. When the state intervenes in agricultural production, as happened in China from the 1950s to the early 1980s, the IIC theory may not explain the performance of the agriculture. Even after the Chinese government partly eased its control over the agriculture sector in the late 1970s and early 1980s, thanks to continued state intervention, the IIC theory does not offer a convincing explanation of agricultural technology and institutional changes in the reform era. This study shows that when inter-regional factor flows are constrained by the state's policies or by other government regulations, technical and institutional change in agriculture is highlighted by considerable inter-regional differences. In fact, cross-country comparisons indicate that holistic diversification of institutional factors (and other factors) give regional characteristics to agricultural technical change. Institutions and local market structures together play a decisive role in determining the local technology selection, transition process and the extent of the technology generation gap between Asian economies.

This work seeks to extend the application of IIC theory to cases in which technological transition occurs under different market institutional conditions. Through a comparison of Asian economies—especially Japan and China in East Asia—we have tried to highlight through observation of different types of Asian institutions and market structures, the decisive role of market institutions in determining the selection and transition of agricultural technologies. Through a comparative analysis of agricultural technical changes in the planting of rice paddies in Japan, Taiwan and mainland China, we find that different market institutions and structures have given rise to considerable diversity of agricultural technical change (even for the same crop variety) between different economies in terms of the nature, timing and duration of the technological transition. Such diversification has, in turn, affected the trajectories of agricultural transition and wider economic growth.

In this work, studies of differences in paddy-rice-planting technological transitions amongst East Asian economies, as well as of the trend of inter-regional agricultural technical changes under different regional market structures in China, provide supplements and extensions to the standard IIC model of agricultural transition.

7.2 Dominant Factors Shaping Differences in Technical Change Between East Asian Economies

Amongst paddy-rice planting economies in Asia, China and Japan represent examples of two different institutional frameworks through which government intervention in agriculture has taken place. In the 1960s, Japan started to implement a transfer payment policy, designed to increase rural income by distributing substantial direct subsidies to farmers. Meanwhile, China used state monopoly controls over grain purchases and sales (including absolute political control by the state over the grain circulation price) to transfer capital—and by implication welfare gains— from agriculture to the urban sector. Under different agricultural institutional arrangements in Japan and China, these two forms of transfer payment (as well as different market structures) were responsible for different evolutionary patterns of inter-sectoral relations between agriculture and industry in the two countries. Further, differences in agricultural institutions led to divergent technology development routes.

From the perspective of inter-sectoral competition, factor competition between agriculture and industry was more intense in China than in Japan. In China, the direct source of labour supply to both industry and agriculture was rural labour. Because of more intense inter-sectoral factor competition and a wider labour price differential, changes in agricultural technology and rural market institutions might have been more flexible in China than that in Japan. In other words, it can be argued that, in theory, the Chinese agriculture sector ought to have chosen a kind of technology and market structure beneficial to its more frequent inter-sectoral labour (factor) flow.

Empirical studies of both countries show that in terms of overall agricultural production, since the 1980s the efficiency of Chinese agriculture has improved much more than that of Japan. This is mainly because while Japan's direct transfer payment has guaranteed return on labour engaged in farm production like its clearing price in the labour market, it has also offset labour price differentials between the agriculture and non-agriculture sectors. According to IIC theory, because of direct transfer payment to agriculture, Japan lost the ability to stimulate agricultural technological and institutional transitions. Meanwhile, under the dual-track pricing system and state control, China's changing grain purchase price concealed the governmental direct transfer payment to the urban sector. However, China's post-1979 agricultural policies neither provided extra subsidies to farm labour nor restricted production factors from flowing out of agricultural production. Thus, in the face of relative price differences in labour, agricultural policies generated a one-way flow of labour from the agriculture to the non-agriculture sector.

Under these two types of market institutions, adjustments of social welfare between agriculture and non-agriculture sectors eventually led the agriculture sectors of Japan and China to follow two different trajectories of technological transition.

7.3 Three Levels to Understand Asia's Agricultural Transition

7.3.1 Level 1: Inter-Regional Differences in Agricultural Growth in Asia

By way of encapsulating all these findings in relation to technical and institutional change in agriculture in China and other Asian economies under conditions of reform and transitions, agricultural growth and technical change under different market institutions can be decomposed into the following three levels of analysis.

First, after WW2, throughout Asia there was a 'convergence' trend of rice production amongst all rice-producing regions, including both paddy and non-paddy irrigation fields. However, it is noteworthy that 'convergence' has different implications for agricultural production than for industry. The fundamental difference lies in the properties of production form between two sectors: the industrial sector faces fewer production uncertainties, whereas agricultural production is much more dependent on external factors—above all, on the vagaries of climate and other natural conditions.

In agricultural production, changes in per capita output of different factors (per unit of land and per labourer) may reflect different trajectories of technical change in different regions. Meanwhile, in comparative studies of Asian agriculture, 'per capita output change' may reflect the process of technology selection when the green revolution was propagated and diffused amongst Asian economies.

7.3.2 Level 2: Influence of Inter-Sectoral Competition for Resources on Technical Change in Agriculture[1]

At the heart of IIC theory, a change in relative factor price results in the existing agricultural technology losing its optimal production efficiency. The IIC model of agricultural technical change highlights a significant difference from *industrial* technological progress: agricultural technological transition is an 'integral sectoral change',[2] which leads to other visible changes of factor demand in the rest of the economy.

The empirical studies of China in Chaps. 3 and 4 suggest that as it has expanded, the industrial sector (but also the service sector) and the agriculture sector competed mainly for labour during economic transition. Because of this factor competition, different types of labour flow occurred between China's agriculture and non-agriculture sectors, thereby affecting

---

[1] For example, competition for resources between agriculture and non-agriculture sectors.

[2] It is a sectoral change in the sense that the input factor ratio throughout the agriculture sector changes.

Conclusion   181

agriculture's technological transition. This represents an inverse path of agricultural technical change, quite different from that implicit in the standard IIC model.

China's geographical conditions dictate that the cost of inter-regional labour flows is generally greater than that of intra-regional flows. Moreover, the cost of both types of flow varies significantly amongst different regions. This cost difference determines whether intra- or inter-regional labour flows will take place, as well as whether the agriculture or non-agriculture sector in the inflow regions will be the net beneficiary of such flows.

All these features have determined the different directions and patterns which regional agricultural technical change has followed in China. For example, in Northeast China, since agricultural production was characterised by a higher marginal product (and return) to labour, technical change did not, to any significant extent, embody labour-saving technologies. However, in some parts of central and western China, the return to labour from agricultural production was even higher than that from industry in neighbouring provinces. As a result, a net labour inflow took place which resulted in 'labour intensification' in agricultural production.

7.3.3   Level 3: Differential Institution-Induced Externalities

Economic externality works as a prerequisite for the research in IIC theory: technologies are always available, and what technological transition needs is an appropriate demand for factors to 'activate' the demand for new technologies. However, empirically, this 'activation' is conditional.

The first condition for the agriculture sector to embark on a process of technological transition is captured in the influence of institutional factors on incentives in farming. In China from the 1950s to the 1970s, as well as in Japan after the 1960s, the association between agricultural output and production incentives was weakened by the impact of government policies (e.g., agricultural subsidies). As a result, the technological transition in agriculture slowed down. Meanwhile, in China the collectivisation thrust of policy almost entirely destroyed production incentives in Chinese agriculture, as a result of which, spontaneous technological progress in the agriculture sector in China virtually halted.

182   J. Du

The second condition lies in the availability of new technologies. In the standard growth model, technological progress in an economy is a result of externality accumulation (such as human capital, research and development, etc.). This hypothesis is heavily dependent on the unhindered transmission of the externality within the economy. However, this assumption does not necessarily hold true in the real economy, especially in developing Asia. In case of China before the early 1980s, individual farmers had no access to major inputs, including fertilisers and pesticides, nor even to the agricultural input market. However, such inputs—i.e., chemicals—were key elements in the green revolution of the 1960s and 1970s. Even so, until the end of the 1990s, the distribution of agricultural inputs (and the market for such products) was still monopolised by China's SOEs. Thus, even when the non-agriculture sector or research and development departments have had the capacity to provide the agriculture sector with new technology-based inputs, the ability of farmers to use them has been dependent on whether the institutional framework has permitted and/or facilitated their use, as well as on transaction cost have been sufficiently low to enable farmers to access the new technologies.

7.4   Summary

On the premise that the initial technology set is exogenous, the technological selection process is a function of the level of factor accumulation and the factor ratio. The existing levels of factor accumulation and factor ratios in the agriculture sector apart, in the short term, the agriculture sector's ability fulfil the conditions required of its transition will likely be shaped by differences in political and/or economic institutions. How institutions constrain or promote the re-allocation of factors during the transition process will determine the inter-sectoral differences of technological transitions, as well as the composition of the economic structure. When the ratio and absolute level of factor accumulation in the agriculture sector are fixed or defined in terms of a sustained non-reversible movement,[3] then the impact of the institutional constraint on factor flow

---

[3] Such as the assumption of continuous labour outflow in the Lewis model (1954).

Conclusion **183**

will become a very significant determinant affecting the nature of the agricultural transition, as well as shaping the process of technological diversification.

This work investigates the process of technological diversification with empirical studies in selected Asian economies. When different economies face the same technology set, differences in their local institutional conditions determine the choice of technologies, as well as the timing and duration of the technological transition process. Through the analysis of agricultural technical changes in China and other Asian economies, this work finds that the examples cited illustrate all too clearly how great technological differences between countries can be. The technology generation gap in the Asian agricultural transitions were determined by the different institutional fundamentals between economies.

In contrast, among major Asian economies, the economy characterised by the most striking regional differences in real rural income has been China under the impact of post-1979 reform. China's inter-regional income disparities of agricultural population have, however, not led to a technology generation gap in agriculture through relative factor price differentials, as has occurred in other Asian economies.

Through its analysis of the process of agricultural technological transitions in selected Asian economies, this work identifies institutional differences to be the factor most responsible for shaping agricultural technology generation gap in these economies. In other words, the path of IIC transition is a special case of agricultural transition, in which a technological transition occurs when given ideal market structure and favourable factor accumulation to start such technology changes.

References

Hayami, Yujiro. 'Sources of Agricultural Productivity Gap Among Selected Countries.' *American Journal of Agricultural Economics* 51 (1969): 564–575.

Hayami, Yujiro, and Masao Kikuchi. 'Inducements to Institutional Innovations in an Agrarian Community.' *Economic Development and Cultural Change* 29, no. 1 (1980): 21–36.

Hayami, Yujiro, and Vernon Ruttan. 'Agricultural Productivity Differences Among Countries.' *American Economic Review* 60 (1970a): 895–911.

184   J. Du

———. 'Factor Prices and Technical Change in Agricultural Development: The United States and Japan, 1880–1960.' *Journal of Political Economy* 78, no. 5 (1970b): 1115–1141.

———. *Agricultural Development: An International Perspective.* Baltimore and London: Johns Hopkins University Press, 1985.

———. 'Induced Innovation Theory and Agricultural Development: A Personal Account.' In *Induced Innovation Theory and International Agricultural Development: A Reassessment,* edited by Bruce Koppel. Baltimore: The Johns Hopkins University Press, 1995.

North, Douglass, and Robert Thomas. 'The Rise and Fall of the Manorial System: A Theoretical Model.' *The Journal of Economic History* 31, no. 4 (1971): 777–803.

———. *The Rise of the Western World: A New Economic History.* New York: Cambridge University Press, 1973.

Schultz, Theodore. *Transforming Traditional Agriculture.* New Haven: Yale University Press, 1964.

———, ed. *Distortion of Agricultural Incentives.* Bloomington: Indiana University Press, 1978.

Index[1]

NUMBERS AND SYMBOLS

1993 Agricultural Law, 87
1998 Grain Purchase Act, 85, 87

A

Above-quota price (*chao gou jia*, 超购价), 67, 69, 140
Adequate factor accumulation, 4, 19, 97
Administrative costs, 75, 84
Agricultural Development Bank of China (ADBC), 80, 82, 83
Agricultural efficiency, 47, 145
Agricultural growth, 7, 8, 10–12, 15, 20, 21, 23, 27, 28, 30, 31, 55, 63, 64, 90, 116, 119, 120, 124, 127n3, 135, 152, 156, 166, 175, 179–180

Agricultural institution, 6, 16, 152, 178
Agricultural labour, 19, 22, 42, 114, 118, 135, 168, 168n4, 169, 172
Agricultural policy, 21, 22, 62–65, 71, 89, 90, 140, 142, 144, 179
Agricultural production, 2, 3, 5, 6, 10, 12, 14, 15, 23, 32, 59, 62, 67, 68, 73, 99, 102, 114–116, 119, 124–126, 128–148, 135n13, 140n19, 155, 160, 168, 177, 179–181
Agricultural productivity, 2–4, 31, 62n6, 124, 126
Agricultural revolution, 31, 33
Agricultural technology, 3–6, 10, 12, 16–21, 62, 89, 97, 98, 116, 118n10, 119–121, 148, 151, 152, 154, 156, 157, 159–161, 166, 169, 173, 177–180, 183

---

[1] Note: Page numbers followed by 'n' refer to notes.

© The Author(s) 2018
J. Du, *Agricultural Transition in China*, Palgrave Studies in Economic History,
https://doi.org/10.1007/978-3-319-76905-9

185

186   Index

Agricultural transition, 2–4, 7, 9, 10,
16–23, 55, 62, 63, 67, 89, 90,
97, 98, 109–111, 120, 121,
123–148, 151–173, 175–183
Agriculture Bank of China, 80
Anhui (安徽), 28, 103, 103n4, 106
Arable land, 23, 29, 31, 40, 103,
112, 114, 118–120, 125,
125n1, 127n2, 131, 132, 135,
138–140, 142–144, 161

B

Bargaining power, 86, 88
Beijing (北京), 15n10, 68n8, 71n13,
72, 74n16, 76n19, 78n27,
81n32, 81n33, 83n35,
101–105, 103n4, 107, 108,
110, 111, 113, 147n23, 170
Biological technology, 156
Boiling Guangxi (*feiteng de guangxi*,
沸腾的广西), 61
Borlaug, Norman, 1, 1n1, 5, 5n8
Budget constraints, 81, 82
Busy farming holiday (*nong mang jia*,
农忙假), 117, 117n9

C

Capital accumulation, 15, 34, 36,
37, 39–42, 44, 45, 47, 55,
154–156
Capital aggregation, 38
Capital flow, 43, 134, 140
Capital intensive production, 39
Capitalism, 5, 33, 49
Capital–labour ratio, 8, 37, 38, 41,
42, 45, 46, 51, 52
Capital return, 125, 136, 137,
139, 140

Capital stock, capital stock per
capita, 34, 35, 37, 38, 40, 45,
46, 51, 52, 155, 169
Central china, 113
Chailai (Indica rice, 在来稻), 137
China Grain Reserves Corporation,
85, 87
Chinese Civil War, 126
Chinese Communist Party (CCP),
2, 3, 68, 70, 70n11, 78, 80,
87, 99
Chongqing (重庆), 103n4
Classical economics, 5, 33–37, 39,
43, 44, 54
Classical economists, 5, 34–36, 43
Coal mines, 32
Collectivisation (*jitihua*, 集体化), 3,
67, 132, 181
Colonialism, 148
Commercialisation, 35, 48–50, 52, 53
Communisation, 3, 99
Contemporary China, 21, 27, 62, 63
Contractual procurement (*hetong
dinggou*, 合同定购), 63
Convergence trend, 11, 39, 153,
156, 180
Cost plus thin profit (*baoben weili*,
保本微利), 83
Cotton, 70n11, 71, 74, 75, 81n33,
99, 141

D

Dazhai model of labour
mobilisation, 62
Decollectivisation (*qu jitihua*, 去集
体化), 63, 68, 131n7
Deng Xiaoping (邓小平), 77
Developed countries, 17, 151,
162, 177

Developing countries, 3–8, 19, 20, 89, 135, 153, 155, 162
Direct subsidy, 75, 85, 87, 178
Divergence trend, 147
Dongting Lake area (洞庭湖区), 108
Double copping, 40
Dual-track pricing system (*jiage shuanggui zhi*, 价格双轨制), 63, 71, 74–77, 179

E

East Asia, 17, 21, 125, 134, 148, 152, 154, 156–161, 163, 165, 176, 177
East Asian economies, 4, 5, 10, 16, 17, 90, 97, 148, 154, 159, 160, 162, 173, 176–178
East China, 119
Economic bubble, 165, 166
Economic crops, 131
Economic equilibrium, 6
Economic history, 28–30, 33, 36, 37, 97
Economic order, 8
Economic taking-off, 97, 127n3, 148
Edo bakufu (江戸幕府), 161n2
Emerging industry, 29
Empirical studies, 8–10, 16, 17, 19, 22, 23, 64, 98, 121, 148, 152–154, 156, 161, 176, 179, 180, 183
Energy deficits, 63
Externality, 19, 47n16, 151, 153, 155, 156, 162, 166, 181–182

F

Factor accumulation, 8, 16, 18, 19, 21, 97, 98, 119, 121, 154, 162, 176, 182, 183
Factor competition, 178–180
Factor endowment theory, 153
Factor equalisation, 155
Factor input, 22, 23, 46, 115, 119, 120, 125, 136, 139, 142, 159
Factor intensification, 3, 9, 115–117, 119, 120
Factor mobility, 17, 20
Factor price, 6, 7, 17, 19, 43, 44, 52, 98, 123, 147, 152, 153, 166, 175–177, 180, 183
Factor Price Equalisation (FPE), 11, 42–44, 43n14, 123, 153
Factor ratio, 16, 18, 98, 180n2, 182
Factor reallocation, 22, 98
Factor return, 23, 123–125, 134–139, 135n13, 144–148
Factor-saving, 115, 116, 119, 120, 157
Farmers associations, 128
Farm productivity, 119
Fertiliser, 3, 12, 20, 22, 63, 72, 72n14, 89, 116, 142, 154, 159–161, 182
Fertility rate, 39–41
Field management, 3, 12
Fiscal pressure, 66, 71, 75, 77, 82
Five Year Plan, 14, 67, 80
Fixed assets, 40, 135, 137, 142, 143
Food circulation, 70
Food security, 22, 64, 87, 88, 99, 147
Foreign exchange, 63
Free trading, 29, 52, 78
Fujian (福建), 103n4, 124

188 Index

G

Gansu (甘肃), 103n4, 104n5, 106
Geographical conditions, 181
Glutinous rice (*nuo mi*, 糯米), 40
Government intervention,
  16, 152, 178
Government subsidies, 124
Grain Bureau, 22, 64, 66, 70,
  70n10, 71, 73, 75–77, 76n18,
  76n19, 77n24, 80, 80n31, 81,
  83, 84, 84n36, 86–89, 99,
  99n1, 141, 171
Grain circulation, 22, 63, 64, 66–88,
  70n10, 80n31, 87n37, 99,
  103, 108, 115, 119, 178
Grain coupon (*liangpiao*, 粮票),
  77n23
Grain crop, 15, 67, 70, 79n28, 99,
  100, 130
Grain pricing based on quality (*anzhi
  lunjia*, 按质论价), 83
Grain procurement purposes
  (*gouliang zhuankuan*,
  购粮专款), 82
Grain provincial governor's
  responsibility system, 79, 80
Grain purchase and marketing
  (*tonggou tongxiao*,
  统购统销), 63
Grain reform, 66, 75, 76, 76n18, 78,
  79, 80n31, 82, 83, 86, 88,
  120, 147
Grain reserve system, 76, 76n20, 82
Grain self-sufficiency, 2, 67, 105
Great divergence, 21, 24, 28–33, 35,
  39, 44
Greater, faster, better and more
  economical (*duo kuai hao
  sheng*, 多快好省), 59

Great Leap Forward (*da yuejin*, 大跃
  进), 2, 3, 14, 59, 61–63, 62n6,
  99, 124, 126, 127
Green revolution, 1–4, 1n1, 11, 23,
  47, 118n10, 148, 151, 152,
  156–161, 169, 176, 180, 182
Gross domestic product (GDP), 113,
  164, 165, 166, 167, 169, 170
Guangdong (广东), 78, 103, 103n4,
  113, 114, 118, 136n14
Guangxi (广西), 61, 103n4
Guizhou (贵州), 103n4

H

Hainan (海南), 103n4, 106, 124,
  142n20
Harvest Song (*fengshou qu*,
  丰收曲), 61
Hebei (河北), 103n4, 104n5, 106
Heckscher–Ohlin–Samuelson
  (HOS), 43
Heilongjiang (黑龙江), 103n4, 104,
  106, 110, 111, 142n20
Henan (河南), 60, 103n4, 104n5,
  106, 108, 117, 127n2
Hetao area (河套地区), 104, 104n5
High inflation rate, 75, 79
High-level equilibrium trap, 12–14,
  34, 54
High yielding variety, 131
Hokkaido, 161
Hongqi (红旗), 61
Household-based production, 53, 131
Household income, 139, 166,
  168, 169
Household registration system
  (*hukou*, 户口), 100
Huanjiang county (环江县), 61

Hubei (湖北), 60, 61, 103, 103n4, 105, 106, 109
Human capital, 6, 46, 47, 51, 115, 137, 143, 153, 154, 182
Hunan (湖南), 103, 103n4, 105, 106, 109

Inada condition, 38n11
Incomplete market, 53, 75
Induced innovation, 7, 10, 49–53, 152, 161, 165, 168n4
Induced Institutional Change (IIC), 4, 7–10, 16–19, 21, 89, 98, 120, 121, 148, 152, 154, 156, 161, 162, 169, 171, 173, 175–181, 183
Industrialisation, 14, 29, 34, 36, 44, 46, 50, 54, 55, 73, 164
Industrial revolution, 35, 49, 54, 55
Inflationary pressures, 74
Input market, 21, 123, 182
Inspection tour to the south (*nan xun*, 南巡), 77
Instant market, 6, 17–19
Institutional arrangement, 7, 9–11, 98, 121, 128, 172, 178
Institutional change, 7, 9–12, 16, 62, 63, 65, 115–117, 166, 171, 175, 177, 179
Institutional constraints, 17, 45, 52, 182
Institutional differences, 153, 183
Institutional distortion, 51
Institutional economics, 38, 49, 52
Institutional factors, 8, 17, 22, 98, 152, 176, 177, 181
Intensive factor input, 97
Intensive-input-based output, 139

International Rice No. 8 (IR8), 1, 2, 2n6
International Rice Research Institute (IRRI), 1, 2, 164, 167
Inter-regional labour flow, 181
Inter-sectoral competition, 19, 23, 97, 98, 178, 180–181
Inter-sectoral labour (factor) flow, 179
Intra-regional labour flow, 172
Intra-sectoral labour flow, 139, 172
Invisible unemployment, 171
Involution, 13, 21, 27–28, 30–45, 31n3, 54, 159
Involution theory, 13, 29–35, 37, 39–47, 45n15, 49, 54
Irrationality, 40
Irrigation, 3, 13, 40, 112, 116, 126, 127, 127n3, 131, 133n10, 142, 154, 160, 180

Japanese occupation, 125, 126
Japonica rice, 104, 106, 127
Jiangsu (江苏), 28, 103, 103n4, 106, 114, 118
Jiangxi (江西), 28, 61, 103, 103n4
Jiangying (江阴), 28
Jilin (吉林), 103n4, 104, 106, 110, 111
Jingmi (粳米), 104

Kiangnan (*jiangnan*, 江南), 28–30, 32, 33, 40–42, 47, 49, 154
Korean Peninsula, 152, 154, 157, 158
Kuomintang (KMT), 127, 129, 130, 133, 138

190 **Index**

L

Labour–capital–land ratio, 153
Labour-intensive, 23, 32, 39, 117, 130, 131, 134, 137, 165
Labour outflow, 19, 102, 110, 112, 114, 117, 118, 120, 182n3
Labour specialisation, 5
Labour supply, 7, 42, 110, 111, 178
Land–labour ratio, 29, 31, 109–113, 109n7
Landlord, 130, 138, 138n16
Land market, 141
Land tenure system, 132, 133
Land-to-the-tiller (*gengzhe you qitian*, 耕者有其田), 130, 133n11
Land use rights, 132, 142
Launching satellite (*fang weixing*, 放卫星), 59–62
Learning by doing, 6, 46
Leasehold system, 133
Liaoning (辽宁), 103n4, 104, 106, 110, 111, 113
Living standard, 12, 31–33, 32n5, 41, 75
Local community, 133
Local condition, 2, 3
Long River (*changjiang*, 长江), 28n1
Low labour cost, 34, 130

M

Macheng County (麻城县), 61
Mainland China, 8, 12, 22, 23, 123–148, 152, 177
Malthusian trap, 13, 34n6
Manufacturing sector, 5
Mao zedong (毛泽东), 2, 59
Marginal output, 8, 19, 32, 37, 38, 41–44, 46, 54, 115

Marginal product, 43, 45, 101, 139, 159n1, 165, 166, 169, 181
Marginal productivity, 154
Marginal return, 38, 39, 44, 119, 136
Market guidance, 89
Market institution, 4, 8–10, 16, 18, 20–21, 24, 30, 48–55, 62, 64, 89, 90, 98, 121, 123, 148, 152, 155, 162, 173, 175–180
Market-oriented transition, 15
Market structure, 17, 20–23, 45, 55, 89, 120, 121, 177–179, 183
Marxism view, 35
Meiji Restoration (*meiji ishin*, 明治維新), 159, 161
Middle and lower reaches of the Yangtze River, 103, 104, 106, 112, 114, 117, 118
Ming, 29, 31, 48n17, 54, 154
Modern Chinese agriculture, 97
Monopolistic purchase, 171
Mu (*mu*, 亩), 29n2, 60n4

N

Natural condition, 134, 157, 158, 160, 180
Natural factor, 109
Needham Question, 54
Negotiated price (*xieyi jia*, 协议价), 80, 83
Negotiated purchase price, 140
Neimenggu (*inner mongolia*, 内蒙古), 103n4, 105, 106, 117
Neoclassical economic framework, 4, 14, 16, 54, 152, 166, 175

Neoclassical economics, 6, 7, 21, 33, 36, 37, 39–41, 44–46, 55, 121, 152, 155, 169, 177

New growth theory, 162

Ningxia (宁夏), 103n4, 104n5, 106

Non-grain crop, 111, 131

Northeast China, 98, 107, 109–113, 119, 120, 181

Northern Zhejiang (*zhebei*, 浙北), 28

O

Output–input ratio, 135, 136, 141

P

Paddy field, 112, 130

Paddy-field rice planting, 4, 97, 113, 116, 118

Paddy rice, 2, 2n5, 2n6, 14, 22, 28, 40, 49, 65, 112, 118n10, 126, 130, 131, 134, 137, 154, 158, 163, 167, 178

Pearl River Delta (*zhujiang sanjiao zhou*, 珠江三角洲), 136n14

People's commune (*renmin gongshe*, 人民公社), 61, 62

People's Daily (renmin ribao, 人民日报), 60

Per capita capital stock, 38, 155

Per capita income, 132, 132n9, 168

Pesticide, 116, 160, 182

Physical input, 6, 123

Policy goals, 64, 88

Policy initiatives, 77, 99

Policy-making, 7, 11, 64, 67

Political institutional, 148

Political intervention, 10

Ponlai rice, 127

Population boom, 12, 15, 31, 53

Population growth, 4, 12, 14, 31, 34, 34n7, 54, 63, 110, 169

Post-1979 agricultural reform, 21, 23, 64, 65, 88, 90, 135n13

Post-war economic boom, 166

Post-war recovery, 144, 165, 168

Price protection, 69

Pricing system, 22, 50, 63, 71, 73–78, 80, 89, 179

Production cost, 140–142, 168

Production efficiency, 6, 128, 133–135, 141, 180

Production potentials, 116, 119

Productivity, 2–4, 10–12, 32–34, 62n6, 114, 117, 119, 124, 126, 138, 154, 164

Product market, 21, 52, 78, 123

Profitability, 36

Property right, 48, 50, 52, 53, 55, 133

Public land (*gong tian*, 公田), 130

Purchase and sales at the same price (*gouxiao tongjia*, 购销同价), 74

Purchase price, 65, 68–76, 79n28, 82, 83, 85–88, 111, 119, 137, 138, 140, 140n19, 142, 143, 147, 171, 172, 179

Q

Qaidam Basin (柴达木盆地), 61

Qian Xuesen (钱学森), 60, 60n4

Qing, 30–32, 34n7, 48n17, 54, 112, 130

Qinghai (青海), 61, 103n4, 104n5, 106

Quota price (*tong gou jia*, 统购价), 67, 69, 140, 140n19

R

Rational individual, 6

Rationing price (*tongxiao jia*, 统销价), 74, 76, 76n19, 76n22, 77, 77n23

Relative price, 7–9, 119, 169, 171, 177, 179

Research and development (R&D), 7, 162, 166, 182

Resource allocation, 20, 50

Resource endowments, 7, 135

Reverse 30:70 ratio (*dao sanqi*, 倒三七), 69

Rice, 2, 30, 60, 99, 106–108, 125, 152, 157–162, 178

Rice bag (*mi dai zi*, 米袋子), 79, 79n29

Rice economies, 23, 97, 148, 151, 152

Risk fund, 76, 76n21

Running costs, 70, 70n10, 75

Rural income, 124, 132, 144, 152, 178, 183

Rural migrant labourers (*nongmin gong*, 农民工), 72, 109

S

Saishike (塞什克), 61

Seasonal agriculture workers, 117

Selling-oriented production, 35

Shaanxi (陕西), 103n4, 104n5, 106

Shadow price, 139

Shandong (山东), 103n4

Shanghai (上海), 28, 103, 103n4, 105, 105n6

Shanxi (山西), 103n4, 104n5, 106

Sichua (四川), 117

Sichuan (四川), 103n4

The Sino-American Joint Commission on Rural Reconstruction (JCRR), 127–129, 127n3

Sinograin, 85

Sino-Japanese War, 126

Small scale, 46, 48, 49, 53, 55, 63, 76, 76n18, 118, 124, 126, 131, 136, 158

Social stability, 79, 129, 132

Solow model, 47, 47n16, 51, 52

Solow residual, 47, 47n16

Solow-Swan model, 38, 42, 50

Song, 30, 31, 154

Songjiang (淞江), 28

Sophisticated (*gao jing jian*, 高精尖), 59

Southeast Asia, 2–4, 50, 152, 161, 166, 176

South-eastern coastal areas, 114

Southern Jiangsu (*sunan*, 苏南), 28

Soviet Union, 2n7, 59, 67, 118, 118n10, 127

Specific assets, 55

Specific physical assets, 35

Sprouts of capitalism, 29

State-owned enterprises (SOEs), 69, 76n22, 81–83, 85, 101, 182

State-owned grain enterprises, 79–81, 80n31, 84–86, 87n37

State procurement (*guojia dinggou*, 国家定购), 73, 80

State subsidies, 75, 85, 87

Subsidies, 23, 67, 74–77, 75n17, 84, 85, 87, 124, 168, 169, 171, 178, 179, 181

Subtropical zone, 106

Suiping County (遂平县), 60

Index **193**

Surplus value, 37, 37n9
Sustainable economic
 development, 33
Suzhou (苏州), 28

T

Taicang (太仓), 28
Tang, 30
Technical change, 5, 7–9, 11, 12, 21,
 23, 24, 38, 46–47, 51, 54, 55,
 63, 102, 118, 148, 151,
 154–156, 177–181, 183
Technical constraints, 30, 38, 45,
 51, 119
Technological constraint, 112
Technological diversification, 183
Technological innovation, 2, 3, 7, 8,
 18, 22
Technological transition, 4, 5,
 16–19, 21–23, 98, 120, 148,
 152, 154, 155, 160–162,
 175–183
Technology accessibility, 4
Technology adoption, 162
Technology diffusion, 2, 4, 23, 151,
 156, 177
Technology generation gap, 121,
 152, 173, 177, 183
Technology innovation, 20, 119
Textile industry, 29, 42
Three links (*san guagou*, 三挂钩),
 72, 72n14
Three Years of Great Famine (*sannian
 da jihuang*, 三年大饥荒), 61
Tianjin (天津), 103n4
Tillage management system, 106
Tokugawa shogunate
 (德川幕府), 161

Total Factor Productivity (TFP),
 10–12, 116
Township and Village Enterprises
 (TVEs), 101, 142, 142n21,
 143

U

'Unified purchasing of agricultural
 products by the state' (*tong pai
 gou*, 统派购), 70, 70n11

W

Weixing Agricultural Producer's
 Cooperative (*weixing
 nongye hezuo she*, 卫星农业合
 作社), 60
Welfare system, 172
Wen Jiabao (温家宝), 66
Wheat, 1, 1n2, 40, 59–61, 60n2,
 60n3, 60n5, 70, 87, 99, 137,
 141, 157, 159, 160
World War Two (WW2), 5, 9,
 124, 126, 127, 129, 133,
 152, 155–160, 163–166,
 176, 180
Wuxi (无锡), 28

X

Xianmi (籼米), 103
Xijianyuan No. 1 Cooperative
 (溪建园一社), 60
Xinhua News Agency (*xinhua she*,
 新华社), 60, 61
Xinjiang (新疆), 103n4, 104n5,
 106, 117
Xizang (西藏), 103n4

Y

Yangtze Delta (*changjiang sanjiao zhou*, 长江三角洲), 28, 31, 32, 106, 107, 109, 114, 118, 120

Yangtze River (*yangzi jiang*, 扬子江), 28, 28n1, 103, 104, 106, 112, 114, 117, 118, 120

Yangzhou (扬州), 28n1

Yellow River (*huanghe*, 黄河), 104, 106, 108

Yunnan (云南), 103n4

Z

Zhejiang (浙江), 28, 103, 103n4, 105n6, 106, 118

Zhu Rongji (朱镕基), 66

CPSIA information can be obtained
at www.ICGtesting.com
Printed in the USA
LVHW07*1920100518
576724LV00014B/285/P